P9-CDV-330

Peace and Arms

Peace and Arms

Reports from *The Nation*

EDITED BY

HENRY M. CHRISTMAN

SHEED AND WARD : NEW YORK

125087

IT IS WITH DEEP SORROW that We note the enormous stocks of armaments that have been and still are being made in more economically developed countries, with a vast outlay of intellectual and economic resources. And so it happens that, while the people of these countries are loaded with heavy burdens, other countries as a result are deprived of the collaboration they need in order to make economic and social progress.

The production of arms is allegedly justified on the grounds that in present-day conditions peace cannot be preserved without an equal balance of armaments. And so, if one country increases its armaments, others feel the need to do the same; and if one country is equipped with nuclear weapons, other countries must produce their own, equally destructive.

Consequently, people live in constant fear lest the storm that every moment threatens should break upon them with dreadful violence. And with good reason, for the arms of war are ready at hand. Even though it is difficult to believe that anyone would dare bring upon himself the appalling destruction and sorrow that war would bring in its train, it cannot be denied that the conflagration can be set off by some unexpected and unpremeditated act. And one must bear in mind that, even though the monstrous power of modern weapons acts as a deterrent, there is nevertheless reason to fear that the mere continuance of nuclear tests, undertaken with war in mind, can seriously jeopardize various kinds of life on earth.

Justice, then, right reason and consideration for human dignity and life urgently demand that the arms race should cease; that the stockpiles which exist in various countries should be reduced equally and simultaneously by the parties concerned; that nuclear weapons should be banned;

and finally that all come to an agreement on a fitting program of disarmament, employing mutual and effective controls. In the words of Pius XII, Our Predecessor of happy memory: *The calamity of a world war, with the economic and social ruin and the moral excesses and dissolution that accompany it, must not be permitted to envelop the human race for a third time.*

All must realize that there is no hope of putting an end to the building up of armaments, nor of reducing the present stocks, nor, still less—and this is the main point—of abolishing them altogether, unless the process is complete and thorough and unless it proceeds from inner conviction: unless, that is, everyone sincerely cooperates to banish the fear and anxious expectation of war with which men are oppressed. If this is to come about, the fundamental principle on which our present peace depends must be replaced by another, which declares that the true and solid peace of nations consists not in equality of arms but in mutual trust alone. We believe that this can be brought to pass, and we consider that, since it concerns a matter not only demanded by right reason but also eminently desirable in itself, it will prove to be the source of many benefits.

> —From *Pacem in Terris*, Encyclical Letter of POPE JOHN XXIII
> April 11, 1963

Peace in the present time is based more on fear than on friendship. It is maintained more by the terror of deadly weapons than by mutual harmony and faith among peoples. And if tomorrow peace were to be broken—which God forbid—all humanity could be destroyed. . . . And, therefore, we urgently beseech all men of good will, yes all men who hold responsible positions in the field of culture and politics, to consider as fundamental the problem of peace. True peace is not that hypocritical propaganda aimed at lulling the adversary to sleep and concealing one's own preparation for war. Peace does not consist in pacifist rhetoric which refuses the indispensable, patient and tiresome negotiations, which are the only efficacious means. It is not based merely on the precarious balance of opposing economic interests, nor on the dream of proud supremacy. But true peace is based on the abolition or, at least, on the mitigation of the causes which endanger its security, as nationalistic or ideological pride, the arms race, lack of confidence in the methods or in the organizations that have been constituted to render the relations among nations orderly and friendly. Peace in truth, in justice, in freedom, in love. This is the peace we pray for!

> —POPE PAUL VI, Christmas Message 1963

CONTENTS

EDITOR'S INTRODUCTION

PEACE VERSUS WAR. Nuclear war. A war that would destroy world civilization in a holocaust so terrible that it defies the imagination. A war that might easily mean the annihilation of mankind, perhaps the extermination of all life on earth.

In comparison, all other public issues threaten at times to become meaningless.

Considering the overwhelming significance of the subject, one would imagine that it would be the most carefully thought about, the most carefully studied, the most written about, the most widely discussed, of all topics. The truth is, however, that the whole subject of peace versus war is almost completely neglected in the mass communications media. When an international crisis develops, there is, of course, extensive news coverage of the crisis and the fact that the crisis may precipitate a nuclear war. When the crisis passes, "things go back to normal." The Cold War continues as before. And, short of such a crisis, there is very little attention given to the question of whether mankind is to survive beyond the moment, much less any sustained investigation of the factors involved.

Comparatively little attention has been given to obvious facts.

First, we live in a completely new world—a nuclear world, with rapidly proliferating nuclear weapons—a world in which any minor conflict can rapidly escalate into a nuclear war.

Second, anything and everything that contributes to the perpetuation and intensification of the Cold War, and to the manufacture and stockpiling of nuclear and conventional armaments, increases the risk of nuclear war. Conversely, anything and everything contributing to the relaxation of international tensions, the reduction and elimination of the arms race, and the extension of international control of nuclear energy, reduces the chances of nuclear war.

These factors, and everything pertaining to them, are priority topics for public scrutiny and consideration. The mass communication media have sadly failed their obligation in this respect.

Among publications, one has succeeded admirably in giving appropriate coverage to this subject—THE NATION. In addition to close attention in its editorial columns, THE NATION has published a wealth of articles. Beginning in the fall of 1960, this highly-respected journal has carried an article on this general subject almost every other week; sometimes the articles have appeared weekly; and, occasionally, there were several such articles in a single issue of the magazine.

These articles came from many different persons, of widely different backgrounds and viewpoints. Their articles all have three vital things in common, however: An obvious conviction about the importance of the subject; a desire to shed light by providing information; and a desire to stimulate wider and deeper public attention to peace versus war.

The book is divided into three sections. Section I deals with the status quo that bulwarks the Cold War and opposes disarmament—the whole military-financial-political-industrial complex that has been aptly characterized as the "warfare state." Section II deals with the response to this situation—the development of the peace movement and its varied activities. Section III looks toward the future.

I have attempted to prepare this book in such a way that it will have a direct, continuing pertinence for some years to come. For instance, during periods of intense international tension, public attention turns to the possibility of nuclear attack. At such times, such subjects as the efficacy of shelters and the whole civil defense program are a primary topic of consideration. During periods of relative tranquillity, it is possible to undertake more constructive, long-range thinking. It is necessary that this book include both types of articles.

In short, I have endeavored to prepare a book that will be relevant regardless of the immediate, short-term political circumstances.

I have included in this book articles that present reportage of specific events, as well as more general and more philosophical essays that are not as closely tied to current events. I do not believe that the articles in the former category will become "dated" in the usual sense of journalistic reportage. First, the reportage deals with truly historic events. The importance of these events cannot be fully appreciated unless one considers what would have been the situation, what would have happened, had there been no public expressions of peace sentiment at the critical periods involved. Second, it was through these events that the techniques of the peace movement were tested and the patterns set; these events will have an indelible effect on the future activities of the peace movement, and also on both the public reaction and the official attitude toward future peace movement activities.

The very fact that it was possible for me to compile such a book testifies to the remarkable breadth and depth of coverage provided in THE NATION. This is a representative selection from that coverage. I have attempted to combine the widest possible range of subject matter with the most penetrating reportage and analysis. Therefore, in one sense, this is an authoritative reference book, a type of handbook, for those concerned with peace. At the same time, this book is prepared with the general reader in mind, with the hope that new audiences will be introduced to this vital information.

In closing, I would reiterate that, of course, the immediate, overwhelming problem is the prevention of nuclear war. However, I believe that the yearning for peace has a potential far beyond this goal. As this book indicates, the peace movement, in the wider sense, is much more than simply a movement against nuclear war. Now that it is obvious even to politicians that war no longer can be used as an instrument of state in the traditional manner, this situation presents a great opportunity for developing a new program of national and international politics. Indeed, there is no alternative. The world must have new and better thinking, planning, and action, or there will be no world.

—HENRY M. CHRISTMAN

CONTRIBUTORS

CLAYTON C. BARBEAU, a free-lance writer, is the author of the novel, *The Icon*.

CHARLES D. BOLTON teaches sociology at the University of California.

RALPH CAPLAN, formerly editor of *Industrial Design*, is a free-lance writer and editorial consultant, and also the author of the novel, *Say Yes*.

JOHN COHEN, Professor of Psychology at the University of Manchester, is the author of *Human Nature, War, and Society* and other books.

FRED J. COOK, formerly a reporter for the New York *World-Telegram and Sun*, is well known as the author of "Juggernaut: The Warfare State" and "Hiss: New Perspective on the Strangest Case of Our Time," and as co-author of "The Shame of New York," all published as special issues of *The Nation*. The author of various books, he received four journalistic awards four years in a row—three Page One Awards from the Newspaper Guild of New York and a Sidney Hillman Foundation Award for "Gambling, Inc.," published in *The Nation*.

BARBARA DEMING has contributed frequently to *The Nation* on various aspects of the peace movement.

CARL DREHER, Science Editor of *The Nation*, is the author of *Automation: What It Is, How It Works, Who Can Use It*.

CHARLES FLATO is a medical journalist in the Boston area.

JOHN M. FOWLER, Associate Professor of Physics at Washington University, is the editor of *Fallout: A Study of Superbombs, Strontium-90, and Survival.*

STEPHANIE GERVIS is a newspaper editor who has written extensively on various aspects of the world peace movement.

MARY M. GROOMS describes herself as a "suburban housewife and mother interested, as all mothers should be, in politics, civil rights and all matters affecting the future of our children."

ROGER HAGAN, editor of the *Council For Correspondence Newsletter,* spent much of 1962 studying the political aspects of the American peace movement on a foundation grant.

CARLETON MABEE, Pulitzer Prize-winning historian, teaches at Delta College, and is the author of *The Seaway Story.*

ROBERT MARTINSON is a member of the faculty of the School of Public Health at the University of California at Los Angeles.

WESLEY MARX contributes to a number of West Coast publications.

STANLEY MEISLER is a wire service newsman now stationed in Washington.

SEYMOUR MELMAN, Associate Professor of Industrial and Management Engineering at Columbia University, is author of several books, including *The Peace Race,* and editor of *Inspection for Disarmament.*

DONALD N. MICHAEL, a social psychologist, is director of Planning and Programs of the Peace Research Institute.

J. B. PRIESTLEY, the distinguished British writer, is the author of more than 60 books and plays.

WILLIAM PROXMIRE, senior U.S. Senator from Wisconsin, is a member of the Senate Banking and Currency Committee and the Joint Economic Committee.

STEVEN V. ROBERTS is an editor of the *Harvard Crimson.*

WILLIAM S. ROYCE is Assistant Director of the Management Sciences Division of the Stanford Research Institute.

EUGENE S. SCHWARTZ is a research engineer in a university-affiliated research foundation.

LOUIS B. SOHN, Professor of Law at Harvard University, is co-author of *World Peace Through World Law.*

1

PROBLEM: THE "WARFARE STATE"

SPENDTHRIFTS FOR DEFENSE

by Senator William Proxmire

IT IS a grim fact of life in today's troubled world that America must rely heavily on military strength to maintain peace. Effective, multilateral arms reduction undoubtedly represents the fervent hope of all peoples. But without United States armed power as the solid basis for negotiation, it will be impossible to achieve.

Peace with freedom is our objective. Our military force is a means to help achieve that objective. Nothing more.

There is an immense potential danger, however, in our reliance on military power, the danger which former President Eisenhower, a lifelong soldier, warned against when he said in his farewell speech to the nation:

In the councils of government, we must guard against the acquisition of unwarranted influence, whether sought or unsought, by the military-industrial complex. The potential for the disastrous rise of misplaced power exists and will persist. We must never let the weight of this combination endanger our liberties or democratic processes. We should take nothing for granted. Only an alert and knowledgeable citizenry can compel the proper meshing of the huge industrial and military machinery of defense with our peaceful methods and goals, so that security and liberty may prosper together.

My own experience in the Senate has shown me the painful inability of our democracy to resist the momentum of excessive spending and waste that accompanies our vast military establishment.

5

On August 3, 1961, the U.S. Senate voted, 87–4, to buy a hundred additional B-52 and B-58 manned bombers at a cost of $525 million. This resounding mandate for bombers was passed in spite of the fact that:

1. President Kennedy had not requested these bombers in his $47 billion defense budget.

2. Secretary of Defense Robert McNamara had testified before the Armed Services and Appropriations Committee of both Houses of Congress that procurement of the additional bombers was not necessary for the national defense.

3. The Defense Department officials responsible for strategy, research and development, and procurement, all testified against buying these planes.

4. In a strongly worded letter to me sent the day before the Senate vote, Secretary McNamara wrote:

I repeat my previously stated opinion that it is not necessary for the Congress to appropriate funds in fiscal year 1962 above Administration requests for B-52 and B-58 bombers. Inherent in this is my belief that the production of B-52s and B-58s is already adequately protected for the period of time involved in our further study of the bomber concept.

Only three Senators joined me in voting for my amendment, which would have eliminated this appropriation. In the Senate debate, we had made an overwhelming case against spending more than half a billion dollars in this way. Yet some 95 per cent of the Senators voting that day rejected the logic of the case, rejected the advice of the President, the Secretary of Defense and his aides, and voted to appropriate the funds. This was more money than was spent in that year by the federal government for medical research; more than was spent for all federal housing programs; more than the budgets allocated to the U.S. Forest Service, the National Park Service and the Fish and Wildlife Service combined.

This episode is worth noting because it is a classic example of providing money in the name of defense which is not based on a solid analysis of our military requirements. It is a symptom of a growing tendency to use defense to justify federal spending that's not really needed for military purposes.

As a rationalization for federal expenditure, national defense has few peers. Programs that wouldn't get a second look from Congress flit through if they are attached to an armed forces appropriation. Yet substantial portions of our military budgets do not provide the kind of specific military strength that is needed.

These extra expenditures often are excused on the grounds that they "strengthen the economy." Undoubtedly they serve to keep assembly lines going and plants running, but whether the production of millions or billions of dollars' worth of unneeded hardware can be described as useful employment of human and natural resources is doubtful.

Defense spending not related to military needs also wins support for other reasons. An influential Congressman, a member of the key Appropriations Committee, put it this way in a recent public statement:

I am convinced defense is only one of the factors that enter into our determination for defense spending. The others are pump priming, spreading the immediate benefits of defense spending, taking care of all services, giving all defense contractors a fair share, spreading the military bases to include all sections, etc. There is no state in the Union and hardly a district in a state which doesn't have defense spending, contracting or a defense establishment. We see the effect in public and Congressional insistence on continuing contracts, or operating military bases, though the need has expired.

I reject these excuses for military spending, not just because they result in a massive unnecessary expenditure of tax funds, but also because I believe that the prime purpose of our military and defense capability should be to make possible meaningful negotiations aimed at securing peace and protecting freedom.

"We arm to parley," said Sir Winston Churchill, and President Kennedy has echoed his words. I do not believe that the present conflict of the interests of the United States and the Soviet bloc in many corners of the world permits any substantial reduction in our military capabilities. Many individuals whom I respect do believe that steps towards disarmament, perhaps unilateral steps, would be useful gestures towards thawing the cold-war climate. I believe, however, that Soviet intransigence, particularly in the difficult Berlin situation, requires the United States to maintain its strength. Only in this way will our negotiators be able to command the respect at the conference table that is essential if effective agreements are to be achieved.

Unfortunately, vast portions of our military expenditure are not based on a sober analysis of the military strength needed to deter Soviet ambitions and to facilitate constructive negotiations. Indeed, most of the lobbying that goes on in favor of increased defense spending bears little relation to our nation's actual hard defense needs. And the lobbying is substantial—often open, sometimes more subtle. It feeds on the "anything goes for defense" attitude that transforms otherwise fiscally responsible members of the House and Senate into open-fisted spendthrifts.

The paradox is that this attitude may be resulting in a weaker defense as well as swollen defense budgets. The heaviest lobbying pressure—and the most potent with Congress—is to hold on to old weapons, keep old assembly lines going and maintain old jobs. In an age when spectacular changes in military technology are routine, such an attitude is dangerous in the extreme.

The most important defense "lobby" is so obvious it is often overlooked since it consists of members of Congress, both Senators and Representatives. In an understandable zeal to aid industry and workers in home states and districts, many Congressmen in effect act as highly potent lobbyists for military spending.

As a Senator, I feel that an appeal from a firm in my state asking for help in getting a defense contract merits my support. Indeed, it is hardly fair to the economic well-being of an area for its legislative representatives not to work to channel defense expenditures to it, since other Congressmen from other states are doing their level best to attract those funds.

An able Congressman from West Virginia, liberal Democrat Ken Hechler, in June of 1959 put it this way in a speech in the House:

I am firmly against the kind of logrolling which would subject our defense program to narrowly sectional or selfish pulling and hauling. But I am getting pretty hot under the collar about the way my State of West Virginia is shortchanged in Army, Navy and Air Force installations. I am going to stand up on my hind legs and roar until West Virginia gets the fair treatment she deserves.

As long as a large military budget is a fact of life in our country, I must agree with Congressman Hechler's contention that due attention should be paid to achieving a reasonable distribution of defense procurement around the country. It would be foolish to overlook the economic impact of defense spending, which can help promote economic growth and employment in areas suffering from severe depression or recession.

But the important point is that this should not be permitted to lap over into the realm where decisions on what is needed to assure adequate military capability are made. It is one thing to use common sense and good judgment in deciding where certain items should be manufactured, taking account of costs, unemployment, strategic dispersal, transportation and so forth. But it is quite a different thing to let non-military factors influence the choice of weapons, and with it the type of military defense and the size of the defense budget to which our nation is committed.

Testifying before a House subcommittee a few years ago, an officer of a major defense contractor said:

Many of the most important decisions in the defense of our country are not made by military technicians. They are made in the Congress of the United States.

I do not think this statement is accurate. But it is obvious that many Congressmen act as if it were true. The case of the Nike-Zeus "anti-missile-missile" is a good illustration.

The first successful proof test of this weapon took place in July, 1962. A Nike-Zeus rocket fired from a Pacific island intercepted a rocket that had been fired from another island, scoring the United States equivalent to Khrushchev's boast that Soviet rockets could hit a fly in outer space. The Defense Department indicated there had been a previous unsuccessful attempt to test this device. The restraint of the public announcement made it clear that there is a long way to go before the Nike-Zeus can be counted on reliably to perform its allotted task of meeting and destroying incoming enemy nuclear missiles.

Yet as long ago as February, 1961—just after President Kennedy took office—a number of Congressmen rose to sing the praises of the Nike-Zeus system, urging that a $410 million production commit- ment be made at once. The speeches occurred after an article ap- peared in the magazine *Army* with a map showing how much of the $410 million would be spent in each of thirty-seven states. Each of the Congressional Nike-Zeus enthusiasts represented one of those states.

More recently, a member of the House Appropriations Committee wearied Pentagon witnesses by his repeated requests that the De- fense Department see what could be done to utilize a costly but obsolete item manufactured in his home district.

The debate on the B-70 bomber (renamed the RS-70, for "re- connaissance strike") this year resulted in Congress' adding a gen- erous ladle of funds for further development and procurement of this controversial plane desired by the Air Force. In the months leading up to that conclusion, dozens of Congressmen expounded on the virtues of the RS-70.

Certainly there is nothing sinister about these kinds of public statements and inquiries. Each of the Senators and Congressmen unquestionably has a right to tout the virtues of products of his state or district. However, the total effect of the utterances is, at best, misleading. It can be more serious than that if it sways the judgment of the military decision-makers. These public enthusiasms for specific kinds of military hardware are not based on an informed evaluation of our defense needs—though garbed in language which makes them appear that way—but rather on the benefits they confer on a particular region or industry or branch of the armed forces.

They also have the effect of encouraging the "anything goes for defense" attitude which makes fiscal responsibility in other aspects of federal policy appear so futile. The competition for contract awards is certainly easier for everyone when there is a larger pie to dish out. The argument is made that we should err on the side of caution. More, it is said, is better than war. The authoritative *Congressional Quarterly* has reported that members of Congress went so far as to telephone President Eisenhower to tell him they were voting for higher defense appropriations in response to local pressures generated by the Pentagon.

In a colloquy with me in the Senate, Senator Richard B. Russell of Georgia, Chairman of the Senate Armed Services Committee and a member of the Defense Appropriations Subcommittee, made the following remarkable statement:

There is something about preparing for destruction that causes men to be more careless in spending money than they would be if they were building for constructive purposes. Why that is, I do not know; but I have observed, over a period of almost thirty years in the Senate, that there is something about buying arms with which to kill, to destroy, to wipe out cities, and to obliterate great transportation systems which causes men not to reckon the dollar cost as closely as they do when they think about proper housing and the care of the health of human beings.

The kind of waste that troubles me is what results from the effort to perpetuate the production of items that are not needed to maintain our military strength. It is this that is so profoundly wrong.

I am confident that Secretary McNamara fully shares my view on this. With great dedication and skill he has pursued a course of deciding on the basis of evidence and logic what military capability is needed, then setting out to procure just that amount of strength in the most efficient possible way.

He is apparently unmoved by the appeals of industry, Congressmen or the service branches that he give special consideration to pet projects. In his determination to continue this policy he deserves full support. In addition, he has undertaken a comprehensive cost-reduction program which in five years is expected to cut Defense Department spending by $3 billion per year.

In fact, due to Secretary McNamara's determination, there was a happy ending to the $525 million manned-bomber procurement that the Senate voted in August, 1961. When the 1962 appropriation was up, the Secretary reported that he had not spent the money and that, accordingly, the Air Force budget request was reduced by that amount.

THE BRASS TRUMPET:
SELLING MILITARISM TO AMERICA

by Stanley Meisler

IN THE SPRING of 1961, Martin Burke, Gilbert Bauer and David Figlestahler, pupils of the Holy Redeemer Elementary School in Portsmouth, Ohio, wrote a letter to Secretary of Defense Robert S. McNamara. In the event of war, Russian troops "will be landing inside our borders," they told the Secretary. If that comes to pass, "the American people will defend this country in a last ditch, to the death stand, along with the military." The civilian population must train itself for this future. "Please send us any available weapons," the schoolboys asked. They listed recoilless rifles, anti-tank guns, bazookas, mortars, machine guns, browning automatic rifles and submachine guns. Martin, Gilbert and David said the weapons would help them learn about arms and would "help us prepare ourselves for our future military service." The boys closed with a compliment: "We the senders of this letter are in full accord with your conduction of your duties so far as Secretary of Defence" [sic].

Although the schoolboys had not learned their spelling, they had learned other lessons well, for they are growing up in a time when all the channels of communication and education overflow with images of war and might and glory, images that tend to obscure the views of death and destruction that linger from other times and other lands. Many teachers have inspired Martin, Gilbert and David to a call to arms and taught them the certainty of war.

12

Perhaps a brother, uncle or cousin, fresh home from a troop-indoctrination course in the Army, has taught them to feel the tentacles of communism gripping their country. Perhaps Elvis Presley, in the movie *G.I. Blues,* has taught them that military life offers pleasure at the same time that it demands duty. Perhaps their comic strip hero, *Steve Canyon,* has taught them the terrible price a country must pay if it lets down its guard for a moment by cutting its defense budget. Perhaps a trip to a nearby military base has taught them the thrill of touching a weapon or hearing the thunderous whistle of a jet. Perhaps their newspapers or magazines or television have taught them the imminence of war. Perhaps an admiral or a general has come to Portsmouth and taught them to beware of effeminate, easily duped diplomats who may try to make us disarm.

In itself, the letter of the schoolboys does not contain much that is objectionable. The boys wanted to affirm their faith in their country and recall the spirit of the Revolutionary Minuteman. But the letter could not have been written in any other peacetime period of American history. In no other time of peace has the military ascended to such influence and power. "The warlords . . . are now more powerful than they have ever been in the history of the American elite," C. Wright Mills has written. "They have now more means of exercising power in many areas of American life which were previously civilian domains; they now have more connections; and they are now operating in a nation whose elite and whose underlying population have accepted what can only be called a military definition of reality."

To a country which spent 59 per cent of its more than $80 billion budget on national security, Dwight D. Eisenhower gave this farewell warning as President: "In the councils of government, we must guard against the acquisition of unwarranted influence, whether sought or unsought, by the military-industrial complex." He added that "the total influence—economic, political, even spiritual—is felt in every city, every statehouse, every office of the federal government."

The path to these heights of power and influence is cleared for the military and its industrial allies by a public relations establishment that has no equal in American public or private life. This establishment uses the press, television, movies, comic strips, civic organizations, veterans groups, schools and troops to sell the military point of view to the American people. No other point of view, save that of the President alone, can reach the people from so many sides at once. Without this military public relations establishment, three Ohio schoolboys would not have picked up their pens to write a letter to the Secretary of Defense.

Public relations is among the newest of U.S. military weapons. Although military commanders and the War Department issue battle reports that were printed or elaborated by the press during the Civil War and the Spanish-American War, the United States military service did not issue its first formal press release until 1904. Even then, military public relations was a minor activity until World War I, when General Pershing set up a press section at his headquarters in France. After the war, public relations in the armed forces lapsed, although the Army Air Force named Major Henry H. Arnold to head its information division in 1925 (his skills are credited with helping to sell Congress and the nation on the need for a separate Air Force). During World War II, the military services, with Arnold's Army Air Force leading the way, built huge propaganda machines. These machines never have ceased grinding. "The information officer has become a key man whose advice is sought and depended upon in the communication of ideas to both the public and the troops," said an Army bulletin issued in 1957. "If there ever was a propitious time for officers to apply for specialization as an information officer, it is now."

During the Korean War, the Pentagon budget listed more than $10 million for public relations. In peacetime, this seemed too high to Congress and, after the war, vague limitations were written into defense appropriation bills, cutting the amount of money the Pentagon could spend on public relations. It is difficult to determine, however, how close the military services are adhering to the limitations.

On April 20, 1961 the Associated Press reported these budget and personnel totals for the 1960 fiscal year: the Department of Defense, which coordinates and, to some extent, supervises all public relations of the three services, has an $824,000 public relations budget and employs 73 civilians and 52 military personnel; the

Army has a $387,850 budget and employs 50 civilians and 65 military personnel; the Air Force has a $295,700 budget and employs 39 civilians and 66 military personnel; and the Navy has a $111,000 budget and employs 39 civilians and 67 military personnel. In total, this meant the Pentagon spent $1,600,000 and used 451 men on public relations during the last fiscal year. But the AP noted that there were two unknown quantities: the budgets did not include the pay of the 250 military personnel; and neither the budgets nor the personnel totals included any military public relations activities outside Washington.

Military pay, particularly in the officer-stuffed Pentagon, could add well over a million dollars to the total public relations budget. The public relations work outside the capital could multiply that several times. Every Army or Air Force base and Naval district has its own public relations operation. In addition, base personnel assigned to other duties sometimes are asked to devote part of their time to public relations. The total military public relations budget is not $1,600,000, but many millions.

At first glance, these millions appear to be spent on a simple mission. Arthur S. Sylvester, Assistant Secretary of Defense for Public Affairs, put down the chief responsibility of a Pentagon public relations program in a recent directive: to "initiate and support activities contributing to good relations between the Department of Defense and all segments of the public at home and abroad." Admiral Arleigh A. Burke, the former Chief of Naval Operations, has said: "There is a vital need for us to have a determined public working with us—an alert citizenry that is conscious of the magnitude of the struggle our country is presently engaged in, and aware of the contributions the military services are making to our nation's cause."

Both statements are candid as far as they go, but neither makes clear that vast sums of money also are spent not so much in selling the public on government defense policy but in drawing the public into the interservice struggles that make that policy, as well as into the individual service rebellions against that policy once it is made. While debate over Department of Defense reorganization goes on, Air Force public relations men work to convince the public and

Congress of its value, while Navy public relations men work to convince them of the opposite. After both Presidents Eisenhower and Kennedy cut back the B-70 bomber program, Air Force public relations men worked to convince the public and Congress of the danger and foolishness of that decision. The channels of communication are manipulated each day with taxpayers' money, first, to implant the general military view of life on the American people and then to sell them on the peculiar prides and prejudices of the individual services.

The services have various targets for their propaganda, and the first, because it is so close, comprises the 2.5 million men and women in the armed forces and the million civilians employed by the services and the Department of Defense. But more than just 3.5 million Americans are affected by this direct propaganda. Short-term enlistments and selective service make the composition of the services fluid: there are always additional young men coming in to soak in the military point of view and others going out to spread it among the people. Then there are the four million men and women in the Reserves, and millions of servicemen's families who read every tidbit of military news they can find.

Almost every Army and Air Force base and Navy district or fleet has a newspaper supplied with weekly news, features and editorials by the Armed Forces Press Service. Magazines like *The Airman, All Hands, Army Aviation Digest, Army Information Digest,* and *Naval Aviation News* also feed the military line to servicemen. But more important for molding a young man's way of thinking are the troop indoctrination courses that fill up a good part of military life.

Five years ago, President Eisenhower and the National Security Council decided on a policy designed to concentrate all the resources of government on the cold war. Under the policy, directives were issued to enlist the Department of Defense in the psychological aspects of the battle. The directives are still classified, but Cabell Phillips, in an illuminating article in *The New York Times* on June 18, 1961 said the directives ordered officials "to take positive steps to alert the troops under their command and the public at large to the issues of national security and the 'cold war.'" Phillips added:

"It is known that commanding officers were allowed wide latitude in applying the directives within their commands."

This latitude permitted officers like Major General Edwin A. Walker to attempt to smother their men with views identical to those of the John Birch Society. Walker, commander of the 24th Infantry Division in Germany, created a "pro-blue program" to indoctrinate troops with an "understanding of American military and civil heritage, responsibility toward that heritage and the facts and objectives of those enemies who would destroy it." Walker, like many other combat officers of the Korean War, had wanted to find out "what went wrong with some of our fighting men in Korea." The answers found by Walker became clear January 24, 1960, when he addressed two hundred men of his division and their dependents. An Army report said that Walker made "derogatory remarks of a serious nature about prominent Americans, the American press and television industry and certain commentators, which linked the persons and institutions with communism and Communist influence."

The Overseas Weekly, an independent newspaper for servicemen, said Walker described former President Harry S. Truman, former Secretary of State Dean Acheson and Mrs. Franklin D. Roosevelt as "definitely pink" and CBS commentators Eric Sevareid and Edward R. Murrow (now director of the United States Information Agency) and columnist Walter Lippmann as "confirmed Communists." Walker continued his "pro-blue program," including the distribution of right-wing material, for more than a year after the speech until an article in *The Overseas Weekly* drew attention to his activities. The Army then admonished him and canceled his assignment to command the VIII Corps headquartered in Austin, Texas.

The Department of Defense moved no further than this admonishment, hoping that the example would prevent other generals and admirals from going too far in their zeal against communism. But all military commanders are still operating under the National Security Council directives to indoctrinate their men for the psychological battle of the cold war. The Walker case may have taught them that John Birchism is too far Right, even for the Pentagon;

but they are free, within this limitation, to employ their own political views in molding the troops under their command.

The services like to use movies in troop-indoctrination programs. Most of the films are made in Pentagon studios; but two, purchased from outside sources, won favor among commanders in the past year until angry cries from liberal groups forced the Department of Defense to put some reins on their use. The movies are *Operation Abolition,* the attempt by the House Committee on Un-American Activities to pin a Communist label on the student riots in San Francisco last year, and *Communism on the Map,* an attempt by the ultra-rightist National Education Program to show how communism dominates Western Europe and certain positions of power in American government, labor, the press and education. *Communism on the Map* was produced by Glenn Green, a member of the John Birch Society.

Soon after *Operation Abolition* was released, the Department of Defense and the services bought copies. John Broger, the Department's Deputy Director of Information and Education, said he authorized the purchase after he noted what he called the resemblance between the demonstrations in San Francisco and the leftist student riots in Tokyo that prevented the visit of President Eisenhower in 1960. The Army alone bought thirty prints. The National Education Program, in a brochure on *Communism on the Map,* quotes laudatory comments from several admirals and claims the Navy bought fifty prints. In a protest to Secretary McNamara on April 18, 1961 Norman Thomas noted that the movie had been shown at the Naval Air Base in Seattle; the Naval Air Stations in Brunswick, Ga., San Diego, Calif., Memphis, Tenn., and Corpus Christi, Tex.; the Navy Air Intelligence Reserve Unit at Floyd Bennett Field, Brooklyn; the Bureau of Naval Weapons in Washington; the Naval Auxiliary Air Station at Whiting Field, Fla.; the Marine Corps Recruit Depot in San Diego; the *U.S.S. Midway;* and the California Air National Guard in Compton. As the two movies reached more and more military audiences, more and more protests began to filter into the Pentagon.

McNamara reacted to the criticism in two ways. First, he removed the two movies from the list of approved educational materials—though leaving them in military libraries throughout the world for use by individual commanders if they wish. Next, the Secretary speeded up production of two films designed to supplant the controversial movies.

One, *The Challenge of Ideas,* was released in July. Cabell Phillips of *The New York Times* described it as a "sober, moving and non-glutinous portrayal of what America is and the kind of threat it faces from communism." McNamara evidently hopes this will prove a non-controversial substitute for *Communism on the Map.* The second movie, not yet released, will be based on *Communist Target* —*Youth,* a report by FBI Director J. Edgar Hoover. Since the report's views on the San Francisco riots differ little from that of the House Committee on Un-American Activities, it seems futile to hope for a "sober, moving and non-glutinous" substitute for *Operation Abolition.*

The same Eisenhower administration directive that ordered commanders to alert their troops to the Communist menace ordered them to alert the public as well. As a result, commanders have spent much of the last few years hopping off base to instill militant anti-communism into the residents of nearby communities. They have participated in, sponsored, even created "Schools on Anti-Communism," "Alerts," "Seminars," "Freedom Forums," "Strategy for Survival Conferences," "Fourth Dimensional Warfare Seminars," and "Project Actions." Often held on base, complete with showings of *Operation Abolition* and *Communism on the Map* and speeches by the local commanders and by imported professional anti-Communists like Herbert Philbrick, these meetings follow a John Birch line. Under the guise of anti-communism, they cry out against all social legislation and mock anyone with different views. The Navy, whose Naval Air Station commanders have been particularly zealous at taking part in such programs, often denies official sponsorship, but it is difficult for any audience to watch a man in uniform declaim against communism and welfare state legislation without assuming he is spouting an official line.

Of late there has been some attempt to hold these militant militarists back, particularly after Sen. J. William Fulbright (D., Ark.) sent an angry memorandum about them to the department. In a July

11, 1961 directive, McNamara delegated authority to Assistant Secretary Sylvester to "provide policy guidance to the commands . . . for . . . the conduct of any informational programs directed in whole or in part to the general public." McNamara also banned any military-sponsored use of *Operation Abolition* and *Communism on the Map* in any public function. His ban is so strict that the Navy refused to let the 11th Naval District band play at a "Coast Cities Freedom Program" rally in Santa Monica, Calif., July 26, 1961 because the sponsors planned to show the two movies.

McNamara's aides have announced the start of careful screening for all material used in community-relations programs. "But," as one department official told Cabell Phillips of *The New York Times,* "this sort of screening doesn't directly affect General X if he wants to make a speech about communism in the schools or play footsie with the Birch Society people. . . . Who is to tell a three-star admiral how right wing—or how left wing—his political outlook can be?" In addition, as another official made clear, timidity often rules the civilian leaders of the Pentagon—they don't want to be tagged as "being against anti-communism."

Another problem along the same line involves the top generals and admirals who always seem to be on a foreign-policy lecture circuit. "The talkativeness of American military men, most of them reading speeches written by professional speech writers who are paid by the government, is an international scandal," says Walter Lippmann. Waldemar A. Nielsen of the Ford Foundation points out that "Defense officials, civilian and in uniform, make several times as many speeches and write several times as many articles bearing on foreign policy as officials of the Department of State." In the four weeks between July 5 and August 2, 1961, Pentagon officials scheduled forty-five speeches to groups ranging from Syracuse University to the Texas Bar Association. Such speeches, while clear of any John Birch tinge, often stress the futility of disarmament and of negotiating with the Russians. "The question must be asked," Nielsen writes, "whether a systematic bias is not being introduced by this branch of government into the stream of American public opinion."

The Kennedy Administration has made some attempts to tone down these speeches. Soon after Inauguration Day, Admiral Burke tried to see how far his new Pentagon bosses would allow him to go. He asked for clearance on a speech bristling with his usual truculence toward the Russians. Sylvester demanded revisions, and the White House backed him up. The situation was repeated three months later, when Rear Admiral Samuel B. Frankel, Deputy Director of Naval Intelligence, planned a speech in Austin, Tex., implying that both former Presidents Eisenhower and Franklin D. Roosevelt had been deluded into negotiating with the Russians. Sylvester again forced revisions. The Assistant Secretary's authority to revise these speeches presumably has been strengthened by the July 11, 1961 directive giving him the responsibility of "policy guidance" over all informational programs directed at the public. A new "guideline"— but not an order—issued by McNamara says:

In public discussions, all officials of the Department should confine themselves to defense matters. They should particularly avoid discussion of foreign-policy matters, a field which is reserved for the President and the Department of State. This long-established principle recognizes the danger that when Defense officials express opinions on foreign policy, their words can be taken as the policy of the government.

But even if the Pentagon could quiet the militant right-wingers who often command installations and the admirals and generals who try to mold foreign policy, this would not stop the military point of view from flowing to the public, particularly to communities near bases. In his textbook, *Public Relations,* Bertrand R. Canfield presents a community-relations case study supplied to him by the Army. It involves the Infantry Center at Fort Benning, Ga., and clearly represents one of the prideful achievements of the Army publicity men.

At Fort Benning, a Citizens-Military Council has been created to maintain continuous ties between the base and nearby communities. Representing the citizens are the mayors of Columbus, Ga., and Phoenix City, Ala.; the chairmen of the commissioners of the two surrounding counties; officers of the local Chambers of Commerce; the president of the Columbus-Phoenix City Ministerial Alliance; the superintendents of schools; the local newspaper and radio officials; the secretary of the Columbus YMCA, and others. Representing Fort Benning are the Commanding General, the chaplains, the Public Information Officer (who is council secretary), and others.

Canfield lists some of the council's accomplishments. The Kiwanis and Rotary clubs invite four military guests to every meeting. A Boy Scout camp is held at Fort Benning. The Army post supplies an average of a speaker a week to the local civic clubs. A group of soldiers helped Union Springs, Ala., build a church. An Army major organized the Great Books discussions at the Columbus Memorial Library. Servicemen receive reduced rates for local high school and professional sports events. Fort Benning furnished "walkie-talkies" to the local Soap Box Derby so there could be communication between the start and finish lines of the race.

Schools are a prime target of the military. The Department of Defense offers film strips, records and discussion guides to school systems asking help in teaching about the nature of communism. The Navy Fleet Home Town Center in Great Lakes, Ill., has a High School News Service Division that supplies news and feature stories about the Navy, Army and Air Force to editors of school newspapers and magazines. In 1960, material was mailed to 16,000 high schools. Last May, the Navy provided the destroyer escort *De Long* for a program called "First Annual Day in the Navy"; forty-five high school boys from Westchester County, N. Y., boarded the warship for a forty-mile cruise on Long Island Sound. The trip was a brilliant piece of long-range planning. "Most of the boys are studying journalism and we want them to understand how the Navy operates," said Lieutenant Commander William J. Roach of the Naval Reserve. The dividends presumably would reach the Navy five to ten years from now, when the boys landed newspaper jobs.

The military establishment, of course, does not confine its influence to the communities that surround bases and naval stations. It courts key Americans wherever they live. Since 1948, the Pentagon has invited men in positions of power or influence to Defense Orientation Conferences. The guests attend briefings at the Pentagon for a few days and then tour Army posts, Air Force bases, aircraft carriers, submarines and naval stations. The guest list for the first conference included Winthrop Aldrich, James B. Carey, Joseph M. Dodge, Al Hayes, David Lawrence, John L. Lewis, Daniel A. Poling, Nelson A. Rockefeller, Arthur Hays Sulzberger and Robert R. Young. Attendance at a conference entitles the guest to membership in the Defense Orientation Conference Association, a kind of alumni association that arranges refresher briefings several times a year. The association now has 1,900 members.

According to the official line, the conferences inform American leaders about military matters and solicit their views on the subject. But Maxine Cheshire, a woman's page reporter for the *Washington Post*, perhaps came closer to the truth on October 1, 1960, when she began a chatty story:

> The Defense Department has a network of high-powered press agents across the country, and fortunately they work for free. It would take an enormous government appropriation to pay for the caliber of civilians who were assembled here this week for the ninth annual meeting of the Defense Orientation Conference Association.

It also would take an enormous government appropriation to pay for the non-official organizations that act as cheering sections for the services. These include the Navy League, the Air Force Association, the Association of the U. S. Army, the Reserve Officers Association, the American Ordnance Association, and the National Security Industrial Association—all financed largely by defense contractors. With these and the various veterans lobby organizations, as Waldemar A. Nielsen has pointed out, "the Defense Department has a built-in system of communication with the American people unequaled in scale by anything available to other federal agencies." Or to any private agency, either.

The capture of military personnel, and of key civilians, is vital to a Pentagon publicist, but his more exciting, perhaps more significant, work centers on the capture of the mass media—Hollywood, television, the press, even the comics. The Department's Office of News Services has an Audio-Visual Division which, among its other duties, sees to it that some movies and television shows have good chunks of military propaganda. The division examines scripts and then lends aid to those deemed worthy of cooperation from the Department of Defense.

Cooperation can save a producer a good deal of money. Indeed, if he plans a movie based almost entirely on the activities of the armed services, cooperation can determine whether he will have a movie at all. For a producer clutching a script blessed by the division, the services may provide military equipment that he can't get elsewhere: modern tanks, weapons, ships, planes. An officer, acting as technical adviser to insure the movie's authenticity, often is sent along. The services will not stage battle scenes for a movie maker, but they will invite him to film maneuvers or naval exercises. If the producer needs a few soldiers, sailors, or airmen for individual scenes, the Defense Department will give them leave to turn actor—at minimum Hollywood rates—for a few days. In addition, the services will supply non-classified documentary films of battles and maneuvers to fill some of the gaps in the movie.

The department has guide lines to determine which movies deserve cooperation; basically, the production must benefit the department and the services. The Audio-Visual Division applies the guide lines with flexibility. Comedies that twit the services usually receive cooperation under the theory that most people in the audience understand the ribbing is all in fun. In serious dramatic fare, the division worries about total effect, rather than individual scenes, and often asks producers for some kind of balance. Should the movie highlight a villainous officer, the division, before it allots tanks, may demand that one or two of the good guys be an officer, too. The Navy, for example, cooperated with the makers of *The Caine Mutiny*. Officials felt that the tyrannical, unbalanced Captain Queeg was offset by some of the young, intelligent and sincere other officers: in total effect, officials decided, the movie was favorable to the Navy. *The Gallant Hours, I Aim at the Stars, GI Blues, Men into Space, Blue Angels,* and *The Patton Story* are other movies and TV series produced with Pentagon help.

It is hard to criticize the Department of Defense for refusing to cooperate with producers who want to turn out movies injurious to the Army, Navy or Air Force. A question arises, however, when the department denies cooperation not because the movie is anti-armed

services, but because its political or social implications are not acceptable to the Pentagon. Here, again, the military drenches itself in
politics. Stanley Kramer was unable to obtain full cooperation for his
movie *On the Beach*. Bertram Kalisch, chief of the Audio-Visual
Division, said the Pentagon felt the movie, based on the Nevil
Shute novel, was "defeatist" and therefore contrary to government
policy. Actually, the movie was more anti-nuclear war than defeatist
and, to this extent, in strict accord with official government policy,
which is that the United States does not want a nuclear war. The
Pentagon objected to *On the Beach* not because it crossed *government* policy, but because its message might stir sentiment for disarmament and thus cross *Pentagon* policy.

Because of Kramer's standing as a producer, the Pentagon did
offer him some minor help, but he did not need it to produce the
movie. With the cooperation of the Australian Navy and the many
millions an artist of his caliber can command, Kramer gave the world
On the Beach. A lesser producer with less money might not have
been able to do so without massive help from the Pentagon. In a
sense, the decision to lend or refuse cooperation, particularly when
some producers alter their script to meet Pentagon complaints, is a
kind of censorship.

Among the millions of men who man our defenses, it is difficult
to imagine any spending most of their time bolstering comic strips.
But Louis Kraar of *The Wall Street Journal*, one of the most perceptive and thorough of all the newsmen who cover the Pentagon,
has reported: "While no military publicity men are assigned strictly
to backing up comic strips, many often spent a lot of their working
hours doing just that. For the services, the 'right' comic strip can do
double duty as an animated recruiting poster and as a vivid support
for budget requests." The right comic strips for the Air Force are
Steve Canyon and *Terry and the Pirates*; for the Navy, *Buz Sawyer*
and *Thorn McBride*. The Army isn't blessed with any.

Milton Caniff, supplied faithfully with Air Force information,
returns the favor by using his hero, *Steve Canyon*, to fight for Air
Force programs. Any Air Force propaganda mouthed by *Steve Canyon* reaches Americans through 625 newspapers. When the Eisen-

hower administration cut back the B-70 program, a Caniff strip read one day:

Steve: Captain, what happened to the BX-71?
Captain: Oh, nothing went wrong with the vehicle itself, Col. Canyon. But I'm afraid your job has been "reoriented." The money boys bailed the bird out from under you. The BX-71 program has been cut back to save money. Your hardware returns to the shelf. I—I'm truly sorry, old man.
Steve: I guess it won't really matter! If the Russians send a few Roman Candles at us some cloudy night . . . we'll make a formal protest in the U.N. the next day—if we can only find the pieces of the building.

Caniff told Kraar that no pressure was applied or needed for him to do his BX-71 strip. "I just knew how important the B-70 program was and that they were fighting to produce it," he said.

George Wunder, who draws *Terry and the Pirates,* has gone even further than this for the Air Force. When the Air Force was feuding with Sen. Margaret Chase Smith (R., Me.), mainly because of her refusal to approve the public relations gimmick of promoting actor Jimmy Stewart to a general in the reserve, Wunder introduced a new character to his strip. She was "Congresswoman Dolores Deepsix," a notorious, penny-pinching, hardened legislator who spent a good deal of her time harassing the Air Force and obstructing some of its most vital programs. The Dolores Deepsix episode was a part of a well-coordinated campaign against Mrs. Smith, which also included anti-Smith comment by a radio commentator and a syndicated columnist. "Unavoidably, Terry's adventures are propaganda for air power and preparedness," Wunder told Kraar, "but these are things I believe in strongly."

Several years ago, the Navy almost lost *Buz Sawyer,* when its artist, Roy Crane, grew tired of sea adventures and decided to take his hero into the life of a private citizen. The fearful Navy publicity men launched a massive campaign, Kraar relates, and persuaded seamen throughout the country to write Crane and tell him how much *Buz Sawyer* meant to them. In addition, the Navy invited Crane to a tour of the Pacific fleet. Crane changed his mind and kept Sawyer in the Navy. Since then, the Navy has been busy supplying him with enough dramatic material to make sure that he doesn't tire of naval life any more. Recently, Kraar points out, Crane had the run of an anti-submarine warfare ship for two weeks. The result was an anti-submarine warfare episode in his strip that coincided with a successful Navy campaign to win more funds for anti-submarine warfare.

Last year a second comic strip emerged to help fight the Navy's battles at sea and in the public arena. The Copley Newspapers started distributing *Thorn McBride,* the story of the commander of an atomic submarine. The Navy League rewarded James S. Copley, chairman of the Copley Newspapers, for this and other favors by presenting him with the Rear Admiral William S. Parsons Award for Inspirational Civilian Leadership.

On the second floor of the Pentagon, facing the Potomac River, a long, rectangular room is filled every day with two dozen men, of varying skills and intelligence, who make up the single most important target of the military public relations establishment. The room is the Pentagon press room, and the men are the few American newsmen who spend all their working time covering military news. They represent the Associated Press, United Press International, *The New York Times,* the New York *Herald Tribune, The Washington Post,* the *Washington Star, The Wall Street Journal,* the Chicago *Tribune,* the Cleveland *Plain Dealer, Time, Newsweek* and a few other newspapers and trade magazines. Although other newsmen nose around the Pentagon from time to time and often come up with an incisive story or two, these two dozen in the news room, by and large, form the image of the military that reaches the American people through the press.

The Pentagon publicity men, who work across the hall, must court these newsmen, answer their questions, direct them to sources of news and, hopefully, instill a military point of view in their stories. One of the best ways to fulfill all these goals at once is to take the newsmen on a "junket." From time to time, with the military paying expenses, a newsman will find himself the guest of the Navy on a cruise of a nuclear submarine, or of the Army on maneuvers of the new anti-guerrilla warfare units, or of the Air Force on the flight of a B-52. For a newsman, these junkets can be invaluable. He has no other way to see the equipment and skills that he writes about every day in the Pentagon press room. At the same time, he may find it difficult to break through the cords of publicity men around him to get a meaningful look at all that is displayed. And, when he returns, he may find it difficult to write anything that might displease his kind military hosts. It takes a perceptive, hard-minded newsman to come through a junket without some bias in favor of his hosts.

In recent years, newsmen throughout the country have received free transportation to visit military installations all over the world. "It may surprise you to learn," Sylvester wrote an editor recently, "that there are cases of editors and newsmen who annually turn up in the spring with requests for government transportation to Europe —including Paris—on the basis of doing stories about our overseas installations. For many years the aviation writers of the U.S. have been carried on government planes to their national convention. . . . There have been many instances of large news-gathering organizations requesting transportation not only for one but two men to various places in the world where, if their news interest is legitimate, they can go by commercial transportation." Sylvester has revived an old directive which prohibits free transportation except under exceptional circumstances.

In summing up defense reporting, Joseph Alsop has said: "The tendency is to take government handouts. This is a very bad thing to do in the area of defense—more than in any other. In this area, government handouts are always and persistently mendacious. All government handouts lie; some lie more than others, I'm certain." The Pentagon's Office of News Services prepares 1,500 handouts a year, whipping them to the newsroom across the hall. Most of these handouts describe new weapons or announce new contracts or describe some upcoming events, and most newsmen in the press room deny that they depend on them. The AP and the UPI may use the handouts to send small stories on their regional teletype-writer circuits for newspapers interested in a particular contract. The trade magazines also use many of the handouts, for their readers in the defense industries want to know about contracts. But the military reporters like to get their stories by talking to people, not by reading handouts.

For some reporters, particularly those representing influential newspapers, the handout often is replaced as a source of news by something far more interesting and complicated—the "news leak," the
name for an exclusive story that comes from a source who can not
be identified.

Because of the news leak, Washington newsmen have found themselves in some lively debate since the inauguration of Kennedy—a
debate that obscures more than it clarifies. The President and his
Secretary of Defense periodically have denounced breaches of security or speculative news stories that, in the view of Kennedy and
McNamara, aid the enemy. As a result, many news columns have
been filled with arguments about security and secrecy and the conflict between national defense and freedom of the press, all ignoring,
in the main, the real irritant and the real problem.

> We have an obligation, a responsibility, to the press and to the public
> to keep them informed on the activities of the Department [McNamara
> told the Senate Armed Services Committee on April 5, 1961]. At the
> same time, we certainly have a responsibility to withhold information
> that would be of great value to our potential enemies. . . . Why should
> we tell Russia that the ZEUS development may not be satisfactory?
> What we ought to be saying it that we have the most perfect anti-ICBM
> system that the human mind will ever devise. Instead, the public domain
> is already full of statements that the ZEUS may not be satisfactory, that
> it has deficiencies. . . . I think it is absurd to release that kind of informa-
> tion for the public.

McNamara's point of view has been roundly denounced by the
press, particularly since it implies that the Secretary wants newspapers not only to refrain from printing information harmful to his
department, but to fill their columns with lies that delude the public
as well as the Russians. In 1958, Joseph and Stewart Alsop, in their
book *The Reporter's Trade*, dealt with arguments similar to that of
McNamara, and their point of view probably reflects the views of
most newsmen in Washington today:

> We have always believed that the American people have an absolute,
> unqualified right to know exactly where they stand at all times. We

have further believed that it is the reporter's highest function to add, if he can, to the American people's knowledge of where they stand. . . . We are further convinced that 99/100s of the American government's secrecy has no other purpose but official convenience.*

Unfortunately, sound arguments like these are wasted now, for much of the current hubbub over secrecy and security is unreal. While Kennedy and McNamara are jumping at newspapers for printing secrets, they really are angry at military leaders for leaking stories. An examination of two incidents that irked the President uncovers the heart of the controversy.

On February 27, 1961, Pentagon newsman Richard Fryklund and State Department newsman Earl H. Voss reported in the *Washington Star* that Secretary of State Dean Rusk had sent a memorandum to the Pentagon advocating a policy that "would sharply restrict the role of nuclear weapons in diplomacy and war." According to Fryklund and Voss, Rusk suggested that "even massive attacks on Europe should be met with conventional weapons." The two reporters had not seen the memorandum, but Air Force officers had given them a summary. The summary actually was a distortion of Rusk's view, which was that the United States must strengthen conventional forces while maintaining nuclear power. The officers had leaked a distorted version in hopes of discouraging the government and public from accepting Rusk's actual views, if he ever advanced them publicly.

This neat dodge gave Fryklund and Voss an exclusive story, the public a false picture of Rusk's views, and the Russians very little. Kennedy ordered an investigation, and the officers suspected of giving the story to the reporters were transferred from the Pentagon.

On July 3, 1961, *Newsweek* published an accurate summary of a plan developed by the Joint Chiefs of Staff to meet the Berlin crisis. The plan included several steps designed to show Russia that the United States would not yield an inch on Berlin: a limited emergency would be called, the draft would be increased, there would be some demonstration of American intent to use nuclear weapons if necessary. Publication in *Newsweek* angered Kennedy, for the plan ap-

* New York: Reynal & Co., Inc.

peared in the magazine before it reached the President's desk. It clearly had been leaked to the magazine by some Pentagon officials to force Kennedy into accepting it—if Kennedy ignored the advice, the public and Congress now would know that the Joint Chiefs of Staff, our top military minds, had advocated a military course that our civilian President had refused to follow.

In an unprecedented move, Kennedy ordered the FBI to investigate the *Newsweek* story and determine who had given it to the magazine. This investigation, still uncompleted, has humiliated the Pentagon and, perhaps, convinced other military men to forget the news leak and find some other publicity device to mold opinion.

The unleashing of the FBI, and several of the McNamara directives mentioned in this survey, make clear that Kennedy is making an attempt to keep the Pentagon and its massive public relations establishment in line. "Our arms must be subject to ultimate civilian control and command at all times, in war as well as peace," Kennedy said on March 28, 1961 in a message to Congress.

The evidence so far indicates that Kennedy's civilian leaders are not afraid to issue orders to the military. But the methods of Kennedy and his administrators are more often oblique than direct. Using the tricks of power learned in Congress, Kennedy does not lash out at military publicity men, but whittles away at their sources of power. As a result, while Pentagon publicity men may be afraid these days to go too far, they do not always realize it is undemocratic to do so.

No one can expect the military to disband all its public relations programs. In the realities of Washington politics, every agency needs to create an image of itself that will draw funds from Congress. Otherwise even the most needed projects will wither for lack of money.

But the military publicity men, while doing their job of smoothing relations between the Department of Defense and Congress and the public, must be curbed far more than they have been by the Kennedy Administration. The dangers are real. According to UPI, the memorandum on right-wing military propaganda prepared for Senator Fulbright and sent to McNamara warned that while the parallel may seem farfetched, the revolt of the French generals in Algeria is "an example of the ultimate danger." The publicity men of the Pentagon are busy molding the thoughts of America to fit a military pattern. If the generals and admirals ever capture all public opinion, they would need nothing as crude as another "Algerian coup" to control America.

THE SAN DIEGO STORY

by Wesley Marx

CALIFORNIA'S RISE to the top of the state population standings has been cheered on by several mass magazines who idolize the new demographic champ as a "look at the future." A look, even a slight glance, at one particular city in California shows that the future is not entirely rosy. Faced with the most critical unemployment problem west of the Mississippi River, San Diego is a defense widow who can't even take care of her own. The city's plight, and California's growing worry over providing, state-wide, a quarter of a million new jobs a year, revolve around the fact that the federal government contributes to a problem it is supposed to alleviate—unemployment.

San Diego is the modern version of a company town. More than one major manufacturer exists in San Diego, but there is only one main financier and customer—the Defense Department. Before the fickle-hearted Big Spender from Washington arrived on the scene, this city marketed its natural resources—a handsome seascape and a sunny clime—as a tourist and retirement center. In 1920, the city fathers began looking for something beyond tourism to swell the municipal coffers. They found what they wanted in the U.S. Navy, which much admired the city's strategic harbor. After the city fathers had offered some shoreline gratis, the Navy established a training center. Today, twenty-one Navy and Marine installations account for San Diego's second largest source of income.

The primary source, the defense business, came in 1933 when Consolidated Vultee Aircraft Company was lured from Buffalo by the traditional offer of a bargain lease on civic land. Consolidated evolved into the Convair Division of General Dynamics, which is now the leading manufacturer in a city where, until recently, manufacturing was the number one industry in point of employment and two out of three workers were in aerospace plants.

Because the city's economic destiny now rests in the hands of Washington, San Diego's attitude toward federal spending has become ambivalent. Briefly, increased federal spending and activity is okay as long as these are in the interests of national defense. Other forms of federal expenditures are often regarded as threats to national defense. Accordingly, the Copley Press—owner of the only two newspapers in San Diego—editorializes: "The only logical way to meet the defensive drain on the U.S. Treasury is to abstain from many of the domestic frills Kennedy would provide."

San Diego's Representative in Congress, Robert Wilson (R.), thinks the same way. Trumpets one San Diego *Union* headline, "Non-Military Expenditures Threat to U.S., Wilson Says." The "threats" are measures designed to give the federal government a more constructive and responsible role commensurate with the government's increased impact on the economy through its $50 billion defense budgets. Wilson has voted against federal aid for retraining workers, the depressed-areas bill and the accelerated public-works bill. But Wilson is always interested in counseling the Department of Defense, i.e., warning it against "shutting down the assembly lines on the world's fastest jet interceptor"—which happened to be Convair's F-106.

The Copley-Wilson brand of defense prosperity flourished in San Diego in the 1950s. Spurred by an economy 70 per cent defense-oriented, the community proclaimed itself the nation's fastest-growing city in the last decade (population: 1950, 334,387; 1960, 573,224). For more class, the city created an Industrial Development Commission to diversify the industrial base with the usual lures. Some 500 acres of civic land would be developed into a research and industrial park and offered at bargain prices to attract outside industry. The Chamber of Commerce portrayed San Diego as a City in Motion, which Thinks BIG (Build Industrial Growth). The Traveling Industrial Drummers spread the civic gospel, "San Diego Has It," throughout the land.

In June of 1960, in the midst of this business evangelism, San Diego became a critical labor-surplus area as aircraft production lines began phasing-out in favor of more automated electronic and missile work. Convair, attempting to prolong its military aircraft capability in the commercial jet field, made public its failure in May of 1961 by laying off workers. Layoffs in San Diego jumped to around 1,200 a month as Convair's work force dwindled from 22,000 to 6,000.

With unemployment over the 8 per cent level (29,000 jobless), the city earnestly reviewed its diversification efforts. In a brochure entitled "Highlights of the 1961 Build Industrial Growth Program," the Chamber of Commerce announced that new industries had added a total of 343 jobs to the work force—about equal to one busy week of layoffs at Convair. Realtors grumbled about City Hall competition as the civic industrial park attracted more San Diego-based companies than outside firms. Retraining offered little relief. "To qualify for retraining, the worker has to find a skill needed in San Diego," explained a local official of the State Department of Employment. "San Diego just doesn't offer a market for a wide variety of skills." Commented Frederick Ryan, Professor of Economics at San Diego State College, in *Frontier*: ". . . the 'Think Big' Scheme is nothing more or less than the expression of a wish that sucker money will appear on the scene. It also has a side effect of possibly convincing some of the citizens that an effort is being made to meet the problem of unemployment realistically."

With its illusions of industrial grandeur collapsing, the city turned again to the source of its economic livelihood—the Department of Defense. A Convair employee wrote a parody of *Roll Out the Barrel* —"Now's the time to roll out the contracts/For the gang's all here!" Aerospace workers telegraphed President Kennedy, urging more defense contracts. "We based our request on competence, not on unemployment," explains John Collins, president of the Machinists' local.

The city was now caught in a trap partly of its own making. In Congress, each state vies to get "its fair share" of the $50 billion defense budget. The "haves" always fight to keep contracts from going to the "have nots," whose pleas for relief are derided as "political." California officials, today assailed by the East for the westward flow of defense contracts, can't afford to use the techniques it has attacked other states for using. Wilson favors the formation of a San Diego "defense lobby" in Washington, perhaps headed by a retired flag officer, which "could help bird-dog government contracts." Meanwhile, San Diego's defense recesssion deepens. Manufacturing employment has retrogressed to six-year-old levels and total employment, responding more quickly now to the over-all results of the cutbacks, is slipping fast to two-year-old levels. *Time* magazine recently introduced San Diego to the nation as "Bust Town," where retail sales are dropping, office and rental space is overbuilt and the influx of new residents is down. Harboring an unemployed labor force that receives up to $2 million monthly in unemployment benefits merely creates further frustration for the city. One councilman, Allen Hitch, unsuccessfully advocated shipping unemployed men and their families to a surplus Marine camp so they could be fed and housed more cheaply, according to *San Diego Magazine.* The State Department of Employment attributes the major brake to a higher unemployment rate (presently fluctuating between 7 and 8 per cent) to "a continuing out-migration of workers from the area"—a serious drawback to a city which wants to Think BIG. The only major category of employment which has shown important gains is government (primarily Navy civilian work); today it is the city's largest single source of employment—and ties San Diego's economic destiny even more closely to the Defense Department.

Brightest hope for the city is not a fat defense contract or an outside firm thinking BIG, but a form of federal spending which San Diego's Congressional representative vigorously opposes. The city is planning a $15 million program of civic improvements, with half the funds coming from the federal government under the accelerated Public Works Program (a Kennedy measure Wilson voted against). San Diego qualifies for the aid under the guide lines set by the Area Redevelopment Agency (another federal agency Wilson unsuccessfully opposed). The agency says San Diego qualifies as one of the four major "recessed" industrial areas in the nation. (Toledo, Buffalo and Philadelphia are the others.) Besides unemployment, the civic projects will combat other detrimental legacies of the defense industry. In *Land Economics,* Professor Ryan listed such legacies as polluted air and water; loss of seaside developments and planned recreational areas; destruction of beauty spots by bulldozers engaged in flattening the land for subdivisions; and an increase in noise, dirt and trash. In the defense boom of the Fifties, the city resisted tax increases for civic improvements because the business community said a low tax rate would attract diversified industry (which never came). The public-works program will help correct such neglect. San Diego is also vigorously expanding its port facilities to service civilian as well as military traffic.

San Diego's mistakes, at most, boil down to lack of farsighted realism which, at best, could only hope to soften, not solve, the effects of mass defense layoffs. In an economy ultimately controlled by Washington, local enterprise has its limits. "We just can't handle these layoffs by ourselves," says Pat Branin, administrative assistant to Mayor Charles Dail. As Al Hayes, president of the International Association of Machinists, said in a visit to San Diego this March, "The government is the primary investor and major consumer in the aerospace industry, but it subsidizes everything except the welfare of the work force." Planning for the welfare of aerospace workers and the communities they work in just does not match the planning or priority accorded to weapons systems.

When the major alternative to defense cutbacks is defense recessions such as in San Diego, no economy—nor the people in that economy—can be called truly free. The United States cannot afford the luxury of postponing plans for defense cutbacks until the uncertain eventuality of disarmament. But the federal government can take steps to avoid forsaking its defense widows. San Diego's accelerated public-works program demonstrates how the federal government can take a constructive and responsible role in an economy which must respond more and more to the demands of $50 billion defense budgets. Utilizing present work forces and facilities, rather than creating new defense complexes and a migratory defense work force, might prove more beneficial, both in an economic and social sense. As Atlas missile workers in San Diego face layoffs, the government is financing a new missile plant in New Orleans, including worker recruitment and training.

San Diego's dependence on a public economy is duplicated in California itself, where a recent study by Pomona College says 30 per cent of the state's gainful employment is now related directly or indirectly to defense spending. A reduction of 30 per cent in military spending in Hawaii would be "disastrous," according to an economic report by Dr. Richard Ratcliff of the University of Wisconsin. In a democratic society, government has a responsibility to fit such an economic factor into the nation's life without the undue social dislocations and hardships occurring in San Diego. President Kennedy stated this in principle when he addressed Congress on his new trade policy: "Just as the federal government has assisted in personal adjustments made necessary by military service . . . so there is an obligation to render assistance to those who suffer as a result of national trade policy." As long as the nation fails to recognize that national security in the cold-war era involves workers as well as weapons, the federal government will continue to forsake defense widows who can't take care of their own.

ADVERTISING DOOMSDAY

by Eugene S. Schwartz

PAGING THROUGH America's papers and magazines, one's eyes are arrested by a profusion of imaginative and colorful advertisements based upon the theme of the missile and space age. These are the advertisements of the military-industrial complex that is nurtured by a cold war that doesn't thaw, an arms race that spirals ever upward, and by a military policy that is based upon the search for an absolute deterrent that is second to none.

Dwight D. Eisenhower, in his farewell address, called the attention of the nation to the "conjunction of an immense military establishment and a large arms industry." While recognizing the need for this development, he warned that "we must not fail to comprehend its grave implications . . . we must guard against the acquisition of unwarranted influence. . . ." At his final Presidential news conference, he lashed out at the spate of advertisements which convey the impression to the world that the munitions business is the main occupation of this country. They were, he said, part of the activities of a "defense lobby" which insists that one or another weapons system is vital to national security.

The kaleidoscopic collages of the defense lobby serve several purposes. First of all, they assure the American public that it couldn't get a better bargain for the more than $40 billion annually it spends on defense—a bargain based upon reliable, fool-proof, creative, scientific achievements. Every company trumpets its patriotic fervor and its creative talent in contributing to the arms race. The larger cor-

39

porations have a larger share in responsibility and creativeness (ten giant corporations in 1959 held 36.8 per cent of the $22 billion in military prime contracts, 25 corporations held 53 per cent, and 100 held 73.2 per cent). Their advertisements are more gaudy, more prolific, more insistent. But the smaller fry, in a-house-that-Jack-built manner, also make their claim to consuming a portion of the defense dollar. The corporation that makes the fastener that fastens the components in a device controlled by a feedback mechanism responding to transducers employing sensors that make a guidance system that steers a missile that is aimed by a mechanical brain, proclaims the role of its fastener in this patriotic and creative undertaking.

Having thus informed the reader of their role in absorbing the defense dollar, the companies proceed to their second purpose—to proclaim and propagate the "strategy of peace through strength." The rationale for this theme is found in an ad by Microdot, a connector manufacturer, that displays a sinister picture of Lenin declaiming, "We have never rejected terror on principle." Beneath the picture there appears the caption: "The words are Lenin's. Remember them . . . particularly when your contribution to defense—to the potential terror of space age war—chafes at your principles. They help you know that what you do keeps fingers off buttons . . . that the real business of the defense business is survival." Whose survival, the company's or mankind's, is not clear. The attrition among the small defense companies and the absorption of others by those who are buying up the glamour arms industries suggest that patriotism by itself does not insure business survival.

While seeking to influence national policy through ads, the companies at the same time extol the virtues of their particular weapons systems. As if to corroborate the former President's criticism, Space Technology Laboratories, systems manager for the Atlas ICBM, proudly proclaimed that with the successful development of its product "the world became aware that the United States had brought into being a formidable retaliatory power for peace." Upon the successful firing of the solid-fueled Minuteman, the Thiokol Chemical Corporation promptly took a half-page ad in the daily press to announce "reliable power for peace at reasonable price . . . the nation's power to restrain war is moving up while anticipated costs come down." The consumer's demand for better products at lower prices and the benefits of a competitive economy are thus brought to the public and are well appreciated, at least in the business community, as indicated by the rise in value of armament stocks following a successful launching.

In their attempts at realism, the advertisers inadvertently reveal glimpses of the war their weapons are intended to prevent, and thereby introduce a terror of their own. Consider, for example, the historical account of a fifteenth-century missile, depicted by the Raytheon Missile System Division: "Flames swept across the open plains as the Mongol hordes ran in terror from the 'arrows of flying fire.' When the smoke had cleared the Chinese had won the battle of Pienking with the first rocket." Modern rockets, the ad states, "have become greatly more sophisticated" than the fifteenth-century bamboo rods and their company is "making significant contributions to the art of missilry."

This is what is disturbing about peace through strength—this and the split-second timing required to maintain the peace. "Response to attack must be immediate," we are warned by General Dynamics. "Minutes only will be available," announces International Telephone and Telegraph, while survival time is further shortened by a Sylvania ad which refers to "Destiny—and the ticking seconds." The push-button warfare necessitated by response measured in seconds is made possible by what ITT has called a "one-second minute for SAC." The SAC Control System is tested in "the imitation real thing," a full-page ad with this realistic text describing a simulated raid:

The first warning alerted posts all over the United States and Canada. Unidentified airborne objects seemed to be approaching at supersonic speeds from many directions. Simultaneously in control centers throughout North America men and machines dealt with torrents of data. Watching blips on radar scopes, crews made decisions which ordered weapons to destroy the attackers. . . . But no rockets were fired. No bombs fell. The blips came from magnetic tapes made by a single high-speed computer. In planning it, System Development Corporation made four billion calculations and six and one-third miles of magnetic tape. To train managers in decision making, to exercise decision under realistic stress, to avoid costly errors in actual operations*—these are some of the purposes of . . . pioneeering work in systems research and development.

One recalls the "terror from the arrows of 'flying fire' " and wonders what would happen if a single critical calculation in the "real thing" went wrong because a speck of dust lodged on the tape. One fervently hopes that we may "keep fingers off buttons"; and one searches the ads avidly for a hint as to what happens to the millions of Americans while the "enemy hordes" are consumed by our armed might. But both science and Madison Avenue are mute on this matter. Is it a muteness of secrecy or a muteness of inability to tell the American people that only a few ticking seconds stand between them and destiny—a destiny which will pass from the probable to the inevitable as the theory of deterrence is pushed to its ultimate of total annihilation in infinitesimal time?

The third role of the advertisements is to extol the scientific prowess of the military-industrial complex. Sometimes the advertisements cancel each other out.

Thus Lockheed, the systems manager of the Polaris missile, proclaims in a two-page ad: "Today it's a Polaris world," and quotes President Eisenhower's characterization of the weapon as a "revolutionary and practically invulnerable ballistic missile system." But Hughes Aircraft Company belittles the idea of the "ultimate weapon": "The ICBM is often called the 'ultimate weapon.' Yet, throughout history, there have been many so-called ultimate weapons.

* The following news item is quoted from the *Manchester Guardian Weekly* of Dec. 1, 1960: "The early warning radar station at Thule picked up signals which were analyzed by the computers there as a flight of missiles coming up over the horizon from Russia and heading in the direction of America. The famous red telephone rang at Strategic Air Command Headquarters. All over the world SAC crews stood to their planes. Someone signalled Thule for confirmation. There was no answer—Thule must have been hit already. What restrained Free-World from launching its retaliation weapons during the next half-hour I do not know unless it was those old fashioned deterrents, incredulity and funk. Whatever it was, it came in handy, for it turned out that Thule had picked up not a squadron of rockets, but a large earth-satellite of whose existence Intelligence had apparently failed to inform them, called the moon. By the time they had discovered this little error, however, they were prevented from passing the correction on because an iceberg had cut their submarine cable link."

Men of science have always found a defense." While Collins Electronics describes the operation of Polaris: "Concealed by ocean depths, these ever-moving missile bases cannot be accounted for by an enemy planning a surprise attack," another vista-colored ad by Sperry Gyroscope Division informs the reader that "a radical new Passive Underwater System apprehends submarine craft almost intuitively . . . with uncanny accuracy. . . ."

Besides a bag of tricks by which missiles can "fox enemy radars" and fly in evasive patterns, we are assured by Eastern Industries, a manufacturer of pressurized dehydrated systems, that an "anti-missile missile radar is kept on the alert" and Sylvania Electronics proudly proclaims that its leadership in electronic warfare is "typified by its advances in countermeasures and counter-countermeasures against all known types of electromagnetic radiation."

And that's the way of science as predicted in the ads. We build a missile-launching submarine that "cannot be accounted for" and at the same time devise a system that "apprehends submarine craft almost intuitively" and develop anti-submarine weapons "that deliver an unerringly destructive missile." Oh, may the Russians and Chinese and all our potential enemies be not as brilliant and creative as our engineers, for if their missiles are as invulnerable as ours and as hard to detect and as full of tricks, then their ads (if they have them) surely portray the "American hordes" in mortal fear before their ultimate weapons! And if their creative genius has created an anti- for all our weapons, then surely, our weapons are not absolute! And what is *vice* is *versa.*

It is this element of weapon and anti-weapon and anti-anti-weapon, etc., that makes an arms race so challenging—and so long lived. As we stand on the "threshold of the future," an imposing ad from General Electric suggests: ". . . Future generation missiles, satellites and deep space probes will require refined or entirely new detection techniques, including many that have not yet been conceived."

We now turn to another major objective of the defense-industry advertisements—recruitment. The hiring and maintenance of scientists and engineers is a problem almost as great as the development of a weapons system itself. It is a problem which transforms the meetings of learned professional societies into adventures in piracy in which the lure is not only money and careers and prestige; it is climate, leisure and culture.

"Scientists and engineers," a technical personnel recruiting agency declaims, "California offers you and your family: A world center of the electronic industry for CAREER ADVANCEMENT, the High Sierra and the Pacific Ocean for RECREATION . . . Major CULTURAL CENTERS. . . ." "Why did I move to Martin-Orlando?", another ad asks. "My wife, the kids love Florida . . . the climate, the ocean, country living. We have everything we need." "Go Middle West . . . for a prime opportunity in missiles!" says Bendix Mishawaka Division, outlining a cornucopia of delights.

In the frantic bidding and pirating for talent, promising talent from all over the world is drawn to America's military workshop. But note this plaintive appeal: "Canadians come home. Salaries are not always equal to the highest. The weather can be miserably uncomfortable. But there are interesting and challenging jobs in companies whose future is geared to the country." Surely, patriotism is the last resort of the desperate.

If a legitimate case can be made for the military-industrial complex, it should be one which simply states: here is an unpleasant task to be done. We don't like it, but it has been forced upon us. We look forward to the day when science may be restored to its pursuit of knowledge to serve mankind, not to destroy it. But in the last fifteen years a whole generation of what the National Cash Register Company aptly calls the "military-oriented scientists and engineers" have become soldiers without uniform, going from the classrooms of their universities directly into military work. A new professional elite has been created in "enlightened prestige organizations" which "offer career opportunities in every area of weapon support equipment and systems management," a "scientific quest . . . as a creative challenge." In a paean of self-glorification, Lockheed states that in its activities men of outstanding talent "find inventive and creative freedom. Here they find a sense of being . . . of accomplishing."

In the "excitement of a pioneering venture," careers are founded on a technology of destruction, and though we grant them the sincerity and integrity of hoping the buttons they are creating will never have to unleash the weapons they are building, their legacy to civilization is one of fear and terror. The military-industrial complex is the crowning epitome of a science dedicated to total war and a generation of scientists whose life work is based upon a technology for genocide.

Those who pay for the arms, as well as the ads that extol the arms, the American public, are told by a missile manufacturer: "Set your sites anywhere." Nothing is out of reach, we are told, and by a process of "scientific fallout," instead of strontium-90 and carbon-14, there will come out of the achievements by government and industry "better living by everybody."

Unless the "sites" are focused on Isaiah's prophecy, "They shall beat their swords into plowshares," the stimulating, challenging and creative efforts of the arms industry will lead instead to Isaiah's warning:

We have made a covenant with death,
and with hell are we at agreement.

The policy of armed strength may make good advertising copy and substantial profits, but it does not lead to peace. The past fifteen years of armed truce do not attest to the success of the policy, but only to the fact it has not yet failed. War today is a deadly game in which mutual suicide awaits all players and the "covenant with death" leads unerringly to what one advertiser inadvertently called the "brief new world."

COMMUNITY SHELTERS:
THE BAIT AND THE TRAP

by Roger Hagan

In January, 1962, the House Appropriations Committee unexpectedly transferred jurisdiction over the funding of the Administration's $700 million civil-defense program from the Defense Appropriations subcommittee, chaired by Rep. George H. Mahon (D., Texas), back to the Independent Offices Appropriations subcommittee, headed by Rep. Albert Thomas (D., Texas). Mr. Mahon's cooperative attitude had induced the Administration, last summer, to give the Pentagon primary responsibility for civil defense; the expectation was that CD funds would then go through as part of the regularly undisturbed defense budget—as, indeed, they did a few months ago, when $207,600,000 was approved for civil defense without any cuts. Now, however, the matter has been returned to Mr. Thomas, who is known to be critical of civil-defense spending (in past years he has cut requests for CD funds by as much as 75 per cent). Thus this decision, made primarily by Rep. Clarence Cannon (D., Mo.), Chairman of the Appropriations Committee, is seen as a blow to the Administration program. CD officials are nervous; CD buffs in Congress have promised to fight Cannon's decision all the way up to the Speaker if necessary. To make matters more ominous, Rep. Chet Holifield (D., Calif.) will be battering away at the program from the other side, charging not that it is wastefully large but that it is woefully inadequate.

Under this kind of crossfire, the bill seems less a shoo-in than it did in December. Holifield's criticism was expected, but Cannon's decision was not.

Yet if the Administration did not actually engineer Cannon's decision (and there is no evidence that it did), it should have. For civil defense is like Frankenstein's monster: once we put the juice of life into it, it will stagger through the community, leaving havoc in its wake. The Administration seems to sense this: the President has pulled away from his CD position of last summer and fall, dropping the family-shelter program and allowing only a minimum of follow-through in the emasculated "Fallout Protection" and "Family Shelter Designs" booklets. Recently there has been very little talk of civil defense by anyone in the Administration, and what little there was has been devoted to flat denials that it is a weapon in the cold war or a component in any weapons system, and to affirm that it has no value in enforcing our will on any enemy. The Administration is undoubtedly touchy about the charge that civil defense is meant to make the use of nuclear weaponry more credible, and the word has gone out to deny it. The word, however, has not reached Rep. Holifield, who is still insisting that civil defense is part of our deterrence mechanism.

Two interpretations of the Administration's delicacy with CD seem likely. One is that it wants to sugarcoat an essentially cynical and manipulative program. The second, made more likely by the decision to put CD funds into the hands of the doubting Mr. Thomas, is that Kennedy now recognizes that he got involved in CD merely by reacting too precipitately to the political thunder of Rockefeller and by listening to the croonings of Chet Holifield, and is now trying to find a way to reverse the process he started. Since the easy way to do this would be to get the CD appropriation killed in a Congressional dicker, one might suppose that Mr. Cannon's decision was not such a blow to the Administration, after all.

This is an unlikely strategy, however; the Democrats would still get the blame. (If only the committee chairmen were Republicans!) Besides, however it happened, the rerouting of civil-defense funds doesn't mean there will be no funds. Too many powerful sectors of our political and economic structure are committed to civil defense by now. IBM is already offering its employees loans to build shelters at home, selling them materials at cost. McGraw-Hill, publishers of dozens of industrial and trade magazines, has made each of its publications carry a special supplement, "Nuclear Attack and Industrial Survival." (At least two of these magazines, *Nucleonics* and *Business Week*, have run editorials indicating that their editors are not entirely enthusiastic about the commitment implied by the supplement.) The Luce magazines have eaten as much crow as they can, and will certainly not back off any further. There is also, according to *Business Week*, a school of thought among some Presidential advisers that the program should be pushed when the economy needs a boost. Sooner or later, then, the money will come through.

Perhaps the most likely interpretation is the third: that the Administration is neither cynical nor engaged in sabotage, but is honestly convinced that CD offers sound "insurance" to the American people—and, at the same time, is unaware of the dynamism implicit in it.

Perhaps it sounds strange to speak of dynamism in civil defense when, to all appearances, the program has already slowed down somewhat. Why should the Administration fear for the future when it has been so widely reported that Americans have reverted to their traditional good sense—that is, to their usual salutary neglect—in this matter? The answer is simply that the worst is yet to come.

The program will start off benignly enough. The last photograph of a man standing gun in hand at his shelter door will have been run to death, the last ringing denunciation of this behavior will have been quoted from government official and clergyman. News of more commendable efforts will soon command our attention. The silliest holes in the program will be plugged. Conelrad stations will be given fallout protection, so that there will be some reason to hope that their personnel can remain on the job. Power plants, now vulnerable because of geographic concentration, will be given interconnecting lines and dispersing switchyards. Licensing procedures will be simplified so that surviving carriers will not have to get licenses from several agencies before transporting priority traffic. Generally the agencies concerned with human health and survival will catch up with the Federal Reserve Board, which had a plan for saving capitalism long before anybody knew how to save people. The counties which have no CD personnel or organization whatever (at present about half the nation's counties) will develop them, and CD personnel will be getting some training at improved federal CD schools. The counties with civil-defense plans based on evacuation (at this writing, most of them: "It's hard to shake them out of it," said one federal CD official) will be brought up to date. The NEAR warning system, with a buzzer in every home, may be sped to completion, although at present estimates we may be depending on our capricious sirens for the next three or four years.

For a few months, in other words, the news will be optimistic, the program grounded in hard work. It will look pretty good.

At the same time, however, something else will be happening. Under the proposed federal program, civil defense will become one of the costliest programs of the New Frontier, possibly involving the expenditure of more than a billion dollars over the next two years. Up to half of this will be used to beef up staffs, train personnel, help states build underground operations centers (fifteen states have begun such projects already), improve warning and communications facilities, hire contractors to survey cities for existing structures usable for shelters, and provide basic food and medical supplies for existing shelter space.

Thus 50 million persons are expected to be provided for. Read "provided for" as meaning five days' worth of wheat biscuit, two weeks' worth of water, and a floor space of 3 1/7 by 3 1/7 feet per individual, an area which the Civil Defense Director of San Francisco, Admiral A. G. Cook (U.S.N., Ret.), terms a "lenient" provision that could be reduced. Also, read "50 million" as really 30 million, since informed estimates propose that one and two-thirds spaces should be built for every person to compensate for uncertainties of location. But read 50 million as 100 million if you ask how many city people will try to cram into these existing-structure shelters if they are needed any time in the next year or two.

The other half-billion of CD funds will be used to spur towns, cities and public institutions (such as county hospitals) to build new shelters. The government would pay about 60 per cent of the costs; or to be more exact, the government will pay up to $25 per man-space, while the total cost per man-space is expected to be about

$40. The cost of the construction program over the next four years is expected to be $3.3 billion, of which $1.8 billion will be federal funds.

Obviously, the latter program throws the initiative to the local community; less obviously the former does, too. In both cases, this is where the trouble begins.

To start with what is already begun: some aspects of the existing-structure survey indicate that the real needs of a shelter program have not yet been faced up to. Once the engineers have decided that the basement of a building is suitable as a shelter, its owner will be invited to donate it for that purpose. But few businesses have empty basements; in most cases, converting the basement into a shelter will involve the owner in building or renting new space to store whatever material he had down there.

To reduce the inconvenience to the donor, however, the contract he will sign specifies that the shelter space shall be used only in emergencies. This means no practice drills, according to CD officials in Washington—a situation that places a rather heavy burden on the qualities of leadership which these officials hope to instill into local CD officials.

Clearly, the cold political realities of a shelter program have not been faced, and no one cares to be responsible for forcing the bitter pill down the commercial-industrial throat. Yet, as Donald Michael of the Peace Research Institute told a meeting of the American Psychological Association in September, 1961, "Any shelter program is only valuable if people are trained to use it under all likely circumstances. Who, then, will take the political responsibility to awaken people at 2 A.M. of a cold, sleeting January morning, to force them to leave their beds and practice taking shelter? . . . Then, too, it's expensive to close down a steel mill, yet if it isn't closed down and shelter-taking practiced, the whole civil-defense system becomes a sham. Who will pay business for the time lost?"

Presumably, some businesses and owners will be reluctant to let the CD men get their foot in the door. But refusals to cooperate may be possible only as long as the community is not paying much attention. The matching-funds part of the program, however, suggests that the community will be forced to pay increasing attention to the matter, and as it does, some unpleasant forms of community pressure may be brought to bear on the reluctant ones.

A sample of this recently came to light in a pamphlet issued by the Civilian Defense Organization of Nutley, New Jersey:

At present, the Civilian Defense Organization is the most obvious and most opportune instrument for recording each individual's committed stand on the question of appeasement or resistance to active, party-line Communism. It is highly important that each citizen participate actively in the Civilian Defense Organization, now. Every loyal, true American should stand at the side of his neighbor wearing an arm band of the Civilian Defense Corps, pledged to support and to uphold the Constitution and the principles upon which our defense rests. There can be no equivocation. Either you belong now—committed to your nation's defense—or you do not belong, and so stand uncommitted. Today, no commitment in this matter is an open invitation to party-line Communist penetration.

Such broadside techniques will presumably not be necessary with commercial organizations, which are much more sensitive than the political sleepwalkers of Nutley to subtle threats. But if the tone will be quieter, the method, and the effect on community atmosphere, will be the same.

The dynamism behind such developments lies in the matching-fund program. Under its stimulus, the ugly battle over the morality and the effectiveness of civil defense must be repeated in every community across the nation. In effect, the government is holding out a lot of money to local construction interests and suppliers, as well as community-function enthusiasts—money that can be got hold of by drumming up from local sources only half again as much. It is unlikely, then, that there will be any way to sweep the topic under the rug. Already a "Civil Defense Market Letter" has begun to appear, advising its subscribers (at $90 per year) how to get in on the ground floor: "Facilities of thousands of companies will be needed to meet the requirements of federal, state and local governments, business firms and individuals. Your company can be one of these firms."

In addition to the local interests, the industries concerned will undoubtedly undertake nation-wide programs to promote community action on shelters. Take, for example, the cement industry, already practiced in lobbying in state capitals for concrete highways. This year the industry has a surplus a million barrels greater than its hitherto unparalleled surplus at the end of 1960. Plants have begun to close because of swollen storage. The industry cannot be expected merely to sit back and wait: shelters can be encouraged everywhere.

The debate, then, will be ubiquitous within a year or so. And then the monster will begin to swing his arms. For debate on civil defense is educative. In each community there will be a faction that will say, in effect, "All right, we buy the insurance argument. So let's see what is needed to give the folks of Abilene the insurance that any government owes its people, as the President says." Unfortunately, and much to the consternation of the federal government, this faction will take the trouble really to find out, and then it will become on the local level what Rep. Holifield is on the national. For whatever one may think of Mr. Holifield's enthusiasm for deterrence and the mobilization of society in pursuit of same, the fact remains that he is closer to correct than anyone else in Washington about what "true insurance" would involve.

Let's go back to the debate in Abilene, Texas; or Wichita or Salina or Little Rock, or Utica, or Lincoln, or Plattsburgh, New York; or Altus, Oklahoma; or Tucson, or Denver, or Marysville, Calif.; or Portsmouth, New Hampshire. In these, as in several hundred other American communities which are the nearest town to an Air Force base or installation, it will shortly occur to people discussing community shelters that the presence of the ICBM complex several miles outside town may have some bearing on the question of what constitutes insurance. It will occur to some that even if one buys the Air Force theory of "counterforce war," in which citizens are not targets (a theory that includes the assumption that the Russians have also bought it), the amount of fallout likely to be produced locally when anywhere from three to thirty large megaton warheads are sent for each emplacement in the complex, will render fatally inadequate the protection factors—and the five-day food supply—of the projected shelters. (The Air Force estimates that if the enemy's missile has a CEP of three miles, he will have to launch fourteen 10-megaton warheads to be assured of knocking out a hardened missile, the number growing smaller as the accuracy increases or the megatonage grows.) In any case the area would experience ground bursts of hundreds of megatons, producing fallout levels from ten to hundreds of times greater than are the operational assumptions of the present CD program—and this not only for the immediate ten to twenty miles around the bases, but in some directions (depending on the wind), sixty miles and more away.

All of this means that for even a single base like Beale in Northern California, the site of only a few of the 234 Atlas and Titan and 600 (soon to be 1,800) Minuteman missiles, the citizens of not just Marysville but also of Yuba City, Olivehurst, Wheatland, Grass Valley, Nevada City, Emigrant Gap, Auburn, Placerville, Folsom, Roseville, Newcastle, Lincoln, Elk Grove, Ione, Davis, Dixon, Woodland, Esparto, Arbuckle, Colusa, Maxwell, Princeton, Willows, Williams, Knights Lodge, Butte City, Durham, Chico, Paradise, Feather Falls, La Porte, Downieville, Alleghany, Biggs, Gridley, and even Mr. Nixon's new frontier, Sacramento, will have cause to wonder just what "insurance" involves.

Worse yet, impertinent characters may inquire into just what "CEP three miles" means. It means that 50 per cent of the missiles fired can be expected to land within three miles of the target. Where, they may then ask, are the other seven or so missiles (per installation: there are eighteen installations around Tucson) expected to land? Oh, randomly outside the three-mile radius. After a bit of cogitation on this, the communities closest in may begin to scurry not for fallout shelters, but for deep blast shelters as Mr. Holifield has been telling them to. The difference will be that they won't be doing it to make our first strike more credible by making retaliation manifestly bearable, but for the perfectly respectable reason, espoused by the most cautious in the Administration at this moment, that they want some insurance against the most "likely" wartime eventuality according to the present theology: that the enemy will go after our striking force, not our cities.

There are other routes by which some will arrive at this same demand. After a moment's consideration of our new intelligence estimates of Soviet missile capabilities, or of the recent superbomb tests, or of the explicit statements of Khrushchev, it may be clear that Russia has neither the intention nor, more important, the *capability* of going after our hardened missile emplacements, which cost so much to destroy. She can only aim at our cities.

In short, we will witness, before long, an escalation of local demands. In most communities, the money to be invested in shelters is going to be raised only by hard sacrifice, and it stands to reason that people will insist that the money not be thrown away. Take, for instance, Norwalk, Conn., where some such escalation has already begun with the Heap Plan for shelters under every school. The proposed plan would bring all capital improvements under the town budget to a halt for three years; or, alternatively, raise the taxes on a modest home by $20 per year to pay off a twenty-year bond issue. In either case, it will probably put an end to expansion and improvement in schools, for, as a former City Councilman told *The New York Times,* "Norwalk for ten years has been in a constant fight to get enough money appropriated for the minimum of services—particularly education." And Norwalk's plan is again only for fallout shelters. As for the effects of blast or fire (the latter being the likely purpose of super-bombs), the money would be all but wasted.

A similar concern that shelters will mean no more classrooms was voiced by school superintendents throughout New York State after Governor Rockefeller announced, on Dec. 6, 1961, his "voluntary" school-shelter plan. The problem facing colleges is the same: as President Gideonse of Brooklyn College said, "It practically means a choice between plans for expansion for growing attendance over the next five years—or shelter plans."

Everywhere, as the pressure grows to get the insurance, spend the money, take advantage of the two-thirds matching plan (and, no doubt, bring new funds and business into economically stagnating communities), the demand will grow, too, that the money be spent *right.* People will gradually be sold on the Administration idea of insurance; but they will also be aware that the insurance isn't worth the premium if the fine print says (as the old insurance business joke has it) that the company will pay off only if the insured is struck down by a cement mixer in a cotton field.

The time will come, then, when a community will send representatives to Washington saying, "We want insurance. We don't know about the rest of the country, but we know that back in Utica insurance means blast shelters, and we want you to pay two-thirds of *that*." What will they get? I asked this question of a CD official in the Department of Defense, which will handle the funds. The answer was that the community would be turned down.

This will make the people back in Utica a bit edgy about the federal government, or at least about its present incumbents. The argument being pressed by some in Washington for making such refusal a matter of policy rather than a matter of refusing to pay more than $25 per space (blast shelters being tremendously more expensive), is that blast shelters are provocative, as indeed they are. But this may not impress the local communities. They want insurance. The more they learn, the edgier they will get. If they learn about the tidal wave a bomb in Long Island Sound will produce, they will wonder about the school-cellar fallout shelters in Norwalk and the $8.5 million it will take to build them. If they look into details like breakage of service lines at terminal points so that yards and streets are flooded and cellars fill up; or like the firestorms for which the larger bombs are designed; or like the several months they will have to spend in damp, crowded shelters even after they can go out for an occasional foray; or like the dope injections that will probably be used for disciplinary problems in group shelters (question: who will have the power to give the shots and to decide what constitutes a disciplinary problem?); or a thousand other things, they will be edgier yet about what is being advertised as insurance and who is doing the advertising. The great shelter debate is going to be much *too* educational.

Nor will political opportunism be absent. Everywhere opposition politicians will be tempted to make hay of the program's inadequacies and the Administration's refusal to support real insurance. This element alone of the shelter dynamic is enough to assure the escalation of local demands. Indeed, it has already been operative in the adoption by the Kennedy Administration of the Rockefeller program. Although this is a fairly mild political escalation, the fact that the President was thus forced to endorse a program for which he is notably unenthusiastic illustrates what is meant. Civil defense is a very vulnerable program, being, unlike military programs, highly visible. The Strategic Air Command may take hours to get its planes into the air, and no one will know it; but everybody can see any muddle in civil defense and make capital of it.

The position in which conservatives will be placed by the shelter program may also give the Administration pause. There are possibilities for vast increases of central power under the program which will make States' Righters and Republicans nervous. This can only aggravate a Congressional revolt against Executive authority that has already begun. In an analysis of the censorship battle entitled "Power in the Pentagon: Defense Secretary's Growing Authority is Called Factor in Clash with Congress," Hanson W. Baldwin wrote in *The New York Times* (Feb. 11, 1962):

> The long-term trend has been the tremendous expansion in size and power of the Executive branch. Moreover, changes in Defense Department organization and procedures of the last decade, particularly those made by Secretary McNamara, have tended toward greater centralization of power in the hands of the Secretary of Defense. The two trends have resulted in a reduction in Congressional power compared with Executive power. It has also led to a reduced capability on the part of Congress to supervise the Defense Department and the Armed Services. Some observers believe these trends are endangering the Constitutional authority of Congress 'to raise and support armies . . . to provide and maintain a navy . . . and to make rules for the government of the land and naval forces.'

What Baldwin did not say, however, was that in the long run the battle is not merely over who will control the military, but who will control Congress. The Pentagon already exercises power over Congress through its ability to allocate defense contracts to or away from companies which, in many areas, are the keystone of economic well-being. The vast majority of defense contracts are not assigned by competitive bidding, but by a judgment in the Administration as to who is best equipped to do some sensitive job. It should be easy, the conservatives may come to feel, for the Pentagon to find reasons for withholding contracts from industries that refuse to cooperate with

CD or from areas that endanger the program either by demanding too much or "volunteering" too little.

The situation grows doubly unpalatable to the conservative when, after the flood of shelter-construction-fund applications have reached Washington from cities, towns and institutions all over the country, he reflects on the power of the Administration to expedite or delay the grants for different areas. Especially in times of tension, Congressmen will be battling to get their area processed first. What happens, then when Albany gets shelters and Utica doesn't? What will it seem to mean? Does Albany have a better Congressman? "Is pork-barrelling affecting the lives of our children?"

The process inevitably bestows vast powers on the President and the Pentagon. But inasmuch as the Right is even more arms-minded than the President, it may not itself be able to oppose CD; its resentment and fear will have to find vent in general opposition-for-opposition's-sake, as well as in resistance to welfare programs which also necessarily entail a degree of centralizing.

What is worse, every international crisis, rather than unifying the President and Congress, will exacerbate their relations and multiply the problems each will face in easing the nation through.

The hardest thing to gauge about the shelter program, but ultimately the most important for the future of our political and social life, is the effect upon the individual citizen and his political attitudes. It is tempting to dismiss such effects as airy speculation, because the crisis does not seem great at the moment; but the quality and dynamism of the whole shelter enterprise are unprecedented to a degree that makes one hesitant to dismiss even the wildest speculations out of hand.

Even harder to ignore are the questions raised by several leading social scientists in a report issued by the Peace Research Institute. In a recent conference on which the report is based, psychologists, sociologists and public-opinion survey specialists expressed, among other things, a growing concern about the effects of a civil-defense program on the government-citizen nexus. Data already available indicate a widespread sense of crisis unlike anything noted by the researchers in the past twelve years. It also shows that people believe, not logically but "psychologically," that civil defense is incompatible with disarmament. (This may be one reason why, in spite of their sense of crisis, people have been reluctant to "vote" for civil defense. In a poll taken by the *San Francisco Chronicle*, only 5 per cent favored family shelters and only 19 per cent favored community shelters even if provided by the government.) The effect of a widespread public commitment to shelters might thus be to reduce what freedom to negotiate the leaders have by aggravating the good-bad imagery that accompanies a sense of crisis ("We can't negotiate with *them!*"). It will also further damage public perception of the cold war, reinforcing the focus upon the Soviet Union and upon nuclear solutions, distracting people from the actual complexities of the situation.

Of course, there are times when governments *want* to increase tension; but the danger, the conferees agreed, is that in the long run this limits the maneuverability of the very leaders who have brought on the peril, and contributes to the store of aggression among people whose sense of a "hostile enemy" has been played upon. The Administration may be reflecting on this pattern even now, as it tries to win approval for the U.N. bond issue, after itself having expressed pique at the neutralist countries following the Belgrade Conference. Such difficulties are a small taste of what may be encountered after a civil-defense mobilization.

Even more to the point than the factors described above is the serious question raised in the Peace Research Institute's report as to the effects on public attitudes toward government of learning too much, of the frustration that will follow the discovery that the hard-bought shelter is unlikely to provide security, and—most important —of the public's growing sense of being victimized by centralization and political deception. Already both clinical data and public behavior suggest a growing sense, among the citizens that they are being "used." The secrecy of the military is felt to be spreading. A civil-defense program is likely to increase the awareness of centralization and to clarify lines of authority in a way never known—perhaps fortunately for American social stability—in the past. Many will react to this with increased fear of deception—fear, it might be added, not totally based on neurotic fantasy. There is just enough real deception inherent in the program to provide what psychologists call "random reinforcement" of such fear.

Another contribution is made by what might be called the increasing obsolescence rate of the incredible: what was beyond belief yesterday is today rumored to be happening. Although this phenomenon begins in technology, it may end in politics.

Thus, as the military ethos of decision-from-the-top is imposed on civilian society, people will fight to keep their voice in decision-making, often in destructive and revengeful ways: they will probe for any weakness in the upper echelons and exaggerate it. The appearance of marchers, counter-marchers and other such outside-of-channels demonstrations, suggests trouble in the society; it shows that the normal routes of protest are felt to be closed. The next step may be short open clashes, sporadic resorts to violence. To one European observer, the situation is already reminiscent of Germany in the early 1930s. One need not assume that we would end the same way to find cause for concern. For the shelter dynamism aggravates these trends, reinforcing the citizens' fear of being helpless before governments which move remorsefully toward a war increasingly treated as "survivable" rather than "avertable."

While wondering about the problems of federal administration in a society losing faith in government, one might also question who will be ascendant in the local cadres. A particular kind of citizen will be drawn into the thick of community-shelter activity, to whom the aura of community discipline and "fitness" appeals. Those who feel guilty about the "soft" openness of American society will be most drawn to the patrician asceticism of such men as Governor Rocke- feller, who is probably shocked that New Yorkers spent $90 million last year on boats when what they need are shelters. Authoritarians will also be attracted by the chain-of-command aspects of shelter planning. To certain persons, furthermore, the idea of nuclear war is morbidly fascinating; they imagine that if only one can prepare and survive, one will emerge into a world cleansed of its sins and gloriously simplified. Such people will be prominent among those urging us to "put on the arm band." Then too, who will go to the CD training schools to become the absolute leaders in the crisis and post-attack world? Policemen and retired military officers, to judge from the local civil-defense cadres of some states. The Southern Negro may well wonder what fallout can do to him that the local police chief cannot.

Perhaps future cadres will be more representative than those in the past, but there is undoubtedly a strong selective process in the very nature of civil defense, and in the psychological stresses and frustrations of the cold war, that will insure an ample flow of recruits eager for civilian mobilization. While it is intriguing to speculate upon the post-attack world such people might create, it is more pertinent to question what consequences ensue from elevating them toward community leadership *before* war, or if no war breaks out.

With bonds to the federal government weakened and headstrong elements in the political ascendancy on the local scene, what happens when less fortunate cities learn their defense problems? Mass migration? What happens when people learn that the military base outside of town makes them a prime target, but that the government will not help them with blast shelters? Immense pressures will be brought to bear to get the bases removed, and Tucson may begin behaving toward the President as Tokyo did a few seasons ago. If these measures have no success, what then? To speak of the possibility of the revival of the nullification and secession doctrines seems the remotest fantasy. Yet again, one cannot be sure just *how* remote. The matters which impelled the South in decades before the Civil War, or today impel the nullifiers on the White Citizens Councils, seem small by comparison with the threat of imminent obliteration which will be raised in every international crisis. What is common to all three cases, however, is the erosion of the moderate position and the reinforcement of the fire-eaters.

Already, according to Dr. Roland I. Robinson, adviser to the Federal Reserve Board, the government is worried that areas left undamaged by attack may try to secede from the heavily hit regions. The idea may arise in areas that are certain to be damaged that there is nothing to be gained by waiting until *after* the attack. And if actual secession is remote, the use of the threat may not be. This would be profoundly unpatriotic, but, seen in the light of the dynamism of the community-shelter debate, not entirely impossible.

That is the curious thing about the program: one can see its beginning, but not its end.

How did the whole thing get started? There is an important lesson
for us here. If adequate staff work had been done in advance, nobody
would have thought of trotting out a Frankenstein's monster in the
first place. If thorough studies had been made of the several bomb
effects on different aspects of the society *as they interact*—communications with transportation with power supply with food sources
with public services, etc.—and all of these considered in the light
of different intensities of attack, under varying strategic assumptions
and on different parts of the country, then civil defense would
probably have been treated with the vague neglect that President
Eisenhower, in his senescent wisdom, always accorded it. But largely
because of inter-departmental jealousies, the Atomic Energy Commission made no such cross-studies. Bureaucrats are jealous of their
bailiwicks, and one can only presume that anyone seen crossing the
hall was considered a meddler.

Only now has the AEC undertaken the staff work which should
have long preceded any high-level decision. This, of course, is the
other side of the coin of Mr. Eisenhower's vague neglect. When an
Administration followed him which had to do everything bigger
and better, the vital staff work needed to support its thumping
clarity was was simply not to be had. What was to be had was the
intricately myopic literature of the several institutes which have
been accepting federal funds in return for hypothesizing types and
sizes of attack that could be survived. On the basis of their fragile
concoctions and little else, the President was encouraged to act in the
way he did during the Berlin crisis. This literature is still being produced, entering into every hearing Representative Holifield conducts.
The most recent example to come under public scrutiny was the reve-
lation of Leon Gouré of the RAND Corporation that the Soviet
Union is well advanced on an extensive shelter program. This was
brought to the public attention, of course, because Harrison Salisbury
of *The New York Times* and other responsible reporters with first-
hand information took the trouble to say that it was not true. But
one senses that this genre no longer carries the weight it once did,
that the lesson has been partly learned, and that responsible studies

are under way which will form the basis for less disastrous ventures in the future.

In the case of civil defense, however, the lesson must be applied still more strictly. People will buy the idea of insurance, particularly when it means enriching the community with nearly two dollars of federal money for every dollar they throw in. Then they will start looking into just what insurance really means. In time they will be angry at having been sold a bill of goods. Opposition politicos will play it to the hilt, political pressures and lobbies will force bigger appropriations, local pressures to conform to the civil-defense mania will be aggravated, regional variations will focus suspicion on Washington, and so on. One sweats to think of it, particularly if he identifies with the better goals of this Administration.

The lesson to be learned from the family-shelter campaign is that a lot of hard thought must be given to long-range goals before the new community-shelter program is given any concrete form. The first thing to do would be to shut up all civil-defense and Pentagon spokesmen who are now answering questions as to what the program will be. Premature statements limit the Administration's freedom to plan. Then, somehow, ways must be found to build into the program a "self-damping" factor. It will not be easy to find a shelter program that actually reduces society's commitment to shelters, particularly when the program is rich in boondoggle possibilities. But it must be done.

The "dual function" idea that may be urged on communities is a small step in the right direction, yet by itself it is not only too little, but likely to aggravate some parts of the dynamism, for example by tempting communities to suppose they can solve the juvenile delinquency problem at two-thirds federal expense. ("Gregarious teenagers often have no after-school hangout where they can relax with sodas and play the jukebox," says the shelter booklet. "This shelter can serve such purposes admirably.") To such giddy hopes and their abuse by shelter hucksters the only available countervailing force appears to be the Right and its fear of federal intervention. Here the mind rebels. Surely a sophisticated appreciation of the dynamism of the community-shelter program will lead us to a more dependable mechanism for undoing that dynamism.

But again the mind reels. What mechanism? How? One is tempted to say that since the Administration got us into this, let the Administration get us out. Unfortunately, though, it wasn't just the Administration, but everybody who acquiesced in a number of things that got us into this: in the rise of the more limited and technocratic forms of systems-design mentality ("What are the inputs, what are the outputs?"); the think factory in which the systems-design mentality is sheltered from public view; the fraudulent bureaucratic publicity utterance; the faith in the chain of command; the assumption that when the Air Force pays a man he'll come up with a plan that serves the long-range interests of the public rather than the short-run needs of the Air Force. Anybody who made the very American assumption that if it took $3 million and two years to produce a study it must be right, got us into this. So did anybody who gave up on the technical questions which underlie public policy and left them to big-name experts on scientific advisory committees and atomic energy commissions.

By now, I suppose, I have included most of us. It follows, emotionally if not logically, that most of us must assume responsibility for reversing the dynamism and, if possible, for presenting proposals that may help others to do the same—nationally, if we can, but at any rate locally.

The atmosphere in a community a substantial number of whose citizens have decided to act on hope will be very different from that in one resolutely deciding to burrow. The reciprocal function of such an atmosphere on the federal policy will be salutary, for where civil defense is rejected, it may often happen, as it did in Lincoln, Massachusetts, that such rejection involves the citizens in a greater commitment to the values of cross-cultural exchange and understanding, arbitration, international order and disarmament. This is the only good outcome conceivable from the great shelter debate, but it will not come about by itself.

WHAT WE KNOW ABOUT FALLOUT

by John M. Fowler and Ralph Caplan

A PROFESSOR OF PSYCHIATRY at the University of Southern California recently isolated a new aspect of mental illness: fallout worry. "Usually," Dr. Isidore Ziferstein explained, according to the *Los Angeles Times*, "the psychiatrist is able to analyze a worry, trace it to an earlier unresolved conflict, and help the patient to overcome the anxiety. But with nuclear anxiety we are forced to realize that much of it is realistic. . . . It is the fear of the unknown and the realization that even the radiation authorities are confused about the exact hazard of low-level radiation that will inevitably lead us to a period of superstition like that of the Middle Ages, when people feared evil spirits because they could not see them."

While psychiatry worried about what fallout could do to the psyche, the Scientists' Committee for Radiation Information worried about what a bomb might do to a typical target area, estimating that a 20-megaton thermonuclear bomb exploded at Manhattan's Columbus Circle would kill five to six million New Yorkers within the first few days, and might inundate a 4,000-square-mile area with fallout.

The fact is, of course, that much vaster areas are already at least *exposed* to fallout, and both the area and the density of the fallout would increase with the resumption of atmospheric testing by the United States. No one really knows all about the dangers of low doses of radiation, but since, as Dr. Ziferstein seems to be saying, ignorance has thus far been anything but blissful, it is worth

64

examining what we do know. In this case, it is possible for any concerned citizen to know almost as much about the hazards as scientists do.

In spite of all the advertising claims for "clean" bombs, the common denominator of all nuclear-weapons testing so far has been radioactive debris that sifts down where we live and becomes part of us. Since the hydrogen-bomb testing of 1954, scientists have tried desperately to appraise the consequences of this debris. The quiet years of 1959 and 1960 made it possible to study fallout in something like the atmosphere necessary to understanding it, and we now have a fair knowledge of how much of it resulted from early tests, of its global distribution, and of what determines the speed at which it is swept from the stratosphere. And we are able to appraise its potential danger a little more accurately than we could two years ago.

What we can learn about the heavy Russian testing that began in September, 1961 (heralded by the small French tests in the Sahara) must be understood in the context of what we know about fallout itself. When a nuclear explosion takes place, matter disappears and is converted into energy. The conversion occurs either when a very heavy nucleus is split, or when two light nucleii are joined. The first—fission—provides the explosive force for an atom bomb; the second—fusion—powers the hydrogen bomb. Although the fusion process produces copious neutrons, it produces little in the way of dangerous radioactive products. But in the fission process, the shattered remains of the uranium nucleus are unstable, and seek to come back into the configuration of ordinary non-radioactive elements by nuclear rearrangements involving the emission of energetic radiations, or high-speed particles. In the fireball of the atom bomb, some 200 different kinds of radioactive elements are formed, ranging in radioactive lifetime from less than a second to thousands of years. In a nuclear war, these would constitute the deadly fallout which would sweep life before it for hundreds of miles downwind from a bomb burst. But when we study the effects of nuclear *testing*, their short lifetimes eliminate most of these elements from our concern, and we can focus on the few that live long enough to reach us.

In about 5 per cent of the fission events, strontium—a chemical

element closely related to calcium—is formed in a way which leaves
it radioactive. The short-range beta particles it emits are relatively
harmless when they attack the body from the outside, but seriously
dangerous inside. At about the same rate, radioactive cesium is formed,
emitting gamma rays whose high penetrating power makes them
dangerous from both without and within.

The "lifetime" of such material is measured in terms of their
"half-life"—the time it takes for one-half of the original amount to
disappear. This is a useful guide to the relative danger of particular
radioactive species. If their activity is short-lived, their effectiveness
can be reduced by keeping bomb debris out of the biosphere for as
long as possible. And if their half-life is very much longer than our
own, that reduces the probability of their decaying inside us in our
lifetime and dangerously irradiating our tissues. The difficult debris
to avoid is that with an intermediate lifetime. Strontium and cesium,
in their radioactive form, have a half-life of thirty years each—
something like our own.

Besides the *physical* lifetime, there is the *biological* lifetime to
consider. A biological half-life is the time it takes for one-half of a
radioactive contaminant to be eliminated from our systems. Stron-
tium-90—one of the radioactive forms of strontium that appear in a
fission explosion—has an extremely long biological half-life because,
like calcium, it gets into our bones. Cesium is less of a hazard. Like
potassium, which it resembles, it stays in our system only about 140
days.

How much fission residue are we exposed to? What kind is it?
And what damage can it do? Radiation is measured in two ways.
Its strength is calculated in "curies." One curie (which is what a
gram of radium measures) of a radioactive material emits 37 billion
particles per second. When these particles pass through matter, living tissue included, some of their energy is lost in passage and
causes chemical changes. This energy deposition is the second
measure of radiation, and is expressed in "roentgens." Very little
energy need be involved. A little exposure goes a long way when it
is exposure to penetrating radiation: although a gram of tissue could
absorb 500 roentgens without a rise in temperature of so much as
2/1,000 of a degree Fahrenheit, the same amount of radiation de-

livered to the whole body in one dose would have an even chance of killing it.

The danger of radiation varies not only with the power of the particles, but with the part of the body exposed. Damage is either somatic (which hurts us); or genetic (which will hurt succeeding generations). When a single living cell is irradiated, it is either damaged or killed. If enough cells are killed, the organ they belong to dies; and if enough—or certain—organs die, the organism dies.

Doses of hundreds of roentgens can cause such death, but the much lower doses that result from test fallout are more likely to result in cell damage than in cell death. In a way we do not wholly understand, cell damage can lead to cancer or leukemia. With reproductive cells, the damage may reach farther, for in these cells is stored man's genetic memory. Radiation can upset this memory, so that reproduction leads to mutation. And that radiation exposure can also cause a general shortening of life is sadly well documented.

To see how much damage we are doing to ourselves, we must see how much we are contaminating the biosphere. Since testing began in the middle forties, we have released fission residue at an accelerating rate. From 1946 to 1951, the United States and the Soviet Union tested bombs at the rate of about 100 kilotons (a kiloton is equal to 1,000 tons of TNT) per year. By 1954, the rate had increased to 20,000 kilotons per year. In 1955 and 1956, the testing rate dropped slightly to 14,000 kilotons per year; but in 1957 and 1958 weapons were tested at an annual rate of more than 40,000 kilotons. In 1961 alone the Russians set off more than 100,000 kilotons. Despite all the talk about clean bombs, the *average* bomb has been half-fission (dirty) and half-fusion (clean). The bomb testing prior to this year has released about 92 million tons of fission energy.

Where has the debris gone? To say for sure, we would need to know the altitude at which the bombs were exploded, the time of year of the testing, and the latitude. But, generally, smaller bombs exploded at the earth's surface contribute most of their debris to the lower atmosphere, or troposphere. Since this is where weather is formed, they lay their fallout products very quickly in a latitude band determined by the prevailing winds.

The products of large bombs and of higher explosions are pushed up into the stratosphere, where they stay a lot longer, and their distribution depends pretty much on the latitude of the explosion and the time of year. Russian tests made in the fall at far northern latitudes deposit their debris in the spring, and concentrate it in the mid-North Temperate Zone. Debris from U.S. tests made near the equator stays in the stratosphere longer; these tests leave some debris in the Southern Hemisphere, but seem also to peak at mid-Temperate Zone latitudes.

How do we know? A global network of soil-sampling stations provides a running account of strontium-90 build-up; and balloons and U-2 planes sample the stratospheric reservoir. Through the end of 1960, the accounts from this bookkeeping balanced. Tests through the fall of 1958 had produced about 9.2 megacuries (the prefix means million) of strontium-90. Perhaps as much as 3 megacuries of this fell out at the testing site, leaving 6 to be spread around the globe. By mid-1959, the natural decay of radioactivity had caused the 6 megacuries to drop to about 5. Soil measurements indicated that some 4 megacuries were already on the earth's surface; air sampling revealed that between 1 and 1.5 remained in the air. All this has settled out by now.

We can translate these figures into terms of local soil radioactivity, then into terms of diet—the major item being milk—and then into terms of the levels of strontium-90 in the bone. In this country, the Midwest generally showed the most soil radioactivity, while the northern part of the country showed more than the South.

The problem in estimating strontium-90 concentration in bone is the difficulty of getting samples that are both numerically and geographically adequate. For five years there has been an interesting project under way in St. Louis. Because of the relationship between teeth and bone, it is possible to learn about one by examining the other. To this end, large numbers (more than 50,000 so far) of deciduous teeth are collected from children (in exchange they receive badges reading, "I gave my tooth to Science") and studied for fallout content.

The two test-free years of 1959–1960 gave us a chance to study fallout effects, but that scientific breather ended in September, 1961. As of November 6, 1961, thirty-one Russian tests had been recorded, with an estimated megatonage of well over 100. Since, on the basis of past tests, we can assume that about one-half of this explosive energy was released by fission, we can expect about four additional megacuries of strontium-90 to have been added to the stratosphere.

The Russian testing was larger in megatonage than any other series. Because it took place in the northern latitudes, the deposition will be maximized at the mid-latitude of the United States. The rains will bring down large amounts of both strontium-90 and cesium-137. Plants will take this into their leaves directly, and absorb some of it through their roots. Since cows will come out to feed on this in the spring pastures, we can expect our milk levels of strontium-90 to reach new and disturbing heights. More than half of the strontium-90 in milk seems to have come from the soil, or at least not to be directly dependent on fallout rate; for in 1960—a year when the rate had diminished almost to nothing—milk in New York City still averaged 8 strontium units (this unit is the measure of strontium contamination), as compared with 11 strontium units in high-rate 1959. Sometime during next April, May or June, milk levels in New York will rise to at least 30, and probably more than 40, strontium units, and we can expect a 1962 average of nearly 15.

Bone levels in 1962 will of course follow the milk levels, most dramatically in very small children in whom calcium will be laid down during the year. Because of the technical difficulties in making bone measurements, the most recent figures available are for 1959, when the average burden in the bones of children up to four years of age was 2½ strontium units. This probably increased to nearly 3 in 1960, then fell off somewhat in 1961. Our expectation that the radioactive strontium content of milk will increase by 50 per cent in 1962 leads us to estimate that, by 1963 or 1964, fallout will send the average levels in children's bones up to 4.5 or 5.0.

What do these numbers mean? Frankly, not much—not, at least, until we have a context for them. We can try to achieve the perspective we need by searching for the minimum level at which radiation has caused damage, and establishing this as a maximum permissible level; or by investigating the radiation to which man is always exposed—from soil, rocks, cosmic rays and X-ray machines—and establishing a minimum of unavoidable exposure.

But a "permissible" limit is extremely difficult to set. Most of our measurable experience with radiation has been at high levels, and to make any statistically valid study of low-level experience we would need unreasonably large numbers of experimental animals —fruit flies, mice or men. It seems more and more likely that there is *no* permissible limit, that any amount of radiation carries with it *some* real probability of genetic damage, cancer, leukemia or life-shortening. In any case, until safety levels can be set, the wisest course is to assume that there are none. This is the attitude of the Federal Radiation Council, officially charged with setting safety standards. The council has established what it calls Radiation Protection Guides (RPG), defined as "the radiation dose which should not be exceeded without careful consideration of the reasons for doing so." The council warns that "every effort should be made to encourage maintenance of radiation doses as far below this guide as practical."

The RPG for strontium-90 is 200 micromicrocuries per gram of calcium—200 strontium units in the daily diet, an intake that would be expected to supply some 50 strontium units per gram of calcium in the bone. The addition of the 1961 Soviet testing will probably bring the average population to one-tenth of the 50-strontium-unit danger point.

But our concern cannot stop with the average, for there are those who—for biological reasons—will take up more than the average amount of strontium-90. And there are parts of the country where the diet levels will be above average in strontium-90 content. Data on this make it reasonable to estimate that as much as 1 per cent of the population will exceed five times the average, and that significant numbers will exceed ten times the average. Thus the end of the latest testing period will find some people carrying in their bones strontium-90 equal to or exceeding the RPG.

It is hard to measure this damage numerically. Biophysicist Walter R. Guild, writing in *Fallout* (Basic Books, 1960) estimates that for each strontium unit in the bone, there will be from two to six cases of leukemia per year per 100 million people. On this basis, the latest series of tests has caused an increase of 3 to 9 cases of leukemia for each 100 million of the population per year. With our population of 175 million, then, we can expect from 150 to 500 consequent deaths.

Although it is just as hard to estimate genetic damage, it is much more certain that such damage will result. For while there is some possibility of a threshold below which leukemia and bone cancer do not occur, no one suggests that there is such a threshold for genetic effects. Every increase in radioactive exposure does some harm to our genetic pool. Geneticist James Crow, in *Fallout*, suggests a world-wide total of 20,000 mutations as the probable result of tests through 1958. The Russian fallout alone should almost double this number.

It is, of course, possible that these mutations will be more, rather than less, virile—better adapted to living. But that a random shuffling of characteristics will produce improvements in the long-evolved and very complicated human reproductive system is considered very unlikely by those who understand either genetics or gambling odds.

The steady Russian cannonading—in effect like a colossal stream of firecrackers—presented as dangers for the first time some of the short-lived activities. The debris-laden clouds, some of them reaching us in less than a week, were rich in radioactive species that had long since disappeared from fallout making its slower way through the stratosphere.

One such material that appeared this fall was iodine-131, a radioactive form of iodine that becomes concentrated in the thyroid, and is dangerous to the sensitive thyroids of young children. It was produced in large quantities but, since it has a half-life of only eight days, it is of danger only during test periods. Luckily for Americans, most of the Soviet bomb debris passed north of us in its first swing around the globe; but clouds from the September 18 and September 22, 1961 tests did deposit significant amounts of iodine-131 on American soil, and high levels of it appeared in milk across the country. In St. Louis, for example, the milk level on September 27, 1961 was 500 micromicrocuries, well within a range of which the Federal Radiation Council has said: "Any intake within this range must be evaluated from the point of view of the radiation protection guide and, if necessary, appropriate positive control measures instituted."

The United States would have been exposed to much higher levels from the Soviet tests were it not for the fortunate coincidence of wind patterns and Russian testing practices. Since the two large Russian tests were at high altitudes, the iodine-131 will have decayed before returning to earth. Present levels here are below the range of concern.

Every megaton of fission creates about 100 pounds of radioactive debris. Even though 20 or 30 per cent of the Soviet fission products came quickly back to earth, there is still a lot of Russia up there—perhaps two tons of her. The winds are diffusing this through the stratosphere, 50,000 to 100,000 feet above the earth, and driving it slowly southward. In the spring, the cold air masses from the stratosphere settle out in the North Temperate Zone, and for the past ten years these settling air masses have carried with them quantities of radioactive debris. This is why April may in fact be the cruelest month: next spring will bring down the heaviest fallout we have ever known.

MEDICINE LOOKS AT NUCLEAR WAR:
IS THERE A DOCTOR IN THE RUBBLE?

by Charles Flato

WHILE PRESIDENT KENNEDY and the American Medical Association continued trading punches over the medical-care program for the aged, a group of Boston doctors concerned themselves with another medicare problem—the possibility of providing medical services in the event of a thermonuclear war.

Taking the 1959 Holifield Committee estimate of the effect of a "mild" (10-bomb, 56-megaton) attack on the State of Massachusetts and the committee count of casualties in that state (2,800,000 dead, 2,000,000 injured) as their yardstick, the doctors have taken a look at the medical consequences, in terms of the kinds of injuries (chiefly burns, trauma, radiation sickness) and their severity, the number of physicians who will be alive and uninjured to take care of the maimed, the number of hospital beds that will be available, the drugs that will be needed.

Their conclusions, which appear in the May 31, 1962 issue of the *New England Journal of Medicine,* are far from reassuring. Even if the attack is restricted to a 56-megaton single strike—unlikely in view of the production of 100-megaton bombs—medical services will virtually be wiped out.

¶Only 1,980 physicians out of the state's 9,440 will escape death or serious injury. Each surviving and functioning physician will have to take care of between 1,000 and 1,700 patients, depending on where he is during the postattack period. "The consequences of a

73

ratio of 1,000 or 1,700 acutely injured persons to 1 physician," the authors of the report comment, "are made clear when one examines the immediate postattack situation in greater detail. If the physician were to spend only ten minutes on diagnosis and treatment of each injured patient, and if he worked only twenty hours every day, it would require eight to fourteen days before every injured patient could be seen for the first time."

¶Fewer than 10,000 hospital beds of the state's more than 56,000 will be available, practically all of them out of the blast and fire-storm area. Moreover, most of them are now occupied by psychiatric patients. "Although these hospitals are poorly equipped to deal with traumatic injury and radiation sickness," the authors point out, "the beds will be needed. It will be necessary to displace their current occupants. If large numbers of psychiatric patients—many of them unable to care for themselves under normal social circumstances—are released, the consequences will be difficult to predict."

¶At best, the drugs now stockpiled by Civil Defense authorities will take care of no more than 15 per cent of the needs of the injured. Drugs and other medical supplies now in hospitals and wholesale drug warehouses, the authors assume, largely will be destroyed since they are in prime target areas. In addition, they point out, many of the drugs that will be critically needed—such as penicillin and the broad spectrum antibiotics, as well as anti-toxins—lose their potency in from three to five years. "Furthermore," the report observes, "narcotics, one of the most essential groups of drugs in the care of seriously injured casualties, have not been stockpiled at all in Massachusetts."

¶The breakdown of elementary sanitation could result in epidemics of massive proportions. Since bacterial and fungal carriers of epidemic diseases are able to withstand radiation injury better than humans, it is considered likely that diseases such as encephalitis, hepatitis and poliomyelitis will become rampant. "The radiation," it is explained, "might also cause new mutant forms of bacteria and viruses, some of which could be highly infective in the absence of immune defenses. Furthermore, the lessening of host resistance by radiation exposure, malnutrition, excessive fatigue and severe emotional stress would render human beings susceptible to bacteria or fungi that are not normally invasive."

¶The hazard of the dead to the living following the attack will be the most difficult of all public-health problems to be coped with. Civil Defense authorities will be faced with disposing of 2,800,000 corpses, about 2,110,000 in Boston alone. "Prompt disposal of corpses will be essential for many reasons," the report comments. "Some of the public health problems are obvious—for example, the need for control of epidemic disease and its vectors, flies and rodents. An equally important, though less apparent, reason is psychological. There is evidence that profound emotional disorders and somatic manifestations follow the sight and smell of decomposing bodies."

The foregoing are highlights of the articles in the *New England Journal of Medicine*. Is there an answer to the medical problems associated with a thermonuclear attack?

"In our opinion," a spokesman for the physician group told the writer, "the only effective therapy for a thermonuclear attack is to prevent it."

The physicians who prepared the report, most of whom are on the faculty of the Harvard Medical School and the Harvard School of Public Health, are members of an organization, Physicians for Social Responsibility, formed in 1961 to alert the medical profession to the medical, as well as the ethical, consequences of thermonuclear war and weapons testing. The organization was started in Boston, but now has members throughout the country. Its major activities to date have been research projects and the dissemination of their scientific findings to other physicians. Like similar professional groups opposed to the thermonuclear-arms race, notably the Committee on Public Information of the American Association for the Advancement of Science and the editors of the *Bulletin of Atomic Scientists*, the organization of physicians also feels it has an obligation to inform the lay public of what the medical sequelae of a thermonuclear war would be.

In the current report, the authors emphasize that their calculations of the medical consequences of a limited, 1959-style attack are based on estimates of destruction laid down by official bodies, including the Atomic Energy Commission. A twenty to thirty minutes' warning is assumed, as well as a single strike, so that fallout, fire and the other bomb effects will diminish relatively sooner than they would following multiple strikes. The general availability of individual or community fallout shelters meeting official standards is also assumed.

"It should be noted," the report comments, "that such an attack, considered realistic in 1959, could be greatly exceeded in the light of recent weapons developments."

Nevertheless, they say that the deaths and injuries that will be caused by blast, thermal and radiation effects in even a "mild" attack will be stupendous, especially from fire-storms. In addition to the already indicated high death toll that will take place within the 16-to-21 mile radius of the center of the attack, the major medical problems facing the few physicians who will manage to survive

. . . will include large numbers of patients with the following: blast injuries, lacerations of soft tissues and fractures; thermal injuries, with surface burns, retinal burns and respiratory-tract damage; and radiation injuries, including acute radiation syndrome and delayed effects. Substantial numbers of patients will present infectious disease owing to lowered resistance and epidemic outbreaks; others will suffer psychologic breakdowns consequent to fear, grief and trauma. In addition, the physician must deal with such pre-existing medical conditions as diabetes mellitus, hypertension and cancer.

Burn injuries will, it is thought, exceed those from the effects of blast and radiation. The authors doubt whether they can be treated with any hope of success:

Optimal therapy for serious burns requires sedation, oxygen administration and large intravenous infusions of fluids, electrolytes and plasma expanders. . . .

Antibiotics, tetanus prophylaxis and local wound care will also be necessary. Even if the individual physician is well instructed in the modern care of serious burns, it is difficult to see how he will cope with hundreds of such patients at once when he is lacking the most essential diagnostic and therapeutic facilities.

Further, the report asks how the physician will be able to identify and rationally treat the many other expected injuries—such as the rupture of internal organs, fractures, penetrating wounds of the skull and thorax, as well as infections, without X-ray and other commonly used diagnostic facilities. "The question is important," the authors state, "since decisions will have to be made to abandon the care of many. Patients with fatal or nearly fatal injuries may be neglected to make care available to more salvageable ones, and primary attention may be assigned to those who have the greatest possibility of survival."

Decisions such as this, the authors comment, raise a number of unprecedented ethical problems for the physician:

When faced with hundreds of severely injured patients, how does the physician select those to be treated first? How does he choose between saving the lives of the few and easing the pain of the many? How does he allocate limited supplies of narcotics and analgesics?

Neither the Hippocratic Oath, the published codes of ethics of the American Medical Association nor the personal morality on which every physician relies provides an easy answer to these questions. In fact, a review of these trusted and cherished guides in the light of the problems of thermonuclear war makes them seem curiously and sadly obsolete, as if they reflected the human innocence of an earlier era.

Depending on the wind direction and other factors, many persons beyond the 16- to 21-mile radius may, the report continues, be exposed to lethal doses of radiation. Those able to reach fallout shelters in time and able to survive in them for the requisite several weeks, will generally be spared. However, many will be unable to reach shelters because of blindness produced at the instant of the explosion. Many who reach shelters will have already been highly irradiated; if they do not suffer acute radiation sickness, they will in any case be subject to the long-term somatic and genetic effects of irradiation. The long-term effects will be a great increase in such conditions as neoplasia, stillbirths and congenital malformations in succeeding generations.

The provision of fully available and effective fallout shelters will,

the authors point out, radically alter the patient-physician ratio
situation:

Under these circumstances, there will be *no* functioning physicians
outside shelters in the immediate postattack period, but the injured-to-
physician ratio will be considerably improved two weeks or more later,
when physicians emerge from their shelters, since large numbers of the
injured will have died in the interim.

The authors of the report make it clear that the medical experience gained in earlier disasters, including the A-bomb attacks on
Hiroshima and Nagasaki, is not applicable to thermonuclear war:

To reason from these models to thermonuclear war is to make the assumption that the problems of H-bomb warfare will be quantitatively
greater, but qualitatively similar, to those of earlier disasters. This usually
unstated assumption implies that since we have survived other catastro-
phes we will survive now—under any circumstances—if we only plan
carefully enough. The present article demonstrates that thermonuclear
war will differ in size and nature from anything in previous experience.

The type, timing and magnitude of the attack, the authors continue,
also will determine the size and character of the postattack medical-
care problem:

There are so many variables and so many imponderables in the complex equation of thermonuclear war that one can reach almost any conclusion by choosing appropriate assumptions. The primary responsibility
of the physician to the medical community and the public, therefore,
is neither to offer sweeping and uncritical reassurances or to cry doom,
but rather to define and study the consequences of a specific possible attack. . . . It is deeply misleading, therefore, to speak of any single
disaster plan as a secure answer to the hazards of thermonuclear war. It
is deeply misleading to focus on radiation shelters while ignoring the
problems of blast and fire-storm.

The report of the Boston group, which is in the highest tradition
of the physician's dual role as scientist and citizen, issues a stern
prescription in conclusion:

Since it is impossible to prepare adequately for every possible type of nuclear attack, the physician's responsibility goes beyond mere disaster planning. Physicians, charged with the responsibility for the lives of their patients and the health of their communities, must also explore a new area of preventive medicine, the prevention of thermonuclear war.

HAZARDS OF CIVIL DEFENSE

by Carl Dreher

THE OFFICE of Civil and Defense Mobilization is the subject. Senator Stephen M. Young (*Congressional Record*, March 8, 1961) is the speaker:

> Since 1951, more than a billion dollars of taxpayers' money has been wasted by the schemes of this boondoggling outfit. Sixty-two per cent of the money requested by the OCDM last year was earmarked for salaries and expenses . . . 40 per cent of the salaried officials received $10,000 a year or more. . . . American taxpayers are 'getting their backs up' and we cannot blame them. . . . Let's stop this nonsense.

Senator Young may have been right in his animadversions concerning OCDM, but he is wrong about the revolt of the taxpayer. This beast of burden may pay no heed to OCDM's behest to build his own home shelter, the thought may cross his mind that OCDM's periodic drills are so much damn foolishness, but sheer force of repetition has convinced him that some sort of civil-defense system is a necessary component of our deterrent strength. Governor Rockefeller of New York was rocked back on his heels when he tried to push through legislation mandating home owners and private businesses to construct fallout shelters at their own expense, but the legislators and their constituents probably agree, in principle, with *Time's* contention that shelters "would blunt the effectiveness of nuclear blackmail, save millions of lives and ensure the survival of the United States itself in case of nuclear attack."

80

On the mechanics of salvation, *Time* is vague. This is not 1775, when a citizen-militia could spring to arms and shoot from behind stone fences. Civilians have absolutely nothing to do with deterrence. Retaliatory capacity, the fear of which constitutes deterrence, depends solely on the missilemen in their hardened bases and, as long as aircraft have a role to play, on the SAC bombers on air alert or able to take off before their bases are obliterated. On the accepted premise of a Soviet first strike, the punishment subsequently meted out to the Russians will be the same whether all American civilians are enjoying Martinis and hors d'oeuvres in their impregnable shelters, or not one remains alive.

The argument that the fate of the Republic hinges on shelters in turn hinges on two assumptions, both dubious. The first is that Khrushchev is bent on a war of mutual genocide, in which he will cheerfully sacrifice 30 or 60 million of his miserable subjects to exterminate 180 million happy Americans, or some lesser ratio, as long as he comes out ahead. Given shelters, after the first strike and the retaliatory strike and the strikes which follow, diminuendo, the survivors will emerge and rebuild the American culture. The second assumption is that the survival of individuals (which, in some degree, under some conditions, shelters may promote) insures the survival of American institutions. Anyone who believes that democracy could survive a nuclear holocaust must believe in fairies.

The most cogent argument against shelters, however, is that while they might reduce casualties, the putative reduction would entail a serious increase in the risk of nuclear war. In 1959, the Special Subcommittee on Radiation of the Joint Congressional Committee on Atomic Energy calculated the possible effect on the United States of a medium-size (1,500-megaton) attack, involving 224 targets, about half of them military. The data presented indicated that roughly 50 million deaths could be expected, about 25 per cent from radiation. Most of the other deaths would be from blast, about which little or nothing can be done. Let us assume, however, that of the 12.5 million radiation deaths half, or say 7 million, could be averted by an extensive shelter program. If there were nothing else to consider, the argument in favor of shelters would be persuasive. But if the shelter program itself adds to the likelihood of war, then we are advised to risk 43 million lives (50 minus 7) in order to save 7 million. A competent bookmaker does not give odds of 6 to 1 lightly. Actually the odds might be even longer, for OCDM shelter designs do not, in my estimation, promise a reduction of anything like 50 per cent in fallout fatalities.

What it amounts to is that nuclear war must have a high occurrence-probability, without shelters, before we should consider building shelters and adding to what would be a lower probability without them. If it can be shown that the building of shelters does substantially increase the risk of nuclear conflict, then the gamble is a rash one.

Suppose, contrary to the willful-genocide theory, that the Russians fear our first strike as much as we fear theirs. In that case, a massive shelter program initiated by either side would be a disequilibrating element in the balance of terror. With only ineffectual shelter measures, the civilian population of each bloc are in effect nuclear hostages of the other. Putting them under protective cover deprives the other side of its hostages in proportion as the cover is—or is thought to be—effective. So viewed, a national shelter program is by no means the innocent, passive, non-military defense measure it is usually pictured as being. It may be regarded as a preparation for attack, and when two blocs detest and distrust each other as deeply as do East and West at the present juncture, it will inevitably be so construed.

Of course this holds for both sides. If the Soviets had gone in for an extensive shelter-building program, the compulsive reciprocity of the arms race would dictate that we do likewise. In fact, however, the Soviets have lagged in shelter construction, even of the public type; in the way of family-type shelters, which are the current stock-in-trade of OCDM, they are doing substantially nothing. By all the evidence available to the American public—and shelter policy is certainly a public matter—the state of Soviet civil defense has not undergone significant change since the Military Operations Subcommittee of the House Committee on Government Operations issued its report on *Civil Defense in Western Europe and the Soviet Union* in April, 1959. The conclusion to be drawn is that while civil defense and indoctrination are certainly more systematic and extensive in the

Soviet Union, neither that country nor the United States has embarked on a shelter-construction program that could be regarded as strategically significant.

Where we rely on OCDM pamphlets, newspapers and magazine articles, the Soviet people are subjected to courses given by the All-Union Volunteer Society for Assistance to the Army, Air Force and Navy (DOSAAF), which also provides mass training in such skills as electronics, gliding, parachute jumping, ship modeling, truck and motorcycle driving, marksmanship, etc.

Barring a deep-seated plot which has been overlooked by our intelligence and publicity agencies, we have little to fear from the Soviet civil defense preparations. The illustrations reproduced from Soviet publications recall nothing so much as those in Agricola's celebrated treatise on mining, *De re metallica* (1556). Shelters are being incorporated in basements of new apartment houses; since shielding depends on mass, these will provide even better fallout protection when the building collapses on them. Smaller shelters are designed as covered trenches or dugouts seating thirty to sixty persons; still smaller types are designed for one- or two-family occupancy in the suburbs.

The general impression given by the shelter phase of Soviet civil defense is the same as that given by the American—one of foggy improvisation, hopeful extrapolation and a pervasive air of unreality. If anything, the Soviet effort is even more absurd in that the trench-type shelters are to be constructed with hand tools only after an "Alert" is sounded. And DOSAAF complains, as does OCDM, of a certain amount of public apathy ("insignificant, it is true").

The most enthusiastic proponents of a big shelter program (or permanent migration underground) are people like Herman Kahn and Edward Teller who, before the event, face the prospect of nuclear war with Spartan-American fortitude. The members of this cabal, with their associates in the Pentagon, envision shelters as an umbrella for a "preemptive" strike. Nor is this line of thought confined to the military-industrial-scientific complex. Congressman Chet Holifield wrote in a paper on "Civil Defense" (*Fallout*, edited by John M. Fowler, Basic Books, 1960, page 130): "We must consider the possibility of extremely provocative action against us or our allies—

but not direct attack on the United States—by the Soviet Union. What action would we be prepared to take in that event? If our civil defenses were no stronger than they are today, a decision to launch a massive retaliatory assault against the Soviet Union might result in loss of 50 million or 100 million American lives in the counter-attack, even if our strike forces substantially reduced the Soviet retaliatory capability." Accordingly, Congressman Holifield favors a national shelter-construction effort as a necessary ancillary to nuclear retaliation against "extremely provocative action" by the Soviet Union. What constitutes extreme provocation, of course, we will decide.

The mass of our citizens, who cannot conceive of the United States' committing aggression, should take a hard look at this aspect of the shelter program. Air Force policy in regard to civil defense will also bear closer examination. Such an investigation was begun in the report on *Civil Defense Shelter Policy and Postattack Recovery Planning* of the House Committee on Government Operations (July, 1960), which dealt, among other things, with relations between General Curtis LeMay, commander of SAC, and Leo A. Hoegh, then director of OCDM. Both Governor Hoegh and General LeMay assured the committee that cooperation was "excellent," i.e., the Air Force did whatever it pleased. "There is no indication whatever," the majority on the committee concluded, "that civil defense considerations have ever influenced the location or relocation of any missile site to minimize the fallout danger. . . . Persons in communities exposed to the fallout danger are understandably bewildered when they find that the civilian commander of civil defense in the United States really has nothing to say about a civil defense hazard which threatens their very survival."

It may be that the siting of missile bases is determined solely by economic factors coming under the heading of "utilization of existing military facilities" (and avoiding trouble wth Congressmen), by supply and maintenance problems, and by the understandable preference of Air Force personnel for stations within convenient motoring distance of cities and recreational facilities. And it is true that the Air Force is consistent: if it has no mercy on the inhabitants of neighboring communities exposed to blast and radiation, neither does

it provide protection for its non-operational personnel or civilian
dependents at missile bases. "I don't think," said General LeMay
about shelters in general, "I would put that much money into holes
in the ground to crawl into, that I would rather spend more of it in
offensive weapons in the first place."

But is it not strange that, under the doctrine of Soviet first strike,
the Air Force should doom its own personnel (other than the trigger-
men on the missiles) and the civilian population which it ostensibly
exists to protect? If, however, the Soviet first-strike doctrine is only a
cover story, and the Air Force is pretty well convinced that its mission
will be to "retaliate," not against a Soviet first strike but against
"provocation," everything falls into place. If the Air Force can get
in the first punch and is hopeful that it will be strategically successful, stateside missile bases will no longer be prime targets. It will no
longer matter much where missile installations are located in reference to cities, whether close in or farther out, upwind or downwind.
The U.S. population, with the possible exception of a few million
victims of enfeebled Soviet retaliation, will be saved and the Air
Force, its savior, having disposed of most of the Soviet missile bases,
can deploy its remaining strength against Soviet cities, if necessary.
On this hypothesis, Air Force siting and shelter policy, while perhaps
too optimistic, may be neither as inhuman (as far as Americans are
concerned) nor as illogical as it appears on the basis of a pledge never
to strike the first blow.

The chief, though concealed, function of OCDM is to front as
the public-persuasion agency for the preemptive war interests. The
fact that this is neither the avowed aim of the organization nor the
conscious intention of most of the staff is of little interest. Publicity
people, even more than others, are to be judged by quite other
criteria than their own opinion of themselves, their social role and
the results of their labors.

OCDM's primary open activity is to arouse religious, educational,
labor, veterans', farm, fraternal, governmental, civic and business
organizations to the existence of a peril and to devise means of meeting it. The peril, though it is of our creation as much as the enemy's,
certainly exists. But, once the enemy's missiles are launched, there is
no way of coping with it. Unless we posit a successful first strike on

our part, the shelter solution is pure quackery. As far as weight-lifting capability is concerned, the Soviets can already put 35-megaton bombs into intercontinental trajectories. Even the 100-pound-per-square-inch missile sites now under construction here will be vulnerable by the time they are finished, if they are not already. There is no foreseeable limit to the size of the bombs and the means of delivery. By all indications the offense is permanently ahead of the defense. The technicians who are plugging the anti-missile missile are visionaries who, in private enterprise, could not raise a plugged nickel for their schemes. The fallout shelters OCDM is promoting may reduce the number of casualties today (though at a considerable discount from the OCDM estimates); tomorrow they will be as obsolete as a 1905 Ford.

OCDM also has a mass-shelter policy. *Civil Defense Shelter Policy and Postattack Recovery Planning* says:

. . . The OCDM shelter-survey program resembles the mass evacuation policy emphasized by the OCDM predecessor agency, the Federal Civil Defense Administration. . . . The evacuation policy led to a simple designation of exit routes and evacuation-reception areas. No plans were made for provisioning these areas with the basic supplies and equipment which would be required to sustain an evacuated population at even the barest level of subsistence. The shelter survey is aimed at identifying shelter spaces in existing structures. Little or nothing is being done to improve the shielding factor of the structure or to make those spaces habitable and to provide essential supplies for emergency use.

These token shelter areas are mostly in the downtown sections of cities. In effect, the business population are told that in the event of an attack during business hours they should stay where they are for two or three weeks, without power, communications, food or water, in the hope there will be enough shielding to enable them, and whoever else crowds in, to survive. The wife and kiddies must shift for themselves.

For one group of citizens, however, quite adequate survival quarters are being provided, at public expense. The favored group is the higher-echelon personnel of OCDM itself, together with their retinues. *The New York Times* (May 14, 1961) reports that con-

struction has begun on a "vast underground fortress" at Denton,
Texas, the seat of OCDM Region 5, to accommodate 500 persons on
an emergency basis for thirty days. Similar underground facilities,
at about $2,500,000 apiece, are projected for the other seven regional
headquarters of the agency. Each fortress, OCDM points out, could
be used as an alternate national capital in the event of unavailability
of the President's shelter, the location of which is classified and
known only to about half the population of Washington, D.C.

The regional H.Q. at Denton will be topped by a "modernistic"
building with offices, a public reception center and a snack bar. The
operation of the fortress beneath will in no wise be hampered should
the modernistic building be destroyed. The fortress will be able to
withstand the blast of a 20-megaton bomb at a distance of three
miles. Hydraulically operated doors of 16-inch-thick concrete will
seal off the underground center. With its own power plant, water
well and other utilities, the two-story, 142 by 172 foot structure will
be a "self-sustaining, buried city," a forerunner of the coming underground culture. Fresh filtered air will be continuously supplied.
Fallout detection instruments on the outside will telemeter gamma
radiation to the inside so that the denizens will know when they can
safely emerge, look at the sun and see how the ordinary citizens
fared. Business will be carried on at the upper level, which will include a key communications center of the civil defense agency's
nation-wide telephone, telegraph, teletype, facsimile and radio networks. The lower level will accommodate the kitchen, refrigerator
and freezer rooms, storage rooms, dining area, men's bunking area,
women's bunking area, sick bay, power plant and maintenance rooms.

Obviously OCDM practices what it preaches—that nuclear war
need not be so bad after all, provided one is well prepared.

If one believes in democracy, one must also believe that the public
is often right without knowing why. The man in the street remains
largely indifferent to the shelter program and civil defense in general. Fifteen million copies of the OCDM bible, *The Family Fallout Shelter*, have been distributed, but the number of private shelters
actually built is insignificant in proportion to the number of private
residences. This is one case where easy credit has failed to move

the goods. FHA will insure Title 1 loans up to $3,500 for improvement of property, which includes fallout shelters. Yet, despite OCDM's preachment that a shelter may save your life, that of your family, and that of the nation, few home-owners have applied for loans for this purpose. Only in a few spots—Southern California, for example—is there a fair amount of activity, and even there swimming pools vastly outnumber shelters.

Of course, even in the affluent society, many householders are already mortgaged to the ears. Others are reluctant to spend for anything except gracious living. But none of this can account for such wholesale abstention. It must be that many who could afford $500 to $1,000 for a shelter or, at smaller expense, build one for themselves, realize that more often than not the shelter will be useless. Where the intensity of radiation is high, the protection factor of the ordinary shelter will not reduce the absorption of the occupants to a nonlethal level. There are all sorts of other risks. Shelters may crumble under blast even at great distances from ground zero. Buildings may collapse on them and burn. A fire storm may leave no air. The ventilating system, if it is operated during the period of active fallout, may suck radioactive dust into the shelter. There are innumerable ways of dying in a nuclear war and probably more people would perish in shelters, or die soon after emerging, than would come out with health unimpaired.

But all these drawbacks cannot entirely explain public apathy, since most people receive a more optimistic forecast and may half-believe it. There must be a large proportion of passive conscientious objectors—persons who have aesthetic-ethical reasons for not buying. They realize that any survivor of an all-out nuclear war will thereafter live the life of Hobbes's primitive man—solitary, poor, nasty, brutish and short. There must also be those who reflect that if men prove capable of doing this to one another, whether we do it to the Reds or the Reds to us, they will have lived long enough in that company.

For those who prefer a more activist role and who can risk a fine or jail sentence, there is an opportunity once a year to join a demonstration against the travesty of civil defense drills. Actually this is a counter-demonstration against the local civil defense politicos who put up a sign designating a building as a shelter, even if it would be knocked over by a bomb exploded ten miles away or has a lobby entirely enclosed by glass. But it is not for the ordinary citizen to argue with the man in the tin hat. Token compliance, such as standing in a doorway, may be enough, but some gesture of submission must be made.

The chief counter-demonstration is held every year in City Hall Park in the City of New York. It drives the Mayor to Times Square, where he poses for the photographers with a walkie-talkie and admires the empty square. But City Hall Park is jammed and the riot act is read by a civil defense police official without result. *Ipso facto,* the regular police, temporarily relieved of the obligation to protect the public against criminals, are pitted against college students, nonconformists, intellectuals, idealists, beatniks and other impotent enemies. To the credit of the police, they go about their duties mechanically, loading the prescribed number of demonstrators— about one in thirty—into the paddy wagons and behaving, on the whole, with unwonted forbearance.

Later, for the defiant ones the day of reckoning is at hand, and for the local Office of Civil Defense the day of vindication and pride in duty well done. The punishment varies, depending on the officiating magistrate, his civic and religious views, and his degree of indignation at discovering a political offender among the usual grist of prostitutes and pickpockets. Some of the magistrates regard a first offense as scarcely more serious than a parking violation, but are wary of appearing to be soft on dissenters. Others can hardly contain themselves. One, who had already been censured by the Appellate Division of the State Supreme Court in another connection, sentenced two college students, a boy and a girl, to sixty and thirty days, respectively, when they refused to avow a belief in divine providence or to swear that they would not participate in next year's protest.

In 1960, fewer than 500 persons stood their ground in City Hall Park. In 1961, the tabloids estimated the crowd at 500, *The New York Times* as 700–800, more sympathetic journalists at 2,000. The actual number was probably between 1,200 and 1,500.

The demonstrators cover a wide spectrum of political attitudes.

What they seem to have in common is a conviction that they couldn't lose. If the holocaust is averted they will have had a part, however small, in averting it. If the holocaust comes, they will have played the part of human beings, and they will be no more dead than the magistrates.

II

THE YEARNING FOR PEACE

THE PEACEMAKERS

by Barbara Deming

IT WAS FROM A GROWING CURIOSITY about this "thing" that, in August, 1960, I attended a sixteen-day training program in non-violence, conducted by a group called the Peacemakers. The site of the training program was New London, Connecticut—where a re-lated group, the Committee for Nonviolent Action, had been pro-testing, since June, the manufacture of Polaris-bearing submarines in nearby Groton. (On November 23, 1960, nine members of this committee were arrested for "trespassing" on the occasion of the launching of the *Ethan Allen,* the newest of these craft.) Both groups propose—as an alternative to the arms race and the cold war—unilateral disarmament (arranged in stages), and national defense, if it should be necessary, through nonviolent resistance. They argue that their means are not only powerful, but the only means con-sistent with our professed belief in the sanctity of human life. They also believe that if we disarmed, there is a very fair chance that the USSR would follow suit.

Peacemaker headquarters were not impressive—or, rather, my first impression was vivid but disheartening. An abandoned three-story tenement had been rented for the occasion—rooms above and two empty shops on the ground floor. The place had been furnished hastily with rented folding chairs, three long tables, a stove, icebox and enough army cots for some (the rest slept on the floor). Plaster dropped from the ceilings in little pellets upon one's head; and now and then drainage water ran down the walls. The first evening, as the group sat about in discussion, a sudden crackling report brought us all to our feet. I thought for a moment that a bomb had been thrown in among us; but it turned out that a beam in the cellar had just given way. Not long after, the building was condemned.

When I arrived, only about a dozen of the participants had gathered. Attendance varied, but usually there were anywhere from thirty to fifty people in the place. These first arrivals were assembled in the larger of the empty shops, their chairs pushed up against the room's four walls. They were young men, for the most part, and shabby as the old building itself. Dirty bluejeans and khakis, T-shirts and rumpled sports shirts were the rule. Flies buzzed about. An older man, gray-haired, mild and grave, dressed in a neat brown business suit, was giving the first lecture. This was Richard Gregg. He was presenting the essentials of nonviolence: respect for the other person, *whoever* he is; patience. "Patience is the recognition that change takes time." He was telling of the struggle of the untouchables in India to persuade the Brahmins to let them use a certain road. For one year and three months they had stood at the entrance to the road. On the 487th day, they had been allowed to enter. Mr. Gregg played with his watchchain, and seemed not quite to look at his audience—his foot quietly tapping the air as he spoke. Did the group seem to him unpromising? I wondered. One young man passed a paperbound book to another, and I noted the title: *Jesus Was a Beatnik. Was* this, in fact, a Beat gathering? What were they digging?

As more people arrived, however, I noted considerable variety among them: there were women as well as men; a number of couples with children; a range of ages, and of dress—though none looked prosperous. Before many hours had passed, the reason for the dismal headquarters became clear: most of those present had adopted a life of voluntary poverty. They had done so lest anxiety about losing what they had should ever make them hesitate; for these were people ready to act. Somewhere in the history of nonviolent resistance, the term "passive resistance" has been picked up. This term should be discarded. During my stay in New London, I was struck by many ironies in the drama I glimpsed of the relation of this group to the larger public. One of the chief was: those who insist on military preparedness are—of necessity now—constrained and passive; the "pacifists" are the only freely active people I have met in a long time.

A large percentage of those present had already risked and served jail sentences for their stand. The majority, for example, refuse to pay taxes, because the bulk of taxes go for armaments. They all stand, of course, for refusing the draft. Those who have been sent to jail for these "offenses" have protested the prison system while they were about it—their battle being with violence wherever it is met. (Many, though not all, are anarchists and object to prisons per se.) And the tales they tell include remarkable instances of prison authorities' bowing to their will. Their stand against violence engages them in protests against capital punishment; against segregation (many were active in the sit-in movement); against imperialism (some had joined a "peace walk" across Puerto Rico, calling for the true independence of that country); against Congressional abuse of investigating powers (many had had to fight for their own lives here; others had picketed for those in trouble). But the most distinctive activity in which they engage is civil disobedience at various war plants. For example, during the summer of 1959, eleven of them trespassed upon the missile plant at Omaha, Nebraska—in symbolic protest, "to reclaim the land for peaceful purposes." (One of the eleven to serve a six-month term for this was a mild-faced mother of four—whose husband patiently coped with the children.) Along with members of the Fellowship of Reconciliation, they have held continuous vigils of protest at Fort Detrick, the chemical and biological warfare plant; have organized protests against the absurdity of civil defense; have demonstrated in various cities on Hiroshima Day; and backed the voyage of *The Golden Rule* into the Eniwetok H-bomb testing area.

In New London, in the summer and fall of 1960, the act of trespass consisted in rowing across the Thames to Groton and attempting to board a Polaris submarine. (They protest the Polaris submarine especially because, in any attempt at a disarmament agreement, it is bound to complicate the problem of inspection infinitely.) The first few times they tried, the submarine turned out to be absent; the demonstrators simply trespassed upon the property of the Electric Boat Company, manufacturer of the submarine. What happened, too, was that the authorities decided that there would be less publicity if they made no arrests, but simply deposited the invaders outside the company gates. The publicity *was* less. On the other hand, the group was enabled to return again and again; and the fact that no one had been jailed encouraged others to swell their numbers. (After I left, they managed at last to board the *George Washington* and the *Patrick Henry*, and on November 23, 1960, the *Ethan Allen*—briefly. These actions did make *The New York Times*. The arrests on the last occasion made the front page.)

There is room in the movement, of course, for those who are not prepared to risk jail. A much larger group of volunteers back up these actions with "vigils" at the scene, with "peace walks" and with "leafleteering." A series of leaflets was passed out among Electric Boat workers at every working shift; lectures were arranged at local churches and clubs, and everybody involved engaged whomever he could throughout the town in conversation.

Many of these conversations took place at CNVA headquarters—a tiny office at 13 Bank Street—where townspeople, throughout the summer and fall, dropped in either to heckle or to ask questions; most took place at Electric Boat, where larger and larger crowds of workers, as well as passers-by, would gather after the acts of trespass to comment upon what had gone on. Over the months, more and more townspeople expressed sympathy, and a handful of workers volunteered to quit their jobs if the committee could find them other work. (A Committee for Useful Work is a CNVA project.) But first responses were for the most part violently hostile. "Why must you make fools of yourselves?"—it was asked again and again, with a tone of horror. There was deeper horror still in the other question asked most frequently: "And why must you break the law?"

Several leaflets reminded the reader of the many examples of civil disobedience in the evolution of this democracy; reminded him that the phrase itself—civil disobedience—had been coined by Thoreau (the group's rowboat is named the Henry David Thoreau). One leaflet quotes him: "If the law is of such a nature that it requires you to be the agent of injustice . . . then, I say, break the law. Let your life be a counter friction to stop the machine." Heads would shake. "But why break the law?" The depth of many Americans' awe of authority astonished me. "Would you have broken the law if you had lived in Germany under Hitler?" I heard one workman questioned. He answered stoutly: "No. I believe in obeying the law." Those who viewed with the greatest alarm the prospect of challenging authority (and who invariably assumed that individual action must be ineffectual: "What can you or I do? It's up to our leaders") were the same people who professed that they would rather die—would rather see mankind itself exterminated—than live "as slaves" under "authoritarian" Communist rule.

The longer I listened to the advocates of nonviolence in conversation with the townspeople, the more I was struck by the difference that marked them off from the majority—a difference, I think, directly resulting from those "foolish" acts in which they are engaging.

One incident, though minor, sticks in my memory as illustrative. The last day I was there, four people trespassed at the submarine base at Groton, and their act was prefaced by a five-mile "peace walk" from New London. Passing motorists yelled "Ass holes!" "Commies!", "Go back to Cuba!" but a few waved and smiled encouragement. A newspaper reporter walked alongside, questioning a woman directly behind me. Like others before him (myself included) he was bothered about the sloppy clothes worn by a few of the marchers. Why couldn't they be more careful of public opinion? Well, she answered, some among the marchers thought it important not to be concerned about middle-class conventions. For some, this was an important protest, too, though for others it wasn't. Did a few beards and a few shirt tails out really matter? The reporter seemed to think they mattered painfully. There was a note of peevish anxiety in his voice —a curious note, considering the fact that it was not, one gathered, *his* Cause the untidy ones endangered. A little later, a CNVA car came along and the driver pulled off at the side of the road for a moment—but not quite all the way off. A police car appeared, and again the reporter began to fret: "Oh, *why* do they do that? Now they'll get a ticket!" His tone was again one of nervous alarm. I turned to observe them both. The young woman looked at him with a calm surprise. "I don't think they'll get a ticket. But why be nervous about it?" she asked him. The police car drove on by. As I turned away, it struck me that here were two people living in quite different worlds, breathing an altogether different air.

The nervous agitation of the reporter was not an agitation peculiar to him. By now it was a phenomenon familiar to me. It seemed to me sometimes in these encounters with those who opposed us, that Fear was tangible in the air between us—a free-floating creature. Often we ourselves, incongruously, were its object. In spite of the fact that one argument used against us was that our acts must be ineffectual, people hardly ever passed us by with a pitying or careless smile. They passed us with eyes averted as though from some obscene or acutely embarrassing sight; or turned on us looks of such venom and such panic that it was hard, at first, to believe; some snatched leaflets from our hands to tear them into shreds—"Get out of here!"; some few got rougher still. By the end of the summer, a great number of the workers were accepting leaflets with open friendliness: "Back again?" "You get up early, don't you?" But I speak of those who were still unsympathetic. When those in the group who had trespassed were deposited outside the gates of the plant (to emphasize both their attitude of disobedience and their rejection of violence, they followed the course of going limp once officials laid hands upon them), onlookers would sometimes yell with fury: "Crack their heads on the sidewalk!" A young Naval officer who wandered into the CNVA office screamed at one of the women volunteers: "When the first Russian soldier rapes you, I hope you remember me!"

The real source of all this panicky fury emerged clearly enough in any prolonged conversation. Most conversations followed a pattern. The man or woman objecting to unilateral disarmament would first declare that war could be prevented if only this country would keep itself strong. (Sometimes one would add the very next moment: "We'll be out there fighting for *you*, if it comes, you cowards!") The risk of war through some accident or miscalculation would be dismissed with a scoff. But at a certain point there would break from their lips some remark revealing the assumption at heart that disaster *must* come, sooner or later; there was just nothing anyone could do about it. Very many added, "Perhaps we all deserve it!" The uniformity of this pattern was striking. The responses of the workers at Electric Boat matched almost phrase by phrase—if one censored a few rough words—the responses I heard from intellectuals. The source is the same acute suffering, arising from an infuriating sense of helplessness—of the impossibility any longer of battle that is not self-defeating, of gallant action; and the same deep sense of guilt from which there is, seemingly, no way out—unless perhaps in that almost-wished-for explosion which would be the End of the World.

A lively admission of the paralysis experienced by so many, but rarely acknowledged, is contained in a statement made by one of the young men who volunteered to try to board a nuclear submarine. CNVA always announces beforehand to the public and to all officials involved just what action it plans; and each individual who is about to commit civil disobedience state his motives in writing. The following is part of a statement by Victor Richman, one of the nine recently arrested:

An awesome specter threatens me now, invading the seclusion of the most precious parts of my existence, carelessly flaunting its meaning and visions, identifying itself, terribly, with my being. . . . It will be at times a dark, inky mist, blocking my path. . . . It appears also as a hard steel chain penetrating insidiously far below my skin, to hold the molecules of my body, to make them . . . cold and uneventful. And I have discovered, eventually, that I am not free. . . .

I have been told that I must not refrain from learning to kill. I have also been told that I must prepare myself in every way for my annihilation. And I have been told that I cannot be present at the places where these conditions are set down.

I have not the right to obey these conditions.

If there is a difference between these people and the majority, this decision has made the difference. In refusing "to obey these conditions," they have found at least a degree of freedom from the bondage the passage above, I think, quite accurately describes. How eventful the actions of these people will be in terms of the world at large, remains an open question—how many others, that is, will finally join them. But there is no question that their actions have changed *them*. The people I saw gathered in New London were people of altogether mixed background: Quakers, Catholics, Episcopalians, Methodists, Jews, atheists; Negro and white; men and women from all over the country, of both humble and privileged birth, and drawn from any number of occupations. They were people, also, of strong temperament; discussions were lively; the group was hardly monotone. Yet the longer I observed them, the more I was struck by a certain enviable air that could be said to distinguish them all—and most particularly those who had experimented with nonviolence for any length of time.

They are marked by an extraordinary spontaneity. All had recovered—or retained—the sense that an individual *can* act, and *has weight.* "If no one else will do it, then do it yourself," a homely, vivid old man said to me lightly—a house painter who had staged a one-man memorial protest in Cleveland on Hiroshima Day. As a result of their commitment to action, almost all were conspicuously hardy—in a very special manner. There was an atmosphere among them both grave and lighthearted. The place was full of wit. The more particular quality and cause of their fearlessness struck me one day as I listened to a group discussion, full of talk of radical changes that should be made in our society. We were sitting in the abandoned store, its windows heavily shrouded (the landlady had insisted on this, for rocks had been thrown through the windows over at CNVA). The shrouding gave the place the air of a gangster's hideout, and as the talk touched upon one thing after another wrong with things as they were, I suddenly asked myself (for I am the daughter of a well-to-do Republican lawyer): What am I doing here? This is talk of revolution. Then I recalled the methods to which they are committed: the rejection of secrecy; their careful advance notice to their adversary of all their plans. If the windows here were shrouded, the door was open to anyone who cared to wander in. I recalled their commitment to the use of persuasion in place of violence (seeing in memory their harmless, though stubborn, forms dragged by Electric Boat officials from the company cars, and dumped on the sidewalk—at which they would rise, brush the dirt from their clothes and address the flustered officials: "We're sorry to have to put you through all this, but it's necessary"). I suddenly recognized the source of their distinctive boldness; the source is innocence. No ordinary misgivings about injuring another person need dilute their resolution, and make them hesitate. The candor and innocence of their actions gives to these people—for all the very great differences among them—a likeness to each other. The actions themselves leave their mark upon them.

Among all those present who had experimented with nonviolence for any time, I encountered the same surprise at the power of the actions in which they engage to bear them up. "There don't have to be big men—just big actions. . . . When you get into it, you discover things about yourself that you didn't understand before you began" —this was a Southern minister speaking, a man very active in the integration struggle. The fact that they marvel not at themselves, but at the possibilities in a certain mode of action, lends to all their stories, a special quality, gives to the teller a dramatist's eye upon events—lively, impersonal, frequently humorous.

One of the most remarkable tales was that told by Eroseanna Robinson, the track star. Arrested for refusing to pay taxes, she refused to cooperate at all: "In conscience I couldn't be part of this drama. . . . Everyone was playing a role. What we have to do more and more is teach them that the script is wrong . . . by ad-libbing in the spirit of nonviolence." So she refused to walk into court, and was carried in; she fasted in jail, and was tube-fed. In the beginning, officials were very rough with her indeed. She was painfully carried along by the chain of her handcuffs ("But I said: I'll just detach myself"). They carried her with her feet carefully angled up in immodest fashion ("But I felt: This is not my indignity"). They put her in solitary; they threatened her with a mental institution; they promised her that the other prisoners would beat her up. But the other prisoners, who had begun by asking "Who is this silly?", ended by identifying solidly with her resistance. In fact, when another inmate was badly hurt, and the prison was slow about getting her to a hospital, a large group, for the first time in the history of that prison, went on a hunger strike—in imitation of Rose—and the prison got the woman off to the hospital with unusual dispatch. By the time Rose left, prison officials themselves were talking to her not "as to a child, but trying to reach courteously across quite a gap, and with apology." She left after ninety-three days of a year's sentence. Other

Peacemakers were by now picketing the prison; all the inmates were stirred by this fact; and it was too much for the authorities.

This story was told with great spirit and wit—the wit impartially at her own expense and at others'. Again, it was not of herself that she boasted, but of these new means she had adopted. The effect of her resistance on the other prisoners occasioned her special wonder. When I went up to her, some time later, and said, "That was a very beautiful story," she answered with simplicity, "I felt that way about it, too."

One constant note recurring in all the discussions was the question of how the nonviolent method could gain mass support. There was much discussion as to whether it was wiser for the group to act on many fronts, or to concentrate time and effort on a single action. The executive secretary of CNVA, Bradford Lyttle, argued with passion that it was essential to forget all other projects and concentrate on protesting against nuclear armaments. As someone paraphrased his words: "Would it matter whether we blew up integrated or segregated?" Another man argued as passionately that "It has always been the folly of pacifism to think of violence and nonviolence as only overt . . . Resistance to war is impossible without resistance to imperialism, to racism, to violence as an everyday pervasive reality." The majority shared this view: "It is all one picture."

It was felt that a considerable impact upon public opinion had been made in New London. When the summer ended, though many had to return to jobs and schools, a few made the decision to pull up roots and actually move to the area. One man has given up a printing business to do so; another has moved his business and his family with him. But various other projects were set in motion, too, before the conference closed—with emphasis on concerted support of the sit-in movement.

The discussions were frankly groping. Those who were most experienced were most frank about admitting how much there remained to be learned. But their readiness to learn it was striking. Perhaps the rest of us have everything to learn with them.

A REVOLT AGAINST SHELTERS

by Mary M. Grooms

WHEN THE BOARD OF EDUCATION of the Greece Central School District, in a suburb of conservative Rochester, New York, decided to include an equipped fallout shelter in its plans for a new high school, it had the best of intentions. According to the board president, Edward Shaughnessy, the members felt "there is a threat [of nuclear war] to our children; we feel we can do something about this at a small cost."

They were encouraged in the plan by state Civil Defense authorities; and, after writing to President Kennedy, they received a letter from the national headquarters of Civil Defense complimenting them for their foresight.

But Mr. Wilho M. Salminen, a fellow board member who had worked at Oak Ridge as a scientist, opposed the project from the beginning. In deference to his opposition, the budget item for the proposed shelter was separated from the $5,960,000 school-construction bond issue, thus enabling the voters to decide upon the shelter separately.

No arrangements were made for public debate on the issue, however. As Mr. Shaughnessy said, "We knew the shelter program was controversial. We didn't make a big thing of it because of its relation to the bond issue." It almost seemed that, while the Greece school board had too much faith in democracy to "sneak the bomb shelter in"—as, according to one member, had been done in four other schools in New York State—it did not have enough faith to let the voters get in on the argument. Members were afraid the voters could not explore the philosophy of fallout shelters without precipitating dissension on the school-construction program.

Five days before the vote, the board held a public information meeting about the building program; it was planned that, at the end of the meeting, questions about the shelter could be asked. The morning newspaper reported that officials from Civil Defense had been invited, as well as members from the "Radiation Group"—the latter an informally organized group of nuclear scientists from the University of Rochester. The scientists volunteered to answer factual questions about radiation, carefully making it clear that they took no sides in the matter.

On the morning of the information meeting another organization, which had been concerned about the shelter for weeks, formally moved into the fray. The Independent Political Forum, formed eight months previously by a group of fourteen veterans of the Stevenson-for-President campaign, asked permission to present its side of the shelter issue. To the credit of Mr. Shaughnessy, the permission was granted, even though the board chairman knew that the forum intended to oppose him and that, legally, he had the power to deny it a voice.

The Independent Political Forum, unconnected with any national organization, is strictly a home-grown phenomenon. From its original fourteen members, it grew rapidly until its mailing list reached nearly 600. As one member said, "It seems as though all the liberals in this conservative town suddenly found each other." Students, ministers, housewives, college professors, industrial workers, teachers, engineers, labor unionists—all kinds of people joined.

The purpose of the organization is "to stimulate meaningful discussion of world, national and local problems and participate in appropriate political action. In practice, this has included the sponsorship of meetings with such speakers as Dr. Linus Pauling and Norman Thomas on problems in disarmament and other speakers on the Cuban revolution; collecting signatures on petitions urging that disarmament negotiations be continued until agreement is reached; successfully supporting a Negro physicist when he ran into

opposition in moving into a previously all-white suburb; distributing
article reprints, books and pamphlets on disarmament, fallout and
Cuba; and keeping a steady stream of letters going to editors, the
President, Senators and Congressmen.

As co-chairman of the forum, I was selected to write and present
our statement at the meeting. After the building program had been
thoroughly discussed, Mr. Shaughnessy read the board's statement
advocating the fallout shelter and presenting an impressive list of
sources of support, starting with President Kennedy and working
down. He then called for questions. It soon became apparent, from
the short answers people were getting, that he hoped to keep discussion to a minimum. At that point, I asked and received permission to
read the statement from the Independent Political Forum.

We first thanked Mr. Shaughnessy for allowing us to speak and
I noted that, as the mother of four young children, I appreciated the
feelings which had led to the inclusion of the shelter in plans for the
new school. But, our statement continued, we had come to the conclusion, after considerable study of the issue, that shelters are a
"form of false security and represent a real danger to our children.
Shelters encourage a war psychology, intensify the arms race and
promote the idea that nuclear war is necessary or inevitable." We
went on to point out that the thinking of Civil Defense is obsolete,
since the shelter plans were predicated on the notion that the nearest
bomb would fall at the Niagara Frontier and that it would take an
hour for the radiation to reach Rochester. Today, however, upstate
New York is the site of a number of "hard bases"—that is, underground launching pads for 9,000-mile ICBMs—and our community
has become a prime target. We suggested, further, that building
shelters would merely lead to the production of bigger and deadlier
bombs or to the use of chemical and biological warfare, in which
case the shelter ventilation system would become an oversized spray
gun loaded with lethal chemicals that would kill the children inside.

We went on to object to the fact that the shelter had not been
publicly discussed and suggested that "this is not the way the citizens
of a free democratic society should approach such a vital issue. To
vote on any issue without full information is not living up to our

obligations as responsible members of a free society." We urged that
the Greece citizens vote against the proposal and perhaps hold another vote on it after the issue had been discussed.

We ended with the statement: "If there is $45,000 in Greece that
you do not know what to do with, it is our hope that you will spend it,
not on a useless shelter, but on books and other equipment for your
children the better to teach them to solve the problems the shelter
seeks to hide from."

After I sat down, the board called upon Warner Weber, New
York State engineer for the design of bomb shelters. Making no attempt to refute the forum's statement, he merely said: "Mrs. Grooms
has valid policies, but I think they are in favor of Mr. Khrushchev."

Surprised, I snapped back, "I resent that!"

Then a young minister seated in the audience rose and said,
"We're told this issue should be discussed, but the first time someone
tries to, they are accused of being a traitor or something!"

At that point, board member Wilho Salminen seized the microphone and, shaking with rage, he attacked both the shelter project
and Mr. Weber: "I came here tonight determined not to say anything about the shelter, although I have been opposed to it from the
start—perhaps because I know something about it. However, even
courts give dissenting opinions, and I guess Boards of Education can,
too. I will have nothing to do with a man who comes here and
bandies words with us as Mr. Weber has done."

He then cited a number of radiation accidents, from the death of
one of the crew of the *Lucky Dragon* to the recent accident at an
experimental atomic pile in Iowa. He told how the bodies were removed by teams of men—one team running in, putting down the
stretcher and running out; another team running in, putting the
bodies on the stretcher, and running out; another team running in,
bringing the bodies to the door; etc. We in his audience could picture
a shelter-full of high school students coming out into a world filled
with hundreds of thousands of irradiated bodies. He ended by saying:
"I object to this shelter because it is inadequate philosophically,
inadequate psychologically and inadequate because it is not sufficient unto itself."

At that, Mr. Weber got up and apologized to the meeting for having been so "emotional."

The remainder of the meeting was relatively calm, with the radiation scientists and the Civil Defense representatives taking turns to answer such questions as, "What would happen here if a ten-megaton bomb fell on Buffalo?"; "Is it likely the Russians would launch a saturation attack?" It appeared, from the answers, that the worth of the fallout shelters depended very largely upon the cooperation of the Russians with the plans of Civil Defense. If Russia would only be reasonable and drop no more than one bomb on Buffalo, fallout shelters in Rochester would be a definite help.

The next morning, one of the board members called me to express his concern at my attitude and that of the forum. He said that the board had encountered no opposition to the shelter elsewhere. We discussed the philosophy of the shelters and related topics for nearly three hours and parted with much good will, though still on opposite sides. He predicted that the shelter would be approved by a two-to-one majority. Actually, in spite of the fact that we were receiving a number of calls supporting our position, we forum members also thought it probably would be approved. So it was as much a surprise to us as to everyone else when the Greece Central School District approved the $5,960,000 building program by a vote of 1,511 to 673, but turned down the $45,000 shelter project by 1,457 to 698.

At this point everyone, on both sides, is trying to figure out why the vote went as it did. In the period between the information meeting and the vote, local newspaper columns blossomed with letters from forum members opposing the shelter; forum members in the school district distributed reprints of Gov. Meyner's article in *Coronet*, "Bomb Shelters Will Not Save Us," and contacted several Protestant ministers; a Presbyterian minister of a large Greece church strongly opposed the project from the pulpit the Sunday preceding the vote; there were long reports in the newspapers of the heated information meeting.

Perhaps these last-minute efforts were successful. Perhaps people are just more opposed to Civil Defense and fallout shelters than we had suspected. Perhaps there was resentment against Mr.

Weber's attempt to "McCarthyize" me (even members of the board who were pushing the shelter disapproved of Weber's tactic).

At any rate, the parents in Greece drew a line on the arms race and said, "No further. You can't make us vote for our own children's burial vaults." Those who believe the American people can be herded like cattle should take note.

THEY WALKED FOR PEACE

by Clayton C. Barbeau

"WE'RE MERCENARIES," one of the pipers told a reporter that October day, "just paid to do a job." And, kilts flapping, pipes yowling, they started out from the War Memorial Opera House followed by over 2,000 non-kilted, non-mercenary marchers. Of no specific age group or type, the walkers yet seemed happily united; smiles were everywhere. "I think the turn-out was better the last time, we had about about 5,000 then," a white-haired, scholarly looking man observed. A little Negro girl of about six or seven walked ahead of him bearing a sign reading: *Mary, Mary, quite contrary/Where did your garden go?* While the white woman holding her hand bore a placard which said: *H-Bombs Kill Kids.*

Monitors with blue arm bands hurried ahead to post themselves at intersections and see that the traffic signals were observed. "Two abreast, please," one monitor was urging, "two abreast, leave room for the passers-by." But there were few passers-by along this part of the route; there were only automobile salesmen, standing in front of the shrines to the latest models, staring at us. *Set the Pace for Peace,* a sign exhorted them. *Join us,* another implored, but without evident success. The salesmen did accept the leaflet that the woman ahead of me was handing out. A young boy was thrusting the same leaflet upon motorists waiting for the green light at intersections.

"Go back to Russia," a voice said near my ear and a man with a

Nixon button on his lapel cut through the procession and hurried on his way.

A photographer dropped to one knee, adjusted his camera and took a pot shot at the marchers as we waited for the light to change so that we could cross Van Ness. A small band of people were stranded on the island in the middle of the thoroughfare and, in their midst, a bobbing poster read, *Frankly, I'm worried.*

The light changed and the monitor stepped into the street and urged the people across. "Don't pay attention to hecklers," he said. "Just smile and continue on your way."

"It's longer than I thought," somebody said, "look."

And I looked back, too, to see that the file behind us extended along Van Ness for at least six blocks. The head of the column, with its bagpipers, was now about six blocks ahead of us.

The woman in front of me proffered leaflets to all whom we passed. About half of them preferred to look the other way, as if our passage embarrassed them. Others accepted the printed sheet. A photographer, balanced on the bumper of a car, snapped the column. We passed a bar. The men standing there already had leaflets and one of them said: "Vote for Kennedy; he'll give you peace." Another shouted at a bearded walker, "Hey, Castro, why aren't you in Cuba?"

We passed a theatre where people were going in for a matinee. They scurried past us, blind to a sign reading: *Radiation means Contamination means Extermination—Ban the Bomb.* Did they fear contamination from us? A stern-looking woman of about seventy, dressed in an expensive black suit and wearing a rhinestone lapel pin that spelled out Nixon, shouted at us: "Go to work! Then you'll have peace." Her young male companion scanned us expressionlessly.

A young man in a corduroy jacket leaned against a car and smiled. "It's really inspiring to see so many rational people," he said. "And all in one place."

"Why don't you join us?" asked the lady handing him a leaflet.

"I will," he responded as he took the leaflet. But he did not look at it. Instead, he continued to stand there shaking his head and smiling happily at the passing parade.

As we approached Union Square, the passers-by were more expensively dressed and shopkeepers stood in doorways to peep out at us. Three women dressed in the peak of fashion were so engrossed in conversation that they entered the column and walked with us for almost half a block before one of them noticed anything. They scampered to the sidelines in confusion.

A matron glanced at the offered leaflet and struck at it violently. "I don't want peace at any price," she nearly screamed. One man glanced up at the sign that read: *Dona Nobis Pacem* and muttered, "Communist dupes." A white-haired woman and her husband each accepted a leaflet from the girl as we paused at another intersection. Then they joined our file, right in back of me. "I don't think they'll mind if we get in here," the old woman said softly.

We passed the front entrance of the St. Francis Hotel. I looked back and saw a sign I had not noticed before: *Peace not Pandemonium.* Across the street, parts of the parade were filing into Union Square. The slogans bobbed up and down among the hedges: *A State with the H-Bomb Is like an Idiot with a gun; End the Arms Race Save the Human Race; A world without war or A war without a world; Destroy the Bomb.*

As the rally assembled in the square, the marchers were led in song by a group on the rostrum. An elderly man in a large, crudely scrawled sandwich board dazedly watched the invasion. *Jesus is coming SOON* his sign read, and cited texts on the need for abolishing Sunday and giving up the eating of pork, fowl and blood, among other things.

After all the participants were settled on the lawn, a Unitarian minister announced that both the local Democratic and Republican headquarters had been asked to send speakers to give their parties' views on disarmament, but neither side had accepted. Each of the two major candidates had been asked to send a statement. Vice President Nixon had failed to respond, but Senator Kennedy had sent a long telegram setting forth his views, which was read aloud.

Then Bob Pickus, executive secretary of Acts for Peace, spoke. Ben Seaver of the American Friends Service Committee and Ross Flanagan, assistant peace secretary, added their comments. Three salesmen in an expensive clothing shop across the street listened from draped windows of their second floor. A Kennedy caravan blasted past.

All of the speakers insisted that there was a path open other than war or surrender, but that our government has not been taking the initiative in exploring this third route: disarmament and the abolition of nuclear weapons. Again and again it was pointed out that the amount of money spent on the pursuit of peace is infinitesimal compared to the amount we spend on war preparation. Our per capita expenditure for the U.N., one speaker said, is $.60 a year; our annual per capita expenditure on missile development and the arms race is approximately $291.

After the speeches, the children were given blue balloons with the words *Voice your vote for Peace* on them and the crowd began to disperse.

The street evangelist climbed upon a bench and harangued the departing crowd, telling them that Sunday was a day dedicated to sun worship and that we were all doomed unless we abolished it. Citing chapter and verse, he smashed his fist into his palm again and again. "The end of the world is imminent," he cried.

Just as I was remarking the absence of the Communists and their newspapers at our rally, a leaflet was handed to me bearing the imprimatur of the Communist Party of California. Now I, too, left, walking the concrete covered hills towards my home. I wondered why I had come. . . .

And then I remembered how Americans had often held the German people responsible for not speaking up when they saw where the policies of the Hitler regime were taking them. I knew now that I had come along because I wanted to do something for peace, if that something was only to walk for one mile through the city of San Francisco on a lovely fall day.

But I am still troubled, because I know that peace will require a greater sacrifice than this.

THE LONG WALK FOR PEACE: NEW MISSION TO MOSCOW

by Barbara Deming

Team members of the San Francisco-to-Moscow Walk for Peace tell how sometimes in the Eastern countries a crowd at the roadside would surge out to meet them, offering flowers, singing songs, expecting from them the kind of talk about peace they were accustomed to. But then the walkers' plea for unilateral disarmament, their plea to resist as individuals the military policies of their own government, would so take people by surprise that there would be a stunned and prolonged silence.

The walk across Europe sharply dramatizes the world's dilemma. As they crossed from the Western into the Eastern world—fifteen Americans, reinforced by volunteers from eight other countries— the team literally stepped out of one perspective of events into another. In the West, fingers were always pointed East: *there* lies the trouble. Crossing the border into the Communist world, they had only to take a few steps and—as though they had walked through the looking-glass—the same image was presented to them, in reverse. All fingers pointed West: *there* lies the trouble.

In the States, the reiterated question, "Why not tell it to the Russians?" had been responsible for the *idea* of the walk. In Russia, they were asked again and again, "Why aren't you back home making your suggestions there?" In meetings in the States, their speeches sometimes brought people in the audience jumping to their feet to cry, "Communist!" The same recommendations now provoked the cry of "Fascist!"

In East as in West the fears they encountered were heartfelt, the bitter experiences cited were real. They became real enough for the walkers; as they were on foot, they covered the actual ground where certain events had taken place—passed the mass graves where the Nazis had used bulldozers to shovel the dead into the ground, spent a day at Auschwitz. At the press conference the team held when it returned home from Moscow, Bradford Lyttle, the team's coordinator in the field, warned: "One thing I would like to emphasize again and again to the United States—that is the horror with which the people of all Eastern countries view our arming of West Germany. The ultimate justification they give for their military policies is that they could take no chance of ever being invaded again by the Germans. . . ."

East and West, fears were real. But to neither East nor West were the fears of the *other* side real. When Brad Lyttle spoke to the American press of Eastern concern about German arms, his words evaporated in the air before him: I saw no subsequent reference to them anywhere, though representatives of all major papers were there that day. And when the walkers spoke to Russian audiences of fears in the United States of a Russian take-over, the response was a great roar of incredulous laughter. (Socialist states fight *defensive* battles, never *offensive* ones—surely this was well known to the world.) A stock tirade would follow, listing the aggressive acts of the Western nations—their own even more successfully overlooked than ours are overlooked when *we* make the speech.

The walk dramatizes for us this condition: East and West confronting each other, each pointing its finger at the other, and arming for "defense"; arming of course more and more heavily—for each tells itself that the other can understand only force. Neither side is able to recall that *no one* understands force; each, for its own part, capable of "understanding" from it only that the other side wants war.

To the walkers themselves, this lesson of the walk was painfully clear. Describing the vigil which they held in Red Square on the day of their arrival, one of them put it: "It was a very sad time, that one hour"—for all the exhilaration of that day, of the extraordinary stint at last completed. They tell first of the march to the square—handing out leaflets as fast as their hands could move (here the speaker would imitate the hectic motion of flicking fingers). The people pressed so thickly and eagerly that "it needed a lot of pacifist technique" to keep them calm. In the square, after the photographers had "finished their gymnastics," they lined up silently with their signs. The crowd of hundreds, who had been so boisterous, moving about, asking questions, pointing, slowly quieted down too and stood, staring intently. Everybody stood there for over an hour. Some of the team members were crying, and some of the Russians were crying, too. One of the walkers explained her tears: "I was thinking how much they wanted peace, and how little they knew how to get it."

The attempted labor of the pacifists was to rouse people from the trance of national self-righteousness. Their role was necessarily a rude one. At evening meeting after evening meeting arranged by the Soviet Peace Council, for example, men and women would rise and—in justification of their government's policies—recount long harrowing tales of personal suffering in the last war. The pacifists had to reply: Your heartbreaking stories are not to the point. Men and women would leap to their feet with long lists of grievances against the Western powers. Their reply had to be: We haven't come to argue with you who is to blame for what. Only one question is relevant now: How are we to escape from the trap in which we are *all* caught? Some one government must make the first move down a new road, giving to others the confidence to follow; and when a new step is needed, on whom should one count if not oneself?

On one occasion in Russia the pacifists received an extraordinary response. This was at the University of Moscow. Here, too, in the hour-long session that had been arranged for them, they heard stock speeches rattled out, the familiar justification of the government position. But they had clear evidence that their own words had made an impression. While one faculty member was replying to them, the students grew so restive that the speaker decided to cut his speech in half. As he talked, the following note was passed up to Bradford Lyttle: "My dear friends, do not believe absolutely this dirty official and his common demagogic phrases. Go your path. We are with you."

After the session was over, Lyttle reports, one of the students who had presented the government position more effectively than any of the others came to him privately and was "an entirely different man. He listened intently to what I had to say." The session lasted rather more than the prescribed hour. As the time drew to an end, and a school official rose to close the discussions, many students rose with him, crying "Let them go on!" The official pleaded that another class needed the room. "Nonsense!", the students roared him down, "this is more important!"

The man was clearly out of control of the situation. The talks continued for another hour and a half. His own last words to the room were a plea that the students there—who were for the most part science students—would always rigorously question the given official position in the light of the facts they had, and of their sense of the new realities of the twentieth century. The reply from the floor was: "We will do this!"

Meanwhile, another note had arrived: "Thank you for your travel and that you went to us. It is not for us to speak as simply as you. The men's kinds of thinking are rather slowly changing." Lyttle sums up his impressions: "One of the most hopeful things to me of anything on the walk was the ferment we saw there, the signs that things are changing—if we can only hold off a war and allow these changes to develop."

It is an astonishing fact that at a time of deep crisis, of near war, the walkers were allowed to enter East Germany, Poland, Russia itself—not only bringing them word of Western views they had not had before, and thus a perspective on their own governments' versions of events, but openly suggesting that if the people really wanted peace, they should disobey their governments, refuse to pay taxes for armaments, refuse to work in war industries, refuse to serve in the armed forces; all this in countries where people had never even heard their governments openly criticized on foreign-policy matters. The walkers quote a foreign correspondent who watched them march into Moscow, passing out their thousands of leaflets, and exclaimed in wonder: "And the police are not preventing

them!" The walk set a precedent for political dissent in these countries.

The walkers themselves, asked why they think they were allowed
in, give as a first answer that the Communists, and particularly the
Russians, have been trying for years to picture themselves as champions of peace. "This made it hard for them to say 'no' to a group
such as ours." They add: The image the Russians like to project is
based on reality. That the Russians do both want and need peace
seemed as clear to the walkers, after their trip, as that the Russians
were trying in all the wrong ways to secure it. *"Mir, Mir, Mir"*
(PEACE, PEACE, PEACE): the signs calling for peace are as
common there as whiskey ads here—though the Russians will declare any day (as we will) their willingness to "defend" themselves
with all the missiles in their armory. Nor was there anyone the
walkers met who spoke of war with the West as inevitable. They
found the people with whom they talked full of their country's plans
for the future ("I have never talked with such confident people")
and full of recognition that peace was necessary for them to carry
out these plans. There was, they report, a good deal more conviction
that they would prosper in a disarmed world than there is here in
America.

Plainly the Russians wanted the walkers to enter Moscow on
their own terms—were hoping and expecting to convert them along
the way to multilateralism. As Lyttle puts it, "They could not really
imagine that we could walk for three weeks in Russia, enjoy their
hospitality, visit their historic places, see the great jump they had
made, see how they wanted peace—all this, without coming to accept
their position." The pressure they exerted was intense. The pressure
of their hospitality was "fantastic." Banquets would appear at the
side of the road as if in a fairy tale: tablecloths spread upon the
grass, set with china and silverware and flowers; and caviar and wine
and decorated cakes; abundant courses piping hot, served by wait-
resses; hot water supplied, too, for them to wash in; towels hung from
the branches of trees! On one occasion, the whole area had been
shaded by a bower specially constructed out of leafy boughs; and
strips of bright carpet were laid out for them to sit on. The log the
walkers kept is full of exclamations on the subject: "Brad gave his

'This is the most exciting meal in Russia' speech, but this time we were astounded and tremble at the thought of future efforts."

Pressures of another sort were exerted at the specially arranged evening meetings. Here audiences would wait patiently for as much as an hour or two, when the walkers were delayed on the road; then would rise to batter and batter at them with their prepared responses. (That they had been prepared in advance was often obvious, as the translations would be written out.)

The Russians did their utmost to change the walkers, and turn the walk to their own use, and yet they failed; and here is the very significant point: In spite of this, the team was welcomed in Moscow. Lyttle quotes one of the members of the Peace Council: "If you work with us, we will give you everything!" The Council is the only peace organization the law permits in Russia—if not officially a government organ, it is virtually so—and *could* have given them "everything." "I've no doubt," says Lyttle, "that if we had been willing to modify our program a little, drop our unilateral sign, we would have had whole villages turning out for us, and a quarter of a million people in Red Square." But the point is: They refused to alter their stand and, even so, were made welcome.

As a matter of fact, before the team crossed the border, the Russians had been given a pretty good idea of what to expect. The East German Peace Council had sent word that the walkers were not very malleable. East German "supporters," walking with the team, had tried to exploit the walk by passing out leaflets of their own—presenting the Ulbricht position. As they had done in West Germany when officials tried to reroute them, the walkers had halted their march and refused to go on until this stopped. Moreover, when they approached Berlin, it had been just at the time of the acute crisis there, and authorities had informed them that they would not be allowed to enter the city—instead, they would be routed round it in buses and taken to the city of Stalinstadt, near the border of Poland. The walkers, although they appreciated the difficulties of the moment, had been given no opportunity to negotiate alternatives to this plan, and considered a simple ultimatum unacceptable; so they refused to cooperate—"defied the authority of the State"—and were dumped, "limp," into buses and driven back into West Germany. *Still* the Russians had made them welcome.

Here, the walkers would agree, another very important point must be made. For all their eagerness to project an image of themselves as champions of peace, the Russians would certainly never have allowed these people in if they had not clear records of challenging Western governments as well. All of them had demonstrated actively against militarism in their own country. Some of them—chiefly among the Americans—had served jail sentences as draft refusers and as conscientious trespassers upon military property.

The team made a point of picketing military installations in every country it passed through, and it made a special impression on the Russians that they had defied the regulations in West Germany and demonstrated in front of four military installations there in one day. (It made an impression on West German peace workers, too, that they got away with it; the officials involved, though—being German—dumbfounded that the walkers would persist in their plans when told they were forbidden, backed down and pressed no charges after the event. German pacifists now intend to be more aggressive.)

This was certainly their passport into the Communist countries— that they came not to reiterate the familiar phrases: *we* in the West are innocent, *you* in the East are to blame, but in a spirit independent of that sad rite. They came as men who reject blind national loyalty, and whose concern is loyalty toward all men. In this spirit they had declared, before starting out, that they would acknowledge no nation's right to exclude them, but in their search for peace would enter each country on their way, legally, if possible, but if necessary, illegally. (It is a sad fact that France alone—a member of the "free" world—tried to prevent their entry. What the walkers did—after clearly announcing their plans—was to jump ship twice at Le Havre, swimming ashore and there distributing their leaflets until stopped by the gendarmes, arrested and carried back, "limp," to the ship. They then proceeded to Belgium, where a group of French supporters marched through France to meet them.)

These people believed that one can consistently maintain loyalty toward all men only if one is committed to nonviolent struggle—as only such struggle can distinguish between another man's policies, which one may wish to oppose vigorously, and the man himself, whom one refuses to destroy. The walk was an experiment in this discipline, and any answer to the question: How does it happen that the team got to Moscow? must seriously weigh the relevance of this fact.

"The nonviolent power developed by this walk," says Lyttle, "went far beyond anyone's expectations in terms of our ability to move the Communists and generate acceptance for ourselves in their countries. I think it was very unusual, very surprising, that we got into the German Democratic Republic at all, considering the crisis the country was in—and that we lasted as long as we did. When they told us we couldn't enter Berlin, I had the feeling that they did so only with the greatest reluctance. Officials at all levels were upset. The ultimatum was delivered at the very last moment, and they came to ask us to reconsider no fewer than half a dozen times—and then retired and said they would just go discuss it with the authorities further. No fewer than six times!" One walker reports that some of the Germans who helped dump them into the buses were crying.

In Russia, says Lyttle, "in those moments when they had the most intense dislike of what we were saying, as when we urged unilateralism upon the Soviet Union, or pleaded with the people to oppose the policy of their government—the same people who called us the worst names in meetings would make it clear to us afterwards: You are our guests, and we honor you for the stand you have taken in the West, and we wish the march well." As a matter of fact, he reports, they put up with some astonishing things. The team was no band of traveling saints, and sometimes were very rude. When the walkers were taken on a tour of Lenin's apartments—an unusual privilege—some of the members were bored and read papers and books while being shown about, which to the Communist officials was the worst form of sacrilege. "They even overlooked that!"

Lyttle came back from the trip, he says, convinced that while it is more than difficult in Communist countries to implant the nonviolent philosophy directly, they respond to it and can be influenced by it profoundly. "They are not cynical, after all, like the Nazis. They think they are doing right. Place them in a situation where they feel they have to use violence to defend themselves, and your treatment will be summary. But avoid placing yourselves in this area, and they find it very difficult. When the conflicts between us got to a serious point, they always backed down rather than regard us as enemies." He gives as an example the following story:

Though there has been a certain effort on the part of our press to picture the Russians as breaking one agreement after another made with the walkers, actually they kept the letter of every advance agreement made—except one. Originally, the walkers were to be allowed until November 1 to reach Moscow. Suddenly, in early September, they were informed that they must be there by October 3. It was pretty clear why the Russians took this action: They had heard from the German Democratic Republic about the team's defiance of authority there; the Twenty-Second Congress was scheduled to convene in Moscow in late October; as the pacifists were obviously not people to be controlled easily, it would be better to have them out of Moscow before the Congress opened. A. J. Muste flew to Moscow to try to restore the original date, but it was soon clear that the Russians would not budge. Which precipitated a crisis.

The team was used to marching twenty to twenty-five miles a day. Now forty to forty-five would be called for. The Russians had their own answer: buses could transport them over those stretches inhabited only by birch trees and rabbits; the walkers could dismount to walk into and out of the towns themselves. But the walkers couldn't accept this arrangement; they had set out on a *walk* from San Francisco to Moscow, and covering the actual ground was important to them. They suggested their own solution. They'd walk in relays; some of them could get up before dawn and some of them could march on after dark if there were miles still to be made. "*Nyet.*" The Russians had insisted from the first on the principle of "togetherness." " '*Vmyesta*'—we heard the word a million times." It was clear that security instructions were involved. And now the team very nearly split up. A few of them (these were mostly Europeans) were for accepting the Russian terms. In fact, some were ready to quit if the other walkers couldn't see that the important thing was simply to *get* to Moscow with their message. A number of the Americans declared that they would quit if the terms *were* accepted.

The matter was discussed most of the night. It was finally agreed that they would try a forced march for a few days, and see how that went—postponing any final decisions. And this they did—all of them rising at dawn (after getting to bed late, because of the usual meeting with the town), some attempting the entire day's walk, some trying their best to sleep for certain stretches of the time in the two Russian buses that went along with them. Tempers soon deteriorated. People began to get sick. On the third day, David Rich, the young man who up to this point had walked every single mile from San Francisco, dropped out, suffering from dysentery and exhaustion. And then a surprising thing happened. The Russians suddenly made it possible for them to continue as an unbroken team and to keep the walk an unbroken walk.

"That evening," Lyttle explains, "Director K., who was in charge of all the arrangements, came and put his arm around my shoulders. 'Mr. Lyttle, tonight we are going to show you how to get from here to Moscow. We will be hunters.'" He pulled out a schedule of days and distances. "I'll show you how we will kill the wolf, the lion and the elephant"—and he pointed to a stretch of 110 kilometers, another of 130, a final one of 150 ("That one is the elephant; I don't know quite yet how we are going to kill *it*"). He then proposed a very complicated schedule which involved walking to the outskirts of a town, taking a bus round it, walking on for some miles, taking the bus back to town for the night, then walking through it—all juggled about to make their arrangements for hospitality possible, but to permit the walkers still to walk every mile.

The team examined the schedule carefully and could find no catch in it; but there was still the problem, Lyttle suggested, of how to walk so many miles in a day's time. Director K. remarked that there was no problem there: they could just send out one group of their people early in the morning, while the others were still in their beds. "All of us just looked at him in amazement," says Lyttle, "for we had been fighting about this for days"; it involved a complete violation of the Russians' own principle of "togetherness." "Oh no, it doesn't," said Director K. quite blandly. "It simply means that some people will be out walking earlier." "We didn't go into it further," said Lyttle, with a large smile.

Both sides, in Russia, wanted the team to get to Moscow, but each wanted it under different conditions. "They were extraordinarily capable and cunning. . . . In many of the bargaining situations," says Lyttle, "I felt I was being pushed harder than I have ever been pushed in my life"; but the team managed nevertheless to retain its integrity and to act in such a way that the Russians always backed down rather than see the project destroyed. "Well, Mr. Lyttle," said Director K. at their last encounter, "together we managed to kill the wolf, the lion and the elephant."

Both Russia and the United States would like to prevent war— though each wants peace on its own terms. Perhaps the walk to Moscow shows the way in which a struggle with the Russians along *this* road could best be carried out.

PROJECT WASHINGTON: "SOMETHING HAD TO BE DONE"

by Steven V. Roberts

MORE THAN 5,000 students from almost a hundred colleges converged on Washington on February 16 and 17, 1962, to express their opinions on nuclear testing, civil defense and other cold-war problems. As several of them entered the office of Sen. John Marshall Butler (R., Md.) to discuss the proposals of the Turn Toward Peace Student Council, sponsors of the project, a secretary in the outer office whispered to a colleague: "They couldn't be with that peace march. They look like such nice kids. They look so respectable."

The secretary was justified in her incredulity. The traditional images evoked by the phrase "peace march"—beards, sandals, guitars, a political philosophy tinged with the rosy hue of the "non-democratic Left"—did not fit these youthful constituents.

There were many new things about this group besides its cleanliness. One was its size: a veteran White House policeman said it was the largest demonstration he had seen in thirty-seven years of duty. Another was its seriousness: even the notoriously hostile Washington police expressed their admiration for the group's demeanor. The project lasted two days, and except for one incident involving two of the demonstrators, the whole thing went off without a hitch. The talk was of nuclear weapons, bomb shelters, the United Nations. The football stadium, the fraternity house, even the twist seemed far away. So in part, did the classroom, whose often stuffy, abstract intellectualism was being here translated into action.

But the major departure of the Washington Project was a re-nunciation of the emotional, over-simplified approach that has characterized so many student demonstrations in the past. The students arrived here with an eight-page policy statement, hammered out at numerous meetings of the group's leadership. The students hoped to present the document to Congressmen, Administration and embassy officials.

The idea for the Washington Project was not, however, the result of any grandiose study. It started with a widespread, almost desperate feeling that, in the words of Todd Gitlin, a Harvard junior and one of the prime movers of the project, "something had to be done."

A week before descending on Washington, Gitlin and his fellow officers of Tocsin, the Harvard student disarmament group, outlined the beginnings of the project. They realized at once that they did not have the money or facilities to conduct a project on the scale they felt necessary. The result was a combining of Tocsin with several nation-wide "peace groups," including the Student Peace Union (launched last year at the University of Chicago), Students for a Democratic Society (youth wing of the League for Industrial Democracy), and the American Friends Service Committee. They united their efforts under the aegis of Turn Toward Peace, an adult organization, and called themselves the Turn Toward Peace Student Council.

But if the participating bodies had a common interest in peace, they represented wide-ranging ideas on policy and approach. The decision to confront Congressmen in a showcase example of democracy at work represented a victory for the more moderate elements; the establishment of picket lines, and the mass meeting that took place at the close of the two days, represented a victory for the more radical elements.

On substantive issues, the leaders were very specific in denying extremism. *The New York Times* quoted David Ottaway, a Harvard senior, as saying "We're the right wing among the disarmament groups. We're not pacifists. We're not for selling out to the Russians."

The policy statement, which was widely distributed, emerged as a confused document. Many observers read into it that the group was flatly against atmospheric testing, but this is not entirely true. Some students merely want the President to weigh factors other than technical ones in making his decision; and they demand that if the decision is for testing, a full public explanation be given. On civil defense, the students are more united: they oppose shelters as offering "almost no protection . . . in the event of all-out nuclear attack," and they consider that shelter proponents ignore the "violence and profound social disorganization" that would exist among survivors. The students further believe that "by creating the illusion of public safety, civil defense encourages public support for the kind of 'hard' foreign policy being urged by extremists."

The Washington Project policy statement also supports the theory of "unilateral initiative" first propounded by Prof. Charles Osgood and later picked up by C. Wright Mills in his book, *The Causes of World War III.* The theory is that the United States should take certain actions, such as withdrawal of bases from Greece and Turkey, in the hope that the Soviet Union would reciprocate, and thereby ease relations between the two powers. The statement is careful not to urge any unilateral action which, if not reciprocated, would injure this country's deterrent capabilities. Among the steps the students propose are a commitment not to give nuclear weapons to countries that do not now possess them; recognition that the problem of Berlin can only be solved in the general context of Germany and Central Europe; and a "vastly expanded United States program of economic, technical and educational aid abroad, channeled through the United Nations."

Many students believe that "there are people now in the White House who will listen to us." They support a great many of President Kennedy's proposals, such as the Arms Control and Disarmament Agency, Food for Peace, purchase of U.N. bonds, cultural and intellectual exchanges with the Soviet Union, and the "opening of communications media on the widest possible basis" with the Soviets. The President's speech to the U.N. in September, in which he had challenged Russia to a "peace race," encouraged them; but they now feel that he is hampered in implementing many of his plans by pressure from the Right. One major aim of the demonstration was to counteract this conservative influence.

Reactions by official Washington closely followed pro- and anti-

Kennedy lines. Rep. Chet Holifield (D., Calif.), Chairman of the Joint Committee on Atomic Energy and one of the leading proponents of renewed atmospheric testing, said the students were "full of baloney." Sen. John O. Pastore (D., R.I.), vice-chairman of the committee, was one of the few Congressmen who would not even see a student delegation. He told a student reporter he was against "emotional outbursts" in place of "well-founded, knowledgeable, democratic opinion" and was insulted at the students' "questioning the ability of chosen leaders to make decisions." Pastore charged that only those who have had the experience of confronting the Russians could presume to offer legitimate opinions as to how to handle them. His comment on "emotional outbursts" illustrates the unfavorable preconceptions of such demonstrations—a problem future projects must consider closely.

Other Congressmen listened, however. Representative Robert Kastenmeier (D., Wis.) spoke with visiting students for almost an hour. He cautioned a radical group from Antioch College to abjure emotionalism, saying, "You cannot allow people to think you are extremists. If they do, it will destroy your effectiveness." He added that foreign-policy machinery is "very hard to change," but urged the students to continue their activities. Recognizing a growing "alienation" among students from the decision-making process, he recommended active support of specific "peace candidates," such as Richard Richards, California Democrat, and Rep. William Fitts Ryan (D., N.Y.).

The students were also welcomed at the White House, where six of the leaders met with McGeorge Bundy, one of the President's top foreign-policy advisers and formerly a dean at Harvard; Mark Raskin, his assistant; Jerome Weisner, the President's chief science adviser, and Theodore Sorenson. The President sent out an urn of coffee to the marchers but declined all requests to appear before them personally.

The White House officials told the students that, contrary to rumor, the decision to resume nuclear testing had not yet been made, and assured them that technical considerations would not be paramount in deciding the issue. Weisner is a vocal opponent of resumption of testing, and many of the students felt the President, too, is personally against the move at this time. Although generally skeptical of the idea of "unilateral initiatives," the officials did indicate sympathy for the withdrawal of U.S. bases from Greece and Turkey, and welcomed the group's support for many of the President's proposals. They expressed appreciation of "the constructive criticism" in the policy statement and seemed especially grateful for any opposition to the "cold warriors" on the Right.

The State Department proved condescendingly neutral—a deadly attitude to assume with college students. In a press conference after the meeting of twenty-three students with five State officials, Peter Goldmark, a senior at Harvard, expressed "amazement" at the attitude of the officials who, he said, treated them as if they were "very, very young, not at all intelligent, and in the dark on cold-war issues."

The 5,000 students who made the trek to Washington did not change any minds; they did not expect to. The reactions of Congressmen, on the whole, were fairly predictable: the Holifields and Pastores are not going to be swayed, the Edith Greens and Kastenmeiers are still friendly. The State Department visit was disheartening; the discussion with the Presidential advisers encouraging.

A large percentage of the students in the Washington Project fit into the general political category of the "realistic liberal." Today the old ideological scale of Left, Right and Center begins to break down; most students do not think in ideological terms. "Realistic liberalism" connotes a wide range of political opinion which is opposed to the emotional over-simplifications found in the Right and Left. It does not submerge all problems into one cause, such as anti-communism or unilateral disarmament. It has the failing of lacking a total world view, but the virtue of dealing with problems, if only one by one, according to the reality of each situation, and not in accordance with any preconceived pattern. Just such a rational, "realistic" approach was the aim of the leadership of the Washington Project. But this type of "approach" has existed since the resurgence of student political activity that began two years ago with the sit-in demonstrations. What is new is the procedure the "realistic liberals" used to promote their views—direct confrontation of their elected representatives and participation in the process of democratic government.

The feeling that "something had to be done," which lay at the root of this particular project, carries in it a fear not only of the spiraling arms race, but also a fear of the broadening chasm between the citizen and the decision-making process. It is this alienation, caused by a complex of factors, including "big government" and "dirty politics," which forced the initial sit-in demonstrators to make a direct moral appeal, rather than a political one. Today, however, whether it be from a growing confidence in their political strength, or a more basic desire to bridge the gap before it grows too large, there is a desperate feeling among politically concerned students that the traditional democratic process must be rescued.

The success of the Washington Project must be assayed on two levels. The "direct confrontation" of Congressmen was at best a limited success. McGeorge Bundy, at the White House, warned the students gently but firmly that "It is very easy to overestimate anyone's effect on foreign policy." Every speaker who addressed seminars and briefing sessions before the Project said the same thing: "Don't have any illusions about the effect you will have." After the first day, spirits were at a low ebb—and yet some still found the will to speak of the "beginning" that was the Washington Project.

The second and final day, Saturday, was different. A bright winter sun shone in a clear blue sky. The busloads kept coming. The pickets were four abreast along Pennsylvania Avenue and ringed Lafayette Park across the street. Students were "doing something." Their faith in what they were doing was renewed.

If they did not convince the State Department to withdraw missile bases from Greece and Turkey, at least they manifested public support for the liberal thrust of President Kennedy's policies. If they did not convince Chet Holifield to reverse his position on nuclear testing, at least they came to realize that they have to support, with hard work, men who oppose him.

Perhaps the greatest benefit of the Washington Project was not in Washington at all, but back on the campuses all over the country. Almost every college newspaper ran stories; almost every lunch table rang with impassioned oratory.

There are still problems for the student "'peace movement." It must not blur the real differences that exist among the various participant organizations. Mass demonstrations, it must be realized, are burdened by public preconceptions that only deliberate planning and education can relieve. But they should be retained, both for their publicity value and the chance they give students for participation in political action.

The outlook for the next few years offers little promise of relief from tensions and deadlock. It will take courage to remain realistic and not seek refuge in over-simplifications, and emotional sloganeering. Students will be ignored, chastised, insulted. They will face frustration, and even moments of total impotence and despair. Yet one feels that this activity must continue, both for the larger and more distant hope of reaching at least partial solutions, and for the immediate imperative of establishing in the American college student and future voter, and in turn the American citizen at large, a renewed sense of his personal place in a living democracy.

WOMEN SPEAK OUT FOR PEACE

by Stephanie Gervis

THE PHENOMENON generally known as "Women Strike for Peace" arose largely out of the fear that Russia's recent series of nuclear tests would mark an "open season" for testing by all the nuclear powers. The movement, already operating in more than sixty cities in this country (with contacts in a score of foreign countries), basically represents a maternal concern; peace with leukemia promises no brighter future for the nation's children than does war with incineration.

The word "movement" is used advisedly, because "Women Strike for Peace" is not an organization. In fact, communication without organization has become one of the women's cardinal principles. Only by preserving the grass-roots nature of their campaign do they feel they can be effective and avoid being written off as just another organized protest group. They are coordinated only in their goals: peaceful negotiation of international disputes and an end to all nuclear testing. Contact is maintained through loose lines of communication—mostly by telephone and mail, together with occasional regional meetings at which joint action, such as the recent demonstrations at the U.N. by women from the New York metropolitan area, may be planned.

To understand the total operation it is necessary to study a local one, since the stress on non-organization makes it impossible for the whole to be any more than the sum of its parts. What has happened at Mount Vernon, N.Y., a city of 76,000 within easy commuting distance of New York City, is more or less typical of the movement.

The awakening of Mount Vernon had its beginnings in a telephone conversation between two friends, Mrs. Dolores Leff and Mrs. Elaine Kuntz, on the night of Wednesday, October 25, 1961, two months after the Russians had begun testing. Their conversation turned to their children and the kind of world, if any, they would have to grow up in. Despair at the prospects was compounded by the feeling that, as mothers, they had a responsibility to do something, but that things had gone far beyond not merely their control, but beyond even their capacity to influence. Finally, after discussing the protests that they heard were being planned for November 1 by women in New York and Washington, they decided to try to organize something in Mount Vernon for the same day.

The following night, seven women gathered at Mrs. Kuntz's home to map a plan of action. For them, the only encouraging development in recent weeks had been President Kennedy's restraint in not immediately resuming atmospheric testing when the Russians did, and his advocacy of a "peace race" in his September 25, 1961 address before the U.N. General Assembly. Representing, as women, a potential majority of all voters, they would let Mr. Kennedy know that he had a political base on which to build the policy he had outlined at the U.N.

Their plan was a modest one—a silent walk through the center of town carrying two signs calling for an end to war and to nuclear testing, and tables set up at four street locations at which passers-by could pen peace messages to Kennedy and Khrushchev as well as to U.N. Ambassadors Adlai Stevenson and Valerian Zorin. They thought it would be a "one shot" deal.

On Friday, three of the women went to see Republican Mayor P. Raymond Sirignano to request permission to stage their demonstration and set up the writing tables. "If less than twenty-five women turn out, we won't walk," they told him. "If more than fifty turn out, we'll be happy." The Mayor granted not only his permission, but his enthusiastic endorsement. The next stop was the local newspaper to arrange for advance publicity and coverage of the walk itself. Friday night and Saturday morning were devoted to preparing fliers announcing the walk and asking local ministers to help in the distribution. Of the twenty-four clergymen contacted, twenty-two agreed either to announce the walk from their pulpits or to distribute the fliers, or both. The two who declined implied that the women might be Communist dupes. Suspicion of motives is a problem the women still face from time to time, and one for which they have no answer except to repeat that they are simply mothers who want their children to grow up and live in peace.

By Monday the working nucleus had grown to thirteen women. At 1 P.M. on Wednesday, the day of the walk, the women began to assemble in front of the City Hall—old and young and middle-aged, Negro and white, Christian and Jewish—until there were 106 of them, including the wife of Westchester's Republican County Clerk, Ed Warren. Many had their children with them. At 1:30, the Rev. A. Kenneth Magner, Jr., minister of the First Presbyterian Church, approached the microphone provided by the Mayor's staff and commended the marchers on behalf of the local clergy for their "courageous act." He then led them in the United Nations Prayer. Following a brief address by one of their number, Mrs. Gilbert Shulman, Mount Vernon's Distinguished Citizen of 1955, the women began their walk silently, two by two, pushing their baby carriages or holding their children in their arms or by the hand. They covered a circular route of twelve blocks in approximately twenty minutes, arriving back at City Hall at 2:10. One of the two signs they carried quoted President Kennedy's U.N. address, "Put an End to War or War Will Put an End to Mankind." The other said, "Join This Walk to Protest All Arms Testing." Seven women did join them as they walked.

The demonstration was received calmly. It was a cold, gray day and not many people were out. But significantly, by the end of the day 600 messages had been written at the street "peace stations." This may not seem like much for a city of some 76,000. But considering the short time the women had to publicize their demonstration and the political complexion of much of the community—exemplified in the editorial comment of *The Daily Argus* that no American will "want war, even nuclear war, avoided solely out of fear of its physical hazards"—the results were considered heartening. Feeling they had done their bit, the women returned to the piles of dishes that had gone unwashed during the week of frantic activity.

They were soon to learn, however, that they had touched a responsive chord. Phones began to ring: "What's next?" "You can't stop now." Most of the calls were from women who hadn't participated in the walk. It was encouraging, but it was also frightening. Most of the women involved had families to care for, houses to keep and no maids. But in their effort to provide a mandate for the President, they had found one for themselves.

So when it was learned that 300 Long Island women who had demonstrated at the U.S. mission to the U.N. on November 1 had pledged to return on November 8, 3,000 strong, the word was passed along. Friday night, November 3, the Mount Vernon women met, decided to participate, chartered two buses and wired Ambassadors Stevenson and Zorin that they hoped to see them on November 8.

Once again the women took to their telephones and, on the day fixed, a Mount Vernon contingent numbering nearly 100 set out for the U.N. Plaza. To pay for the buses, each passenger gave a dollar. Some of the women drove their own cars. The number of demonstrators that day—from New York, Long Island, Westchester, New Jersey—was closer to 2,000 than 3,000, and they were met by neither Stevenson nor Zorin (the Russians were celebrating the anniversary of the Bolshevik Revolution). But there were enough of them to command attention from both officials and the press, and they were addressed by Ambassador Arthur Dean, chief U.S. negotiator at the Geneva test-ban talks. Splinter delegations visited the Japanese, Canadian and West German missions.

Two days later a delegation, including representatives from Mount Vernon, met with a first secretary at the Soviet mission. He read a statement repeating Soviet charges that the Western powers had provoked the Russians to resume testing. The women replied that they were not interested in laying the blame; they were interested only in stopping the testing once and for all. They presented the secretary with statements for both Premier Khrushchev and Mme. Khrushchev.

After a weekend off, Mrs. Leff and Mrs. Ann Phillips attended a meeting of metropolitan area "peace women" at the Hotel Paris in

New York on Monday night, November 13. Word of this meeting, like all the meetings—local, regional and national—got around via the grapevine. The idea of formal organization was discussed and rejected, as it had been at a national meeting in Washington, D.C., the preceding Wednesday. Two women from neighboring Briarcliff who had attended the Washington meeting reported on the suggestions that had come out of it. One was that demonstrations be held the first of every month. Another was that demonstrations be held on December 1 which would focus on the contamination of milk by strontium-90 and other poisons produced by nuclear explosions. They were offered as only suggestions; it would be up to local communities to decide whether to accept them or not.

That Thursday night, the Mount Vernon women met and decided they did not want to "contrive" monthly demonstrations. They proceeded with what they thought would be the wind-up of their campaign, at least until something new and "critical" came up. They ordered photo-offset copies of the newspaper accounts of their activities printed and sent one to every member of Congress.

But the problem of milk contamination bothered the women. "We decided that we would at least find out about it," Mrs. Leff recalls. So they began wading through reports of the Atomic Energy Commission, the Public Health Service and the Federal Radiation Council. They found out that even if all nuclear testing stopped right now, by spring the strontium-90 content of milk will reach the level at which continuous monitoring and decontamination will be necessary. This, they agreed, was critical; with the aid of a chemist and a science writer, they put together a fact sheet for public distribution. They heard from the chemist that one of the Great Neck women had come to him for similar help. They arranged that the Mount Vernon women would complete the fact sheet and the Great Neck women would see that it was printed.

On November 30, a committee was named to work out a plan for distributing copies of the fact sheet locally. It was the first committee of any kind set up by the Mount Vernon women, and it will exist only as long as it takes to do the job for which it was set up. (None of its members were among the original thirteen who worked on the November 1 demonstration.) The following day, December

1, the Mount Vernon women again joined others from the New
York area in a peace walk at the U.N. The Great Neck contingent
brought 25,000 printed copies of the fact sheet and handed them out
to the demonstrators for distribution that day and later in their
communities. Mount Vernon took 10,000.

Mrs. Leff presented the fact sheet, with some explanation of its
content, to a regional meeting held in New York the following day.
It was announced that office space at 750 Third Ave., in the city,
had been donated and that the Manhattan women would operate it
as a "clearing house" for information, mail and material.

But the Mount Vernon women feel that they can be most effective
within their own community, at least for the time being. For the
next month or so, they expect to be occupied with educating local
citizens to the dangers of milk contamination. They are also in
demand as "consultants" to other peace groups throughout Westchester County.

As for the future, they feel they must stay in existence until there
is complete disarmament. But this poses problems. In the first place,
they are growing (those connected with the Mount Vernon movement now number about 100), and they all want to be kept informed
of what's going on. The grapevine method of communication is no
longer adequate. Absolute adherence to non-organization may have
to be abandoned and a communications committee set up. This is a
question the women are still pondering. There is also the question of
time. Most of the women are wives and mothers, which is why they
became involved in the first place. A system of rotating responsibility,
which began when new blood assumed the task of educating the
public on milk, will have to be developed so that children can be fed
and husbands reassured.

Newcomers to the field of public action, so far they are doing all
right. They surprised not only the community, but themselves by
proving that the voice of the average citizen can still be heard.

PEACE AT THE POLLS

by Roger Hagan

TWO YEARS INTO THE NEW DEAL, just as we were two years into the
New Frontier, the trial marriage of native American radicalism and
the Roosevelt administration appeared to be over, and an insurgency
that seemed to promise a fundamental reconstruction of American
politics began taking shape. The promise was not fulfilled, but it
might have been; and since we now stand at a similar point in the
political cycle, there is more than nostalgic interest in recalling the
mood of that period. The only radicalism with any grassroots strength
today seems to be the peace movement, which had its meaningful
political baptism in last November's elections. Does it hold forth
more promise, or less, than the insurgency of the early thirties?

Discussing results of the 1934 elections, *The Nation's* lead editorial
ventured to wish out loud:

There is genuine cause for rejoicing in the striking triumph of the
new Progressive Party in Wisconsin . . . as well as in the splendid victory of [Farmer-Laborites] Governor Olson and Senator Shipstead in
Minnesota. If the independent parties in these two states can get together,
it is possible that they may yet grow into an effective national third party
movement.

The next week's *Nation* warned that the ugly defeat of Upton
Sinclair's "End Poverty in California" Democratic gubernatorial
campaign "shows what will happen to any radical who attempts to

137

challenge the existing order through the medium of old party politics." Before long an extended discussion was under way in the
letters column about the possibilities for a new United Liberal Party.

The Nation was not unique with these speculations. Many liberals
and radicals had concluded that a Democratic administration would
never make the serious, deep-reaching changes in the economic and
social structure that they felt the times demanded. John T. Flynn had
written in *Scribners* in late 1934 that if the proper kind of economic
planning were to be undertaken, it would be because radicals had
seized upon the "historic moment" that was developing for "the
launching of a powerful third party upon modern radical economic
issues." John Dewey and Paul Douglas' League for Independent
Political Action had resolved, at a conference in late 1933, that the
people must "rise up and win economic and political control" to
achieve "a new social order, a scientifically planned system"; and as a
beginning, the conference had formed the Farmer-Labor Political
Federation and called for a new political party. Wisconsin's Progres-
sives also called themselves a new national party; and Phil La
Follette, who won the governorship on their ticket in 1934, insisted
that radical state parties could spread on their model and bring about
"a national third party—a real leftist party" by 1940.

The elections of '34, adding nine Democrats to the House and ten
to the Senate, were much more a mandate to the New Deal than
those of 1962 were to the New Frontier, but the hopefulness of the
insurgents was undiminished. Governor Floyd Olson wrote in *Common Sense* in 1935 that "a third party must arise"; Montana Senator
Burton K. Wheeler looked forward to one; the American Commonwealth Political Federation, led by Congressman Tom Amlie (Prog.,
Wis.), Alfred Bingham of *Common Sense*, and (now Senator)
Paul Douglas, constituted itself a crypto-party to jell, if necessary, by
1936. In the State of Washington, the Democratic Party, captured
by the Commonwealth Builders movement between 1934 and 1936,
committed itself to the radical goals of public ownership and produc-
tion-for-use. In short, entirely apart from the activities of the American Marxist parties, there was a ferment of native radicalism after
two years of the New Deal, a mood of insurgency apparently ready
to coalesce into a significant political force to bring about structural

changes which the New Deal evidently had no intention of attempting. People with radical goals had found themselves still outside the system, and they were devising bold new strategies to get back in.

Currently the equivalent of these native insurgents is a strongly nonpolitical collection of candidates and groups, largely middle class and without serious domestic discontents, whose disillusionment with the Administration is over foreign, not domestic, policy. To a veteran of the thirties, peace politics is no politics at all: no view of history, no domestic agenda, no idea of structural changes that might reach causes rather than symptoms, hardly even a clear idea of what to do to replace what is protested. It seems more a mood than a program, an *affaire des femmes,* a native cry of anguish against the hard ironies of contemporary life. Viewed overall, it had no strategy in 1962, no political base, no popular cause to compare with the condemnation of greed and injustice of yesteryear, no strong allies on the inside like Senators Wheeler, Norris and La Follette, Congressmen Amlie, Maverick, Lundeen, Boileau, Walgren and Marcantonio, no strong-rooted politicians like LaGuardia; and, most to the point, no significant victories. After the elections, it looked even less like the making of a third party than before—when to be sure, it had looked little enough like it.

None the less, the problems and prospects of the new peace politicians are not so different from those of the insurgents of the 1930s as it may appear—indeed, their prospects may be better—nor is their weak showing and relative silence since the elections a safe guide to their future potential. To an extent, their weakness may be an advantage and their silence a good omen. They start with fewer illusions and may, as a result, evolve a more practical strategy for affecting American life with their concerns than proved possible for the radicals of 1934-36.

On the other hand, although their demands seem more circumscribed than those of the thirties, they have an immensely more difficult task. For if the 1962 elections taught them anything, it was that significant blocs of votes will not swing their way simply upon the intelligent articulation of peaceful alternatives and initiatives to reduce tension. Tension and polarization, they learned, are not recognized evils like starvation and injustice. Rather they are built into the system, integral parts of present-day life—for all classes.

In other words, the burden of peace politics is not merely to alter a small segment of public policy, but to undertake the most awesome task of reforming popular attitudes ever attempted by a minority in the history of American politics. How far this realization will lead' them to extend their critique back into the focus of politics as the older generation of insurgents regarded it—into the structure of American society—remains to be seen. Their experience in the campaigns of 1962 was varied, and the strategy to which it may give rise is still much in question. Vague and incomplete as it is, however, that experience itself is, at the moment, their most valuable asset. Does it add up to anything?

There were thirty-two campaigns in 1962 in which the peace movement took particular interest. The table on page 141 ranks the candidates according to the importance they gave the peace issue. Several other candidates, like Senators Clark and McGovern, supported by National SANE or the Council for Abolishing War, would be below those at the end of the list. The table is only a rough indication of how much initiative the peace movement took in the campaigns, however. The second group of candidates generally received less aid from peace groups than the third group because of their poor chances or because of disorganization of peace groups in their areas. Some in the fourth group won strong support because of their credibility as politicians. The list excludes candidates for state and local office who got help from peace groups, such as Assembly candidates Reed Searle in California and Manfred Ohrenstein in New York.

There were ten "pure" peace candidates; or, by a slightly broader definition, seventeen (comprising the first two groups in the table). None of the seventeen won office. Four were nominees of major parties, six ran as independents either on the ballot or as write-ins, and seven more lost primaries seeking major party nomination. One of the latter subsequently ran as a (N.Y.) Liberal. All but two of the remaining fifteen candidates were regular Democrats who could only loosely be called peace candidates. Curiously, these two—Pacht and

Results of Candidacies Supported by Peace Groups

"PURE" PEACE CANDIDATES

Name, Office Sought and Party*	District	% of Vote
Harry Purvis (H., Ind.)	N.Y. 4th	1
Harrop Freeman (H., Lib.)	N.Y. 33rd	3
Elizabeth Boardman (H., R.)	Mass. 3rd	48 P**
Helen Bliss (H., D.)	N.H. 2nd	27 P**
William Hefner (H., D.)	Mass. 1st	28
H. Stuart Hughes (S., Ind.)	Mass.	2.4
Sidney Lens (H., Ind.)	Ill. 2d	1
Robert Cosbey (H., Ind.)	Ill. 13th	1
Alva Tompkins (H., Ind.)	Ill. 9th	1
Herbert F. Hoover (S., R)	Iowa.	15 P**

OUTSPOKEN CONCERN FOR PEACE

Name, Office Sought and Party*	District	% of Vote
William O. Hart (S., Ind.)	Wis.	1
Elizabeth Weideman (H., D.)	Mich. 16th	14 P**
Caroline Ramsay (H., D.)	Md. 7th	30
Alice F. Bryant (H., D.)	Wash. 1st	27
William Meyer (S., D.)	Vt.	45 P**
James Youngdale (H., DFL)	Minn. 6th	49 P**
Knox Mellon (H., D.)	Calif. 24th	30

SYMPATHETIC BUT NOT OUTSPOKEN

Name, Office Sought and Party*	District	% of Vote
John O'Connell (H., D.)	Calif. 6th	42
George Brown (H., D.)	Calif. 29th	56
Edward Roybal (H., D.)	Calif. 30th	57
Jerry Pacht (H., D.)	Calif. 31st	P***
William Stewart (H., D.)	Calif. 12th	38
Jerome Ziegler (H., D.)	Ill. 14th	40
Martin Dworkis (H., D.)	N.Y. 17th	32
Bob Wilson (H., D.)	Ill. 22nd	39
Tom Payne (H., D.)	Mich. 2nd	42

GENERALLY LIBERAL, CAUTIOUS ON PEACE

Name, Office Sought and Party*	District	% of Vote
Blaine Whipple (H., D.)	Ore. 1st	48
Lionel Van Deerlin (H., D.)	Calif. 37th	51
Frank Kowalski (S., D.)	Conn.	****
Robert Kastenmeier (H., D.)	Wis. 2nd	53
Charles Weidner (H., D.)	Calif. 14th	37
William Fitts Ryan (H., D.)	N.Y. 20th	73

*H., House; S., Senate; R., Republican; D., Democrat; L, Liberal; Ind., Independent.
**Primary vote; never reached General Election.
***Primary vote; ran second to winner in field of nine.
****Defeated in convention before Primary.

Kowalski—were opposed by Democratic chieftains on grounds other than their foreign-policy views.

Of the thirteen Democrats who reached the General Elections in the lower half of the list, five won House seats, including two incumbents. In the entire list, fourteen candidates lost to incumbents in November, and of these, six cut the incumbents' percentages below the 1960 showing. But only two of these were in unaltered districts, and only one of the eight whose opponents increased their percentages was in an unaltered district. Redistricting has made it impossible to draw conclusions from the figures about such candidates' ability to threaten incumbents on the basis of the peace issue alone.

There was no consistency among the seventeen peace candidates on domestic policy. Excluding Hughes, the first group discussed domestic issues only as related to the arms race; the second group had a broader platform. Three of the seventeen were Republicans and two others more conservative than most of their workers. Ramsay, on the other hand, was by any standards liberal. As to background, the candidates included four professors and three other educators, two bank presidents, an accountant, a lawyer, two farmers, two newsmen, a printer, a manufacturer, a forester and several professional politicians.

This suggests the variety of persons and styles that made up the "peace" campaigns. A focus on candidates such as this can be misleading, however. It is not the candidate or the size of his vote that might ultimately affect the politics of his district, but the people working for him. The vote was unquestionably disappointing, but the experience of politics may count for more in this first year of the peace movement's cautious insurgency.

"I told these peace guys you've got to make up your mind what you want to do: elect Wilson to Congress or use his candidacy as a platform for peace education." The Democratic chairman of a downstate Illinois city was getting hot under the collar just remembering his warning. "Now if you want to build a twenty-foot cross and nail him up there and put footlights on him, go ahead and do it, but if you want to get him elected to Congress then you've got to just shut up. And work like hell ringing doorbells."

He was speaking of Robert Wilson, candidate for Congress from Illinois' 22nd District, a farmer and owner-editor of a string of country weekly newspapers. Wilson is a well-informed liberal with roots in his section of Illinois that go back for generations, and his editorials have made him well known in much of the district. He was, therefore, the best political material the Democrats had laid hands on for years. But he is also a practicing Quaker, and his pacifism made him want to differ with the Administration on defense policy. Around the University of Illinois, in the eastern part of his district, there were some local peace groups eager to support him if he would begin to build a policy on his good instincts.

As it happened, he never did. The peace groups came into his campaign too late with too little. They had also insisted on interviewing the Republican incumbent, who had held them up for weeks. Wilson's closest advisers and managers, while not professional politicians, were predominantly concerned about the problems of winning and turning him into a credible, respectable candidate. Many of these advisers were themselves liberals who had long been engaged in discouraging battle with the entrenched down-state pros. But the chance to hitch a ride with a strong, hard-campaigning candidate with real roots in his district and a mind good enough to explain the Administration to the cautious, prosperous farmers of the 22nd District was enough to turn them into hard-nosed professionals when confronted with the idealists of the academic and women's peace groups.

The pattern here was a familiar one. The Democratic Party official himself expressed the primary dilemma of the peace movement in politics. "Me," he said, "an old NAACP, ACLU, ADA liberal, I have to talk like a real conservative Republican to keep from hurting the poor guy. You've really got to change roles in a hurry if you want to get anything done." The new militants of the peace movement are not about to change roles in a hurry: although, be it said in their favor, they did, here and elsewhere, accept compromise positions and work ringing doorbells, watching polls, distributing literature, raising money, running mimeo machines and licking stamps. Not often, however, did they "shut up."

When it was over, those who *had* held their tongues for a while and immersed themselves in the machinery of a campaign had to ask if the sacrifice had been vindicated. Where they had worked for a regular party candidate who merely showed sympathy for their concerns, such as Wilson in Illinois, Payne in Michigan, Pacht, Weidner or the more outspoken O'Connell in California, or Whipple in Oregon, the results were often discouraging—no victory, and not much public education. And in the few places where their man won, victory seemed attributable to factors other than themselves. Edward Roybal in the 30th District of California (Los Angeles), for example, seemed most indebted to a lackadaisical opponent and to his Mexican-American nationality. He won with 57 per cent of the vote in a district which includes 35–40 per cent Mexican-Americans. But here at least peace people were useful in getting the Democrats registered, a particular problem in such a district. Elsewhere their aid was even less clearly a benefit.

George Brown's 29th District in Southern California was safe in terms of party registration (62 per cent Democratic) and Brown, as a former city councilman, mayor of Monterey Park and state Assemblyman, was well known to the electorate. Even so, his vote, at 56 per cent, was lower than expected. His opponent had hit hard at Brown's pro-SANE views, and this apparently had cut into his margin. Brown publicly acknowledges the helpfulness of SANE, the women's peace groups and Californians for Liberal Representation (CLR), an offspring of the California Democratic Club movement (CDC) formed to aid candidates strong on disarmament, civil liberties and civil rights. In terms of what campaign managers call "bodies"—precinct workers—and money contributed, the peace groups gave Brown more help than his most important labor support, and more than the national and state Democratic Committees. Privately, however, he wonders if peace-group support did not do enough harm to offset the gains. The consensus of the managers of the few regular party candidates about whom the peace groups were enthusiastic was that their help was fine if restricted to "bodies" with no strings attached. But public endorsements were not always welcomed.

Many in the peace movement knew that working for a party candidate would involve them in compromises without any opportunity for open criticism of Administration policy. The demand to retain their clarity was argued out in local meetings from Boston to Los Angeles, and the decisions were never final. In Boston, the result was a high mortality rate of advisers and campaign managers in the Hughes campaign, some being eased out because they were too rigid for practical politics, some because they were too practical to inspire volunteer energies. In Los Angeles, years of experience in the Democratic club movement made some leaders of CLR and SANE wary of the unknown candidates with good platforms but no organizational base who turned up to contest primaries; there was an unusual abundance of such people in California. Yet the same experience made others wary of formal linkage to the Democratic Party of Jesse Unruh and John F. Kennedy, because they valued their program and their identity. They preferred to adhere to a clear set of policy demands and promised support to whoever agreed with them.

Essentially the same arguments, in other words, took place in Los Angeles on the basis of experience as took place in Massachusetts on the basis of inexperience, only at a different level of possibility. There was little hope of success for the Political Action for Peace (PAX) candidates: Hughes, Hefner and Boardman in Massachusetts, and Bliss in New Hampshire. Of the three seeking regular party nomination, all in districts securely in the opposite camp, only Hefner reached the general election—no other Democrat wanted the nomination—and he took only a quarter of the vote from incumbent Representative Silvio Conte. Los Angeles, on the other hand, presented a choice between allocating resources among all candidates who expressed good views or restricting them to a few real politicians with good sentiments whose districts showed 57 per cent or better registration in their party. Because the latter course was chosen, outspoken candidates like Knox Mellon and William Stewart went unsupported, even though their districts gave them far greater strength than most House candidates elsewhere in the country whom the peace movement would support. The political experience gained by amateurs in the California Democratic Clubs (CDC) made such hard choices possible (much of the peace movement would not have made them); but beyond the primaries, where concentration of resources was clearly fruitful, the choice was not fully vindicated.

Since it was impossible to say whether peace-group support helped or hindered them, the victories probably did not strengthen the peace movement's bargaining position in California politics, which had been one hope of those arguing for practicality over ideology. The most extreme case was that of Lionel Van Deerlin of San Diego. In spite of CLR support, he said nothing about most key peace issues, but discussed only economic planning for reconversion, an obvious need in defense-contract-bound San Diego. He won with 51 per cent of the vote after being attacked vigorously by his opponent for taking CLR support (the group gave him over $1,000, but no workers). His debt to the peace groups was far from unequivocal.

The California groups around Brown, Roybal, Van Deerlin and O'Connell opted for success. They did not entirely abandon clarity, since they published their own platforms and secured some explicit agreement from the candidates they supported, but they saw little made of their issues in the campaigns. As George Brown put it, he saw no value in excessive candor. Nor did they secure any assurance that their men would vote in a particular way when they got to Washington. Elsewhere in the country, groups which followed a similar path had even less satisfaction from their candidates; such was the disorganization of the New York groups that no statement could be agreed upon for the candidates to support, and peace-concerned liberals supporting William Fitts Ryan, Bentley Kassal, Martin Dworkis, Frank Montero, James Scheuer and David Levy did so mostly because of their reform status and their generally liberal outlook, not because they had them on the line for peace.

For many members of peace groups and liberal organizations in Chicago, the story was the same; SANE and the Independent Voters of Illinois (IVI) suported Kennedy Democrats such as Sidney Yates for Senate or Barratt O'Hara for the House with little to show for it in terms of foreign and defense policy agreement except that, as one leader of Chicago SANE said of Yates, "He reads all the literature I send him." But one Chicago organization made the opposite decision. For Voters for Peace and its intellectual entrepreneur, Sidney Lens, a writer and labor official, a political campaign seemed the one opportunity to say what needed to be said and have somebody besides the faithful brethren listening. Lens hoped to begin building a bloc of electoral strength rigorously committed to new policies in foreign and defense affairs, a bloc that would not fall apart at the last minute. Since many Congressmen win by margins of less than 5 per cent, Lens thought that, as candidates, they should be sensitive to small, well-organized blocs of votes. In such districts the peace voters might make the incumbent or a strong candidate jump even if they could not replace him with their own man.

The problem with this theory, of course, begins when the price for peace-bloc support is agreement to policies which alienate larger blocs. An example of its abuse was seen in the 8th and 9th Congressional Districts of North Carolina, where Negro leaders, rather than aiming at a two-party South, urged their people to vote for conservative, segregationist Democrats in close races with conservative, segregationist Republicans on the theory that the winning Democrats, recognizing that their margin of victory came from the Negro, would support the President on civil rights. But what would happen to the larger Southern white bloc after the Congressman had voted for civil-rights legislation? Clearly, the interest of the politician lies in remaining unresponsive even to a crucial Negro bloc except when everyone can be pleased at once. This problem applies equally to peace politics. If not related to an intensive and prolonged program for changing the attitude of the general public, small peace "pressure blocs" will not work wonders on Congress—unless the bloc grows immensely bigger than the peace movement seems able to make it.

Voters for Peace never reached a point where that problem concerned them. They had another: how to build such a bloc with which to influence incumbents. Paradoxically, the answer seemed to be running candidates against unsympathetic incumbents in order to demonstrate strength for next time (if strength there was), or to rally voters and workers for the future. Lens and two other VFP candidates ran as independents.

Unfortunately, in Lens's district, blocs would not make a difference; the incumbent had won by 50,000 votes in 1960. Worse, he was Barratt O'Hara, the most liberal of Chicago's Congressmen, a man Lens could take no pleasure in unseating. For VFP, the presence of a good but cautious liberal like O'Hara posed the challenge to the political hopes of the peace movement in its starkest form. Must basic points of opposition to the arms race give way before the demands of domestic liberalism? O'Hara was undeniably good on labor and welfare causes, had been one of the six Congressmen to vote against the appropriation for the House Un-American Activities Committee in 1961, and had supported the Peace Corps and worked actively for the Arms Control and Disarmament Agency. On the other hand, he was an Administration man who would not take a position opposing the White House lest he lose influence. He voted for all major military bills, extension of the draft, military foreign aid and the amendment to increase the current military allotment by $200 million, and all of the basic defense appropriation bills. Worst of all, he favored the nuclear-testing program and supported the shelter program.

Lens had no chance to run against O'Hara in the Democratic primary because of the early filing date in Illinois. (VFP, like all the peace-politics groups except PAX in New England, was formed during the spring of 1962.) If Lens were successful in drawing many votes, therefore, he would merely put a right-wing Republican into the seat. Perhaps the decision was made easier by the size of O'Hara's 1960 plurality; but before Lens and two other VFP House candidates were ruled off the ballot, it appeared that VFP could do considerable damage by drawing away some O'Hara precinct workers. The old Congressman and liberal leaders of the 2nd District were clearly disturbed at this prospect, and for a brief moment there was a gratifying response: thirteen prominent Democrats of the district, most of whom disapproved of Lens's candidacy, sent O'Hara a telegram urging him to declare his opposition to further nuclear testing and his support of a gradual, phased reduction of the arms budget.

Lens, to his credit, agreed to withdraw from the race if these two minimal points were met, but O'Hara stalled until past the filing deadline. Lens was forced to file, and subsequently to battle in the courts for his right to be on the ballot without the requisite number of signatures (on the grounds that redistricting had made the number uncertain). O'Hara's strategy did not win him any affection among the peace-oriented liberals of Chicago, and although the city-wide Independent Voters of Illinois supported O'Hara, some IVI officials worked for Lens and helped him with the court case. In fact, the Fifth Ward IVI, in the University district which is the core of IVI strength in the city, had to be overruled by the city-wide organization after it had resolved to designate Lens and O'Hara as equally qualified so that its workers could support either.

But at the same time, Lens's willingness to jeopardize one of the ablest liberals in Congress won him little affection among Chicago liberals and officials of the labor movement. Lens was aware of the problem: "Sure, this creates divisions. It's a dangerous thing and we may be making a mistake. We're going after a fairly good liberal here, and the only thing is that he won't break with the Establishment. But then, that's the big thing, isn't it?"

In the opinion of some professionals in peace education, it was not. Many, such as the leaders of Turn Toward Peace and SANE, believed that the peace movement's task is to work with liberal groups long enough to lead them out of the embrace of the Administration on matters of defense policy. Voters for Peace may have lost its chance to do so in Chicago. Not only IVI but Lens's colleagues in the labor movement and the older peace movement were badly split on the merits of the effort. His own and other VFP tactics angered many who should have been its allies. In the two remaining districts, where independent write-in candidates were run, the interviews which VFP held with both candidates before refusing them support were conducted a bit like military inquisitions, the interviewers hewing closely to a demanding set of policy proposals and all but insisting that the Democratic candidates declare their opposition to the President on many vital matters. One candidate with a tough district was anxious to get workers and requested a second chance after failing his first "exam." At the next session, he showed signs of having read Blackett and Melman, but the eternal questionnaire was pressed on him in such a way, by some reports, as to force him to disagree. Thus an opportunity was passed by to influence and develop a possible winner and Robert Cosbey was run against him.

Perhaps it was a case of adhering to the check list too strictly—a mistake that only experience and a dose of pragmatism could have corrected. But one can also sympathize with VFP activists who were asked to pour time, money and shoe leather into campaigns on the basis of off-the-cuff agreements, "in principle" concurrences and a few good sentiments. Uninformed politicians do not inspire issues-oriented people. Some will respond to patient briefings, but it is slow work with few immediate returns. One of VFP's explicit goals was public education, and it appeared at the time that they could get more said to people in their district with their own candidate speaking their own message.

In retrospect, it seems that one of VFP's problems, one widely shared with other peace groups, was having two incompatible purposes: exerting pressure on candidates and incumbents, and educating the voting public by inserting issues into the campaigns. Another was their failure to recognize the kinds of pressure and influence available to them, focusing, perhaps too early, on political pressure of the least subtle sort—voter strength—without any clear prospect of achieving it. A third was to alienate some of the groups it would need to gain such strength in the long run.

Paradoxically, this least compromising of peace-political organizations also gave financial aid to a Democratic candidate in the 14th District (a semi-rural district west of Chicago) who was among the most cautious of all "peace candidates." Jerome Ziegler, an old friend of Lens who had long worked with the Chicago American Friends Service Committee, concluded early in his campaign that politics and peace education were not at all as "inextricably interwoven" as VFP believed them to be.

Although his name appeared among the sponsors of Voters for Peace, Ziegler made no call for any of the proposals in the VFP platform. Nominated by the regular Democratic Party organization in a newly reorganized district, he refused to jeopardize his chances by making an educational effort. In part it was a matter of time. Ziegler aimed to meet a thousand people a day for the last ninety days of his campaign. "I can only spend a few seconds with each person, and there is simply not time for education. The most I can hope to do is identify myself with some good cause in the right direction." But his reluctance to get into the tangled web of foreign and defense policy was also related to his conviction that peace groups make a mistake in talking slogans rather than events and specific issues with which people can identify. He felt that by discussing the Peace Corps and getting across the spirit it represents he could make at least as many points about international reconciliation that an audience might carry away with them as he could have by discussing initiatives, as H. Stuart Hughes did in Massachusetts.

Ziegler lost; his opponent's plurality of 63.8 per cent in 1960 was cut to 60 per cent, but the addition of Will County to Ziegler's district may account for that. None the less, he doubts that he would have spent his energies more fruitfully running an educational campaign on the VFP or the New England model. In any case, to do so would have contradicted his sense of responsibility to the party which nominated and helped him. Ziegler stressed the problem that once people like himself go into party politics seriously, they take on responsibilities to others who may not share their views.

There are both gains and losses in such a course. The apocalyptic sense which compels the peace movement could be silenced by politics as usual, and this would be a serious loss. Ziegler's kind of politics offers an experience which the peace movement needs. One cannot watch the serious candidates like Ziegler, O'Connell, Brown or Blaine Whipple of Oregon without coming away with a certain respect for the awful rigors of democratic politics. A Congressional race is, on the one hand, a silly, superficial sort of popularity contest which makes fearsome demands upon the endurance of the candidate; but on the other, it is a programed contact with the mood and concerns of the people that cannot be had in any other pursuit. Such experience could be an antidote to the tendency, characteristic of peace groups, to over-polarize the community, as well as to over-optimism. It is also an education in the ways of power and influence in our society, a lesson that leads many to cynicism but a few to a rare ability to do good.

In the opinion of George Brown, whose victory in California is the primary source of hope to the new insurgents, the peace movement badly needs to learn that neither social change nor attitude change are simple matters:

Ray [Sebens, Brown's campaign manager] and I have a hell of a job educating the peace groups. I've been in peace work longer than most of them [Brown is one of the founders of the Friends Committee on Legislation and has long been active in the War Resisters League and the

Fellowship of Reconciliation] and I want them to learn the complexity
and depth of the problems. Now they have awakened to these problems
and want to do something big. Some of them want to take credit for elect-
ing me to Congress. I want them to know this didn't come about so
simply. They have to learn politics from the bottom up, and what it is to
be a politician, and how to build their own politicians.

Most of the peace groups that entered the political arena in 1962
have concluded pretty much the same thing. In California, due in
part to Brown's urging, the Californians for Liberal Representation
will try to find persons with political potential and develop them as
candidates from the city councilman level upward, so as to give them
political roots. Voters for Peaceful Alternatives, the group in Ithaca,
N.Y., which ran Professor Harrop Freeman for Congress, has also
resolved to work on a local level. The debate is now whether to aim
at capturing the stagnant Democratic Party machinery by finding
people to run for town committees or to build the Liberal Party.

In Massachusetts, the disappointing showing of Stuart Hughes has
led his campaign organization and the PAX organization from which
it emerged into a similar train of thought. Their effort will now be
to hold together the considerable network of town coordinators,
workers and donors that the state-wide campaign developed, and
make it a recruiting ground for town committee and state legislature
candidates aiming at having good people ready for the primaries in
1964. The interim activity designed by Campaign Manager Jerome
Grossman to keep the organization active and increase its role in the
political life of the state, and to "wean" the organization from the
attractive and highly popular figure of Hughes himself, consists of
state legislative action—the introduction of bills into the legislative
session written by the Hughes campaign organization, making use of
the right of petition and the help of interested legislators.

The Chicago VFP organization also intends to involve itself further
in traditional politics the next time around. It is aware that by beginning too late to enter the primaries, it missed its best opportunities for
improving community contacts and having political effect. Its main
effort in 1963 will be to develop promising political material and to
enter the primaries of both parties as a disciplined caucus.

There is other evidence of a willingness to attempt a more organic growth and careful allocation of energies. In Ann Arbor, Michigan, a student-faculty group supported a local Democrat with good instincts but little substance in foreign-policy matters. By working closely with him and securing expert academic aid for him on policy proposals, they managed to insert the issue of peace, disarmament and economic reconversion into his campaign. (The candidate lost, but by no more than he had two years previously.) Research being conducted by Students for a Democratic Society (led by the Michigan group) and other organizations promises to locate a number of Congressional districts where such effort may show results. Projects are also under way in Massachusetts and elsewhere to measure the effectiveness with which issues were presented.

All this cautious resolve will amount to nothing, however, if the message of peace politics continues to seem basically wrong to most Americans. In the thirties many flirted with socialism from hunger, anger or because it was intellectually attractive. It had a dynamic and a vision of the future as well as of how to get there. How much of this can be said for the cause of the new insurgents?

On election eve, when the returns were coming in from all over Massachusetts, there was a particular misery in them for a few people in the Hughes campaign like Chester Hartman, who had directed the earlier, vastly successful signature campaign which gathered more than 147,000 signatures to put Hughes on the ballot. Hartman knew the precincts by heart, and he noticed that it was frequently in the precincts most heavily canvassed that Hughes made the poorest showing. The negative correlation was most pronounced in lower-income precincts and disappeared or reversed as the income and education level rose.

Hartman pursued the question of impact with a telephone poll which further revealed the difficulties of delivering a complex issue in politics. It was as Ziegler might have predicted. Nine out of ten persons called had heard of Hughes, but some of them had to be pushed: "Who ran for Senate?" "Lodge and Kennedy." "Was there anybody else?" "Oh yes, Hughes. . . ." In a lower-income precinct, however, few had heard of Hughes, even after a campaign costing nearly $150,000. When asked what they liked about Hughes—most

who knew of him liked him—the respondents listed personal qualities: honesty, courage, personality, "a professor." Few mentioned
issues. Just over half the respondents knew that Hughes had a platform concerned with disarmament, but most of these knew only
labels. They considered his views "nice but impractical," "visionary,"
"way out," "twenty years ahead of his time," those of a "dreamer."
Interestingly, India was mentioned as a factor discrediting Hughes
more than Cuba; for although Hughes is not a pacifist he was associated with pacifism because he opposed war, and India's need to
fight against China was said to prove him wrong.

   With such results, the handwriting was on the wall. Hughes
was as articulate a spokesman as the peace movement would ever
find, and while his somewhat donnish appearance may have contributed to these results, it was hard to avoid the conclusion that the
issues themselves were to blame—unpopular, unpleasant, touching
on deep sources of anxiety, in some way they seemed to be their own
obstruction.

   In part, being "Independent" was a hindrance. Whatever the cor-
ruption and nepotism of the two parties, the poll showed that it
seemed worse to be outside the system, particularly after Cuba.
Hughes himself had recognized the extent to which this disrupted
communication long before his organization did. Often, after shaking
hands through a factory and being well received, as was usually the
case, he would think to himself, "Well, there are two or three more
votes—maybe," while his aides made rosy predictions. After the election, he advised SANE not to encourage further independent candi-
dacies like his own unless all possibilities for supporting a party man
were exhausted.

   The basic problem was not in being an independent candidate
but in saying what Hughes said. The defeat of the O'Connell campaign, the most outspoken of all the regular party campaigns, well
staffed with peace-movement and other volunteers, operating in a
district newly favorable since redistricting, came as a harsh surprise
to most observers. Those running the campaign blamed the issues
themselves. This is the hard lesson. To build from the bottom as the
peace movement now intends, it will be necessary to confront as

never before the basic unpopularity of the cause—and more than
that, to do something about it.

This unpopularity is no news to the old peace movement, but
politics is no place for people who readily accustom themselves to
being in a losing minority, and the new activists of the peace campaigns will not rest easily with the popular verdict. The question of
how far to accommodate to popular attitudes will therefore be an
increasing source of tension within the movement.

What I have called "peace people" and "peace groups" are in
almost all cases not old-line pacifists or seasoned dissenters. They are
unhappy outside the system of accepted values. They are liberals
who most properly should be called peace-concerned, not pacifistic.
They want to change the trend of events, to find alternatives to military solutions, to calm the hysterias of the cold war, but not to dump
weapons in the sea all at once. Only the failure of the Kennedy
Administration to change the trend towards militarization alienates
them from the Democratic Party; if things were moving in a hopeful
direction, most of them would return to the fold. With few exceptions, their candidates demanded only such hopeful steps as ending
testing, strengthening the Arms Control and Disarmament Agency,
beginning serious study of the economics of disarmament and—
where they went at all into the specifics of defense policy (as did
Hughes)—opposing counterforce doctrine. Most accepted the need,
at least for the time being, of a minimum deterrent nuclear capability.
This was a significant break from the policies of the older peace
movement, and one still not accepted by many community peace
organizations.

In short, much of the traditional pacifist peace movement that
knows, perhaps too well, how to live with failure was not active in
the campaigns. The ranks were filled with the new peace movement
which SANE was first to develop: a middle-class, college-educated,
issues-concerned rank and file reminiscent of the Stevenson troops of
1952 and 1956. The hardest work was done by the women's groups
and by students, with support from young professional and academic
men. The trajectory of these people has been rapid, from apathy
through signing protests to demonstrations to political action. Each
stage had its rapid disillusionments, and the danger is that the dis-

appointments of politics and the realization of the size of the task ahead may propel them on into cynicism on the one hand, or by the persuasion of numbers, to doubt their own cause on the other. The new peace movement is not inured to failure, nor should it be; yet, to an extent, it has to be.

The early signs after the elections were favorable. After a few weeks of dejection following November 6, a surprising number of campaign workers bounced back into meetings to plan how to keep their organizations functioning and make use of what they had learned ("how not to spend money," as a coordinator put one of the chief lessons). A graduate student at Cornell who had done the hard, door-to-door precinct work of Freeman's campaign in the small cities of New York's 33rd District summed up the hopeful side of the experience for a campus political magazine: "There are many who go to rallies, to Washington and New York. It is not so much fun to go door to door; it's not a social event to the tune of folksongs. Guitars are to be left at home. It's hard work, and a day of campaigning means ten hours. But it is rewarding, and it works."

But many will ask: does it? It works to overcome the campaign worker's sense of political alienation, but what else? Freeman's was perhaps the most successful independent campaign (Liberal Party support in upstate New York means nothing more than a place on the ballot) in terms of injecting the issues of disarmament and reconversion into political discourse. He was invited to all gatherings where the Democratic and Republican candidates were to be heard, and usually succeeded in making them look pale and ill-informed on foreign policy. The regulars were forced to discuss Freeman's issues and insist that they were for peace too. Furthermore, Freeman's showing in the Democratic primary, which he lost very closely, shook the Democratic leaders of Elmira and Binghamton who had been drifting along in the profit-by-losing pattern so often found among minority party politicians with a little urban strength and a federal Administration of their party.

But only extremely sophisticated techniques of analysis could determine whether or not the campaign had changed the politics of the district for the future or softened the ground for new ideas in foreign and defense policy. Aside from identifying allies around the district, no early gains were discernible.

Before the campaign, many of these people showed signs of having thought about forming a third party: but the way they showed it is by insisting that that is not their intention, that they intended to work within the two-party system. Some said this because they were Democrats and had hopes for reforming their party (in the South, this is a nearly total distraction among peace and civil-rights advocates), some because they wanted to retain leverage on both parties by entering primary fights, and some because the experience of 1948 taught them that it is a mistake for many reasons to form a party too soon. The rejection of third-party plans was even more pronounced after the election. This is probably just as well, for the third-party effort of the thirties broke up over the prospect of throwing the election of 1936 to a Republican President: because it had aimed too high for what its people were ready to dare, it fell apart.

None the less I think it safe, in spite of their disclaimers, to call the veterans of the peace campaigns a third force at this point. They have not evaporated since the elections, and the trend of their thought is toward avoiding commitments or alliances with either party, even though it is also toward working with party candidates. This edging away from the kind of commitment which characterized the older club movements is true even where ties to the Democratic Party have been strongest and most rewarding, as in California.

The likelihood is that "leakage groups" will form to catch those who find themselves edged out of the system. Their structure and methods will be fluid, and they will "flow" to whatever candidate or tactic promises them increased effectiveness. In the process they may begin to operate in a "professional" manner, ready to make deals or apply pressure and to play the same games the pros play with skill and without rancor. The California club movement is already confronting the need to do this. As one officer of the CDC put it, only half jokingly: "We were dealt out of the L.A. County Committee by paper clubs, maybe we will have to build a few paper clubs of our own." Means unquestionably matter to men like Hefner and Hughes, but there are a lot of tactical lessons short of dishonesty and manipulation that can be learned.

Not only do peace people in politics recognize themselves increasingly as outside the parties, but, unlike the liberal reform movements of New York and Chicago, their groups are linked: intellectually by sharing a primary concern with national policy, and physically by informal communications networks: newsletters, SANE personnel, occasional conferences and organizations such as the Committee of 1,000 and the Council for Abolishing War formed to raise and distribute campaign funds.

This "third force" quality is an uncertain trend, however. The internal debate between those who hope to establish a role for themselves within the traditional parties, at some cost in "ideological clarity," and those who value this clarity above all, will not quickly be resolved.

Many are certain that the hope of politics lies in reforming the parties. They may be right; but they must ask themselves how the struggle for "citizen" politics will fare against the professionalization of the activists as they move up in the party as CDC's former leaders have. They will be racing against the new national machine which Kennedy is building to replace the dying city machines, a machine of which Jesse Unruh is a characteristic "new man." They must be aware that the effort to work as a caucus within the old parties may be doomed to perpetual frustration by the President's famous victories and the "restriction by partial incorporation" which perpetually undercuts the foreign-policy Left. And they must recognize that most real candidates will go Ziegler's way, staying respectable and supporting the President; that the President's strongest point with the voters, on which the candidate will differ at greatest peril to his electoral chances, is foreign policy, the one place where the peace groups will most want criticism; and that if their men win they will go to Washington with obligations to the Administration and to crucial war-economy elements at home which will further mute their critical stance.

Are they then right who, like Hughes or Lens, insist that only a politics not committed to winning, a politics based on the young and what Lens calls the "left-outs" (those who have a sense of having lost their vote in the direction of domestic and foreign policy) can retain the clarity to contribute a new position to our political dialogue? This is the politics of losing so familiar to the Left and un-palatable to the new insurgents. Its danger is that, never needing to compromise, it falls into sectarian bickering over fine points of theory. If the "leakage groups" lose contact with the major parties, they run this risk.

At the moment, then, the debate comes down to this: will it be necessary over the next decade to try once again to reconstruct democracy within the parties on the lowest level, as reformers have repeatedly tried to do, and thus to battle head-on the accelerating trend toward centralized policy formation? Or must the peace move-ment build from small beginnings and early disappointments a new force with a radically critical program which links the problem of cold-war escalation to the organic problems of the domestic society and economy as no standard politician can dare to do? In a way it comes down to whether one believes in power or in ideas. The ques-tion was not resolved in 1962, but fortunately, it did not have to be. The political insurgency of the peace movement has the benefit of a pragmatism new to the American Left which may enable it to unite many who would fall apart over this question. The decision can be suspended for some time to come.

EUGENE, OREGON:
A CITY CHOOSES PEACE

by Robert Martinson

ON DECEMBER 19, 1961, a terse proclamation was issued in the city
of Eugene, Oregon, signed Edwin E. Cone, Mayor. It began simply,
"WHEREAS" and then proceeded with laconic brevity to the blunt
and rather startling conclusion that "the United States must take the
initiative for peace."

In a world of 50-megaton bombs, this admirable little document
may go unsung and unanalyzed. Yet it deserves to be broadcast
across the country as a worthy example of community courage and
local initiative. Coming in the midst of the great debate on civil
defense, it is a pungent reminder that the anxieties of the atomic
age have begun to penetrate every city, village and hamlet in America and that the issues must be fought out and won on the community
level. In this instance, Eugene, Oregon, is *Anywhere*, U.S.A. Millions of Americans and tens of thousands of communities share its
problems. The step it has taken in the direction of sanity may help
reveal the essential ingredients of a peace effort adequate to the
American scene and politically effective.

Eugene is not a small town. With a population of 52,000, it is
considered the fifth largest commercial center in the Pacific North-
west. Its main industry is lumber. It is the home of the University of
Oregon and is the professional and medical center for a good part of
the state. Its local newspaper, the *Register-Guard*, has a circulation
of about 40,000. Its Mayor, Edwin E. Cone, is known to the citizens

160

of Eugene as a conservative and prudent man not given to making inflammatory pronouncements. Until recently, Eugene was not a center for peace activity, and its local political history does not sufficiently account for Mayor Cone's action.

The academically trained scientist, both government and lay, has played a remarkably prominent role in recent times, especially in the debate over shelters. The more concerned and well informed a person is, the more likely he is to seek scientific advice before making up his mind on the facts of the case.

In Eugene, this advice was supplied by two sources: Dr. Willard Libby's serialized articles on fallout and shelters, and a sizable protest against the articles, in the form of letters to the editor, which called them "fraudulent" or, at best, inaccurate. According to George Streisinger, a research biologist at the University of Oregon and a key figure in the Eugene story, Dr. Libby's articles provoked "considerable community interest" and a continuing and "vigorous debate." Critics of Dr. Libby gave talks before the Oregon Psychological Association and at the Unitarian Church, and the editor of the *Register-Guard* was personally approached with a more rounded view of the facts. The *Register-Guard* interviewed various members of the science departments at the University of Oregon, most of whom were critical of Dr. Libby. The paper then carried a series of four articles prepared in cooperation with biologist F. W. Stahl and George Streisinger that presented "realistic estimates of the effects of atomic war" and ended with a call for "more study in the area of achieving disarmament."

Thus far the story is probably quite typical. Dr. Libby may have provided the unanticipated but inestimable service of prodding a good number of American scientists into performing their elementary duty: informing the public. However, what followed was not at all typical. Not content with merely setting the facts straight, a local peace group, the Eugene Peace Information Center (EPIC), seized the opportunity presented by these events to move into the area of community action.

EPIC was set up in 1960 with a mailing list of 150 persons. It limped along in the usual doldrums, mailing out occasional bulletins

on the Berlin crisis, U.S. intervention in Cuba, civil defense and disarmament. It had one virtue, however. Its leadership understood that
the problem of the peace movement in America is to break out of the
charmed circle of convinced pacifists and to make its policies relevant
to the great mass of the American public. To this public "peace" is at
best a synonym for a kind of muddleheaded idealism; at worst, it
suggests appeasement or even treason.

EPIC's evolution on a local scale was both mirrored and aided by
the recent formation of Turn Toward Peace on the national scene.

Turn Toward Peace is a rather complex affair. It seems to be more
in the nature of a miracle than an organization. It is a kind of combination coalition and campaign, at the core of which are the traditional American pacifist and peace-oriented groups such as the
American Friends Service Committee, the Fellowship of Reconciliation, the War Resisters League and the Women's International
League for Peace and Freedom, together with such associated organizations as SANE, the American Association for the United Nations
and the Committee for World Development and World Disarmament.
But Turn Toward Peace has reached out beyond this core and now
includes as "communicating" organizations the American Veterans
Committee, the United Auto Workers, Brotherhood of Sleeping Car
Porters and the National Association of Social Workers. A whole
conglomeration of additional organizations have been invited to associate themselves in this venture.

The model for TTP was worked out over a number of years by
Robert Pickus, founder of the West Coast group, Acts for Peace, and
one of the most original talents in the pacifist camp. Pickus' aim was
a related national peace effort servicing "community peace centers"
that could provide a continuing base for local education and action,
as well as coordinate the activities of the cooperating organizations. A
Policy Proposal Committee, composed of leading intellectuals, sends
suggestions to the "communicating" organizations, which in turn
agree to inform their memberships of TTP activities and proposals.
TTP provides for cooperation on many levels, both organizational
and personal, and hopes to weld some kind of politically relevant
force out of its constituent parts.

In Eugene, EPIC made the decision to associate itself with TTP in September, 1961. Immediately, new interest was aroused. Attendance at meetings increased, a mail appeal for funds netted $500, and TTP received a good deal of publicity through an organizational tour by Northwest regional coordinator, Anne Stadler. At this point, a series of crucial decisions were made which led directly to the proclamation making the week of December 24 through 30 Turn Toward Peace week. These decisions were so startling in their effect that they deserve the closest attention.

The first decision may be illustrated by a letter sent to 380 "key community people" inviting them to a luncheon to hear Robert Pickus, TTP National Coordinator. It was signed by Melvin O. Dahl, president, Eugene Chamber of Commerce; (Mrs.) Catherine Lauris, president, City Council; The Reverend Clarence J. Forsberg, First Methodist Church; and George Streisinger, Coordinator, Eugene Steering Committee for Turn Toward Peace. The letter said in part: "Mr. Pickus will be in Eugene to describe some of the proposals being advanced that could diminish the threat of war, avoid surrender and further the spread of American values of freedom and democracy."

The Eugene Steering Committee deliberately, almost provocatively, broke with the traditional conception that peace is the monopoly of the Left. Naively or not, they assumed that everyone is for peace unless proved otherwise. Instead of weighting their pronouncements with the tone and style of an embattled minority, they tried to speak for the community as a whole. Instead of pushing the conservatives in Eugene into the camp of the arms-racers, they deliberately set out to recruit them.

The invitation was sent to Rotarians, Chamber of Commerce people and key community leaders in all fields. The chairmen of the Lane County Democratic and Republican executive committees were asked to invite members of their committees, as well as local officeholders, to a morning coffee. Invitations were sent to ministers for a morning breakfast. In a forty-five-minute "interview" program on television, six local businessmen thoroughly questioned Turn Toward Peace and its program.

The results surpassed expectations. One lunch was attended by

about seventy people, among them the first vice president and
manager of the First National Bank in Eugene and president of the
Chamber of Commerce; the manager of the Chamber of Commerce;
the owner of Eugene's largest furniture store; the president of the
City Council; several Councilmen; two deans of the University of
Oregon; heads of several departments at the university; the president
of Eugene's frozen-food concern, and the superintendent of Eugene's
public-school system. The audience listened attentively and many of
them signed the Turn Toward Peace Roster and made a contribution.

Of course, there is no appreciable war industry in Eugene and it is
not a key target. Nevertheless, it is representative of thousands of
similar communities. Many of the city's community leaders are well
aware that if the bombs fall they will make no distinctions as to rich
and poor, Left or Right, young or old. Fallout is the universal
leveler and faces all mankind with the same terrifying danger. This
fact can be turned into a powerful political force. By its tone and
nonpartisan appeal, the Steering Committee proved that the real
minority in Eugene (and elsewhere) are the advocates of preemptive war and the unquestioning supporters of the arms race.

Another crucial decision had to do with policy. Many levels of
ideas exist within TTP, but they move within a framework "clearly
different in tone from efforts that dwell on the horror of war in a
way that encourages a climate for surrender, or which consistently
and uncritically rationalizes Soviet behavior. . . ." Though the emphasis is on reaching the whole community, the message is a radical
one: the need for unilateral American action not dependent upon
prior Communist agreement which will actually move toward a
"disarmed world under law safe for free societies."

A TTP advertisment in the *Register-Guard* put it this way:

We believe the best defense against communism is to strengthen our
commitment to freedom and democracy. Freedom and democracy cannot
survive nuclear war, but they can flourish in peace. To preserve our way
of life and safeguard our future we must:
¶Turn Toward Peace
¶Support the President's appeal for total and complete disarmament

¶Strengthen the United Nations
¶Accept and develop world law
¶Establish non-military solutions to international conflicts and take new initiatives toward peace.

This approach strikes a novel note quite at variance with the "Better Red Than Dead" partisans. It obviously speaks directly to a real local audience and is at pains to prove that the measures it favors will in fact defend what the audience holds dear. It tries to make visible alternatives which are "neither war nor surrender." It is clearly a movement for peace and has nothing in common with appeasement.

Thirdly, the Eugene Steering Committee made a complete break with the politics of Armageddon, a modern equivalent of the medieval belief that the end of the world is just around the corner. TTP takes the position that we are in the post-atomic age and we must come to terms intellectually and spiritually with its dimensions. The usual methods lie ready at hand: discussion, debate, demonstrations and political action.

Peace advocates must win over that vast, uncommitted, but politically decisive middle ground which will only respond negatively to hysteria, alarums and mindlessness. (For example, civil disobedience is a responsible and appropriate response for the civil-rights struggle in the South, but may become gauche and self-defeating when carried over uncritically to the peace field.) The style is the man. Eugene illustrates the effectiveness of a quiet, thought-out approach which resolves hysteria through concrete action.

Finally, it was quite inevitable that Turn Toward Peace should be countered in Eugene by the formation of a new local group—Turn Toward America. The group's secretary, a Mrs. Florence Reed Cook, told the *Register-Guard* that "the new group is particularly interested in giving out information contained in the California committee report about some of the leaders of Turn Toward Peace."

A January 8, 1962 editorial in the *Register-Guard* indicated that the old, shopworn methods of the ultra-Right fringe were having little effect:

It is folly to think that one can't be for both America and peace. Indeed, how can one be for America, for the healthy America we know and love, without being for peace also?

A new atmosphere exists in Eugene. Peace has become a respectable political force in community life. Discussion can now begin on the merits of those "alternatives"—neither war nor surrender—which desperately need to be made visible to the American people.

III

LOOKING TOWARD THE FUTURE

QUIET, PLEASE!

by J. B. Priestley

ONE REASON why life is difficult today is that many of us are compelled to live in two quite different worlds. Moreover, it costs us about a thousand times as much to live in the world we don't trust, don't like, don't believe in, as it does to live in the other world that has our liking and confidence. Another thing is that while one world, the expensive one, cannot have a future, because it must soon either fade away or end itself—and us—with a bang, the other world already shows us a possible and promising future. It can do this because it is very much *our* world, belonging to our age, and not a dubious legacy from the past, a monstrously magnified inheritance.

This world, the one that doesn't cost much and never makes the headlines, is known to most artists, scientists, scholars, technologists, athletes. It is a world of coexistence and cooperation. It covers the round earth, and is peculiarly suited to a time in which jet aircraft can cross any frontier in a few hours. It does not think in terms of good people versus monsters. It talks instead of screaming hysterically. It is not secretive and enjoys swapping pictures and passing out information, but is not engaged in propaganda. It is not moving towards war, but always away from war; not talking about Peace as if it were a golden egg a mile long as people in the other world do, but creating peaceful conditions, the global civilization of the near future, simply by going along with what interests it.

Because it is flexible and easy, I shall call this the Loose World. And now that it has a name, I can reveal one remarkable fact about

169

it. Intelligent young people *in all countries* accept and try to live in this Loose World. This is the one they believe in, not the other. They move into it and around in it quite naturally and easily. It is their world. And this I believe to be true of the intelligent and most promising young people, whether they live in Baltimore or Odessa, Manchester or Belgrade, St. Louis or Tiflis, Kiev or Lyons, Chicago or Warsaw. They are all, so to speak, Loose-minded.

The other, the magnified inheritance, I shall call the Stiff World. It costs us about ten dollars for every cent we spend on Loose. It could easily cost us everything we have and are. But though it demands so much and could kill us all, somehow it is far more unreal and fantastic than Loose, which is one reason why the young turn away from it. In this Stiff World, everything is out of scale and proportion. It is as if an old game were being played in an immensely exaggerated form, baseball teams a hundred strong playing with immense steel bats and explosive balls on a field sown with mines. It is crowded with tough-minded realists who are, in fact, more than half-crazy.

The Stiff World never stops declaring that it is guarding democracy. But the democracy it guards never allows people to vote on anything important to the Stiff World. This is in fact a strangely secretive, authoritarian, liberty-removing kind of democracy, which tells most of us to keep quiet and mind our own business. And indeed, some of us are sufficiently cynical to believe that many Stiff types, although they pretend to deplore the state of the world, cannot help enjoying the authority and importance lent them by the Stiff setup, and would not know what to do if we stopped having so many crises. They are themselves power-hungry types, and so they cannot help seeing everything in terms of power. It is a weakness of our age, which has largely rejected any inheritance of power, that we are led by men who have been hungrily ambitious for years. I have often thought that our international affairs might be better managed by any random collection of chess players or bird-fanciers.

The Stiff World is forever announcing that it is looking for a lasting peace; but this is just a tape-recording. It maintains, at our expense, huge state departments working day and night to make mischief. Sometimes they are trying to put into effect policies that are not only out-of-date now, but were shaky and dubious fifty years ago. The new foreign secretaries start where their predecessors left off. They are all too busy and anxious, as one crisis follows another, to ask themselves and their staffs what the hell they think they are doing. No flexibility is tolerated; all is rigid; this is the Stiff World.

Here the characters are as fixed and typed as they were in the crudest old melodramas. They are seen in black and white. It is sheer goodness defying appalling wickedness. It is Truth versus The Lie. This is, of course, the world of propaganda. And most of this propaganda is curiously rigid, pedantic and unreal, for in it are opposed a communism that the East hasn't got and a capitalism that the West hasn't got, as if we were all staking our lives on a debate on a ouija board between Adam Smith and Karl Marx. It is only if we go into the Loose World that we can begin to discover what West and East really have got.

But then of course the chief product of Stiff World propaganda is fear. And some curious things have happened. In the old world, from which the Stiffs inherited their power complex, armaments had to be increased to meet a new danger. But in the Stiff World this has been reversed. Because, once we were in the atomic age, the new armaments were so terrible, so monstrous, that the danger, the menace, had to be hugely magnified to match them. Clearly if we had such things, then we *must* be in a desperate situation. And now indeed we are, though we weren't when all this nonsense began. What was unthinkable has now become thinkable—that is, if you call it thinking to suggest that a nation halved by nuclear casualties can still function as a nation, and begin organizing itself for World War IV. It would, in fact, consist of a lot of radioactive lunatics, not ready to organize anything except the immediate lynching of any World War III experts they could find.

To show what propaganda can do, I take an example from behind the iron curtain, as the Stiffs like to call it. We were recently in Soviet Armenia and Georgia, where my wife, an archaeologist, was visiting digs and sites and ruins, and I was tagging along, trying to capture some of the mountain scenery in *gouaches*. Our guide and interpreter was an extremely intelligent, youngish anthropologist, who knew several oriental languages as well as sufficient English to interpret for us. He was in nearly everything a Loose World man, but as soon as disarmament came up as a topic, the shadow of the Stiff World fell on him. He said if the Soviet Union took a unilateral disarmament risk—"Tomorrow, American paratroopers would be in our streets." This is what propaganda can do to a nice, quiet, intelligent scholar, quite sure his own people had no intention of attempting world conquest, suddenly turning up with machine guns in Dallas or Cleveland, Ohio.

Sometimes I read those stories of international espionage and counterespionage that exist entirely in a Stiff World atmosphere. They are often the work of men who know something about Intelligence, spy-catching and whatever else makes for what is called "security." And nearly always, reading these stories, I feel I am being given a glimpse and a whiff of hell. It is not only the inhumanity, the ruthlessness, the cruelty, that make me feel this; it is also their suggestion of an appalling underlying idiocy. The harder you look at the Stiff World, the more you realize that behind its solemnity, its unceasing activity, its dark secrets, its daily waste of millions, there is nothing but a bad mental legacy and a few false assumptions. If it kills us, as it easily might, we shall not have died for freedom, for our country, for our children's sake, only for silliness—tragic figures in a planetary farce.

Now I believe that the Stiff World, which is organized for conflict and war and not for understanding, mutual help and peace, has no future to offer us and our children. It is bound for nowhere except catastrophe. It has been given a good run, together with more money than all the tyrants in world history have demanded, and all it can offer for tomorrow is a lot more of what we dislike today. This is why all intelligent young people—and, I repeat, *in all countries* —want no part of it, are already rejecting it by the millions, are turning hopefully towards the other, the Loose World. And with them, I believe, are nine-tenths of the most gifted persons on earth, the real public benefactors. So now I will venture a suggestion on their behalf.

It is this. The Stiff World, which has been laying it on, thick and hard and fast, for years, should now consent to lay off for a year or so, just to give the Loose World and the future a chance. If only as an experiment, it should instruct its huge mischief-making departments to stop plotting and planning. It should give its spies and counterspies a sabbatical. It should arrange for its pet maniacs to take a twelve-month narcotic treatment. It should lend some—let us say, a fifth—of the money it wastes annually to the Loose World, to help finance better coexistence and more cooperation, the start of real global civilization. But even if it refuses to lend anybody or anything a cent, it can benefit us all just by laying off for a spell, by trying not to whisper for six months in order to shout and scream for the next two crisis weeks, by behaving for a year as if it was not important and did not do what it had been doing.

Anyhow, it has been working too hard; let it give itself a holiday. For even with such a brief respite, the Loose World, the real world, the only one with a future, might begin to take over. It seems to me worth trying.

WAR AT THE ARMS TROUGH:
THE COMING POLITICS OF DISARMAMENT

by Fred J. Cook

IN THE AFTERMATH of the Cuban confrontation in a year in which the military budget has so escalated that even $50 billion seems like the piddling commitment of a simpler past, it may seem the height of paradox to suggest that the basis is being laid for a politics of disarmament. But such is the reality.

While no politician worth his salt at the ballot box would, as yet, dare to embrace disarmament, the hidden forces that eventually move even politicians to rationality are beginning to operate. The fact is that the prolonged arms race has started at last to commit a form of economic hara-kiri. Recessions come with increasing frequency; unemployment rates continue disturbingly high; the growth rate limps. These are symptoms that clearly say all is not well, and the inquiring mind, probing behind them, quickly discerns two facts: (1) military spending is a drag on the overall economy of the nation; (2) it represents a financial drain to most of the states and awards its beneficences only to the few.

These are hard, economic facts, only now becoming apparent, that in time may well become the cornerstones for a new politics of disarmament.

The first hard fact favoring the new politics is that the billions spent on arms do not build up the domestic economy; in the long run, they debilitate it. Of course, military expenditures have provided millions of jobs, and still do. But the end-products of these

174

jobs are mostly waste: Minuteman, once finished, is sunk in its silo and there it sits, waiting for Doomsday. The billions spent to produce it and its kindred flock are dead; they have not created useful goods, they have not opened up new lines of endeavor, they have not stimulated and regenerated the economy. Economists, analyzing the prosperity of Western Europe, where the growth rate outstrips ours, where unemployment runs far lower, have been struck by the fact that this prosperity seems to bear a direct ratio to the proportion of the national income that is plowed back into the domestic economy instead of being buried in the silos of modern war.

Coupled to this first fact is the second: Though an entire nation is being bled by onerous taxes to finance armaments, the immediate economic benefits are distributed with gross inequality. A Department of Defense analysis of the distribution of procurement contracts, issued September 29, 1962, tells the story. Military prime contract awards in the 1962 fiscal year totaled $25 billion. Of this amount, 57.2 per cent was distributed among just seven states. California, with $5.9 billion (for 1963, the figure is expected to be $6.2 billion), led all the rest, gobbling up 23.9 per cent of all major orders. New York, which has been fading in this competition, nevertheless benefited to the extent of $2.6 billion, or 10.7 per cent of all contracts. Only five other states—Massachusetts, Connecticut, New Jersey, Ohio and Texas—managed to wangle their way into this exclusive billion-dollar club. By contrast, twenty-six of the fifty states obtained contracts totaling only fractions of 1 per cent of those war-industry billions.

The armament race is keeping a select few of the states in a style to which they never previously were accustomed; the rest are getting only crumbs. In many of the latter, unemployment has become endemic; businesses fail; hard times clamp down cruelly in the midst of the bounty of the Warfare State. The picture spells the potential. For years, these comparatively deprived states, their businessmen and their politicians, have tried to cut for themselves a larger slice of the munitions pie. They have failed; and it must soon dawn upon them that they must continue to fail, for the bulk of military procurement will continue to go to the states that already have the vital installations, the major research centers, the key production plants.

These two facts, then, offer the broad economic base for a new politics of disarmament. One foundation stone is being laid by the dragging national economy, hampered by its abnormal devotion to military interests; the other, and politically the more explosive, lies in the inevitable—and inequitable—economic consequences of military procurement: the rich getting richer, and the poor poorer, and there is nothing much that can be done about it.

Let's take a closer look now at that first weakening pillar of the Warfare State: the health of the national economy. Statistics now show that economic pump-priming through military expenditures, a device that was seen in Harry Truman's day as the guarantor of unending good times, can no longer insure perpetual abundance for all the people. Unemployment statistics in America, compared with those of Western Europe, are one graphic barometer. The President's Committee to Appraise Employment and Unemployment has come up with an adjusted schedule of unemployment rates in which the United States shows at a sharp disadvantage.

This analysis, based on 1960 figures, put our unemployment rate at 5.6, a figure that has held distressingly constant over the years despite the steady rise in the military budget. Other nations of the free world, spending far less on military hardware, exhibited strikingly lower unemployment figures. Great Britain had a rate of 2.4 per cent; France, 1.9; West Germany, 1; Italy, 4.3; Sweden, 1.5. In the Far East, Japan had a rate of 1.1.

Gardner Ackley, a member of the President's Council of Economic Advisers, testifying before the Senate Committee on Banking and Currency last July, was asked by Senator William Proxmire (D., Wis.) to explain why Western European economies were growing at a much faster rate than ours. The witness replied:

> I would certainly also stress the fact that in the United States we have been devoting a very substantial chunk of our resources to military purposes during this period. Those same resources in most of Europe are being devoted to productive investment, and it is not surprising that this productive investment should permit a much more rapid growth of total output than we have.

Senator Hubert H. Humphrey (D., Minn.), in a hearing on August 29, 1962 before the Senate Small Business Committee, noted that, in America, the government finances about 65 per cent of all research and development and that by far the larger portion of this is devoted to the needs of military and space. On the other hand, as the Senator pointed out:

In Germany, 85 per cent—85 cents out of every research dollar—is private, and less than 15 per cent goes into military and space. Eighty-five cents of that goes into the civilian economy, so that today the German plant competition for world markets of civilian goods is being automated, modernized, equipped in the latest and best fashion, and new products are developing, while we are developing new wrappings. We are the greatest packagers in the world. . . . In Japan, it is about 85 to 15 again. . . . In England, which also has a low rate of economic growth, as does our country, 60 cents out of every research dollar is governmental and goes into military and space, atomic energy. . . .
What is happening to our civilian economy as we plow more and more of our scientific personnel, our brains, into the military and into space and into atomic energy for military purposes? Where are we going to end up in this trade competition with these Belgians and these Dutch, who are clever, and the Germans who are very clever, who are spending more money for civilian aspects and will develop products cheaper, better and more serviceable?

It was a good question, and it is significant that it is being asked, even if it is not yet being answered. For it is becoming increasingly clear that our economy is beset with deep-seated problems that are not being tackled, much less solved, while our brains and energies and resources are devoted to the creation of new and more ghastly implements of war. The new world of electronics is bursting upon us like a cataract. Its flood is such that not even multi-billion-dollar boosts in the already bloated military budget can prime the economic pump. For not only are military end-products an economic waste; they are also now being produced in an automated world that calls for ever fewer workers. Analyzing this trend, Gerard Piel, publisher of the *Scientific American*, said in delivering the Phi Beta Kappa oration at Harvard last June:

The arms budget is losing its potency as an economic anodyne. It is concealing less and less successfully the underlying transformation of our economic system. Progress in the technology of war, as in all other branches of technology, is inexorably cutting back the payroll. . . . Expenditure on armaments has begun to yield a diminishing economic stimulus.

Yet our fixation with the cold war and military demands has so hamstrung us that we have not even recognized the true nature of our economic problem, much less considered what to do about it. Perhaps we can understand better if we ask ourselves the question: Is this much-heralded "affluent society" of ours really affluent?

Gunnar Myrdal, the distinguished Swedish economist and sociologist, recently pointed out in a lecture to a convocation of The Fund for the Republic that 20 per cent of all Americans in this "affluent society" live below the poverty line—and another 20 per cent barely above it. He stressed that the technological revolution is making the unemployed unemployable, for jobs increasingly depend on the education and skills needed to cope with the sophistications of a new age. This means, as Myrdal sees it, that a massive federal effort must be made to educate and to train if this wasted 40 per cent of our human potential are ever to become full partners in the tasks, and to share in the rewards, of our society.

Myrdal's figures are not to be challenged; but his solution is one that the Warfare State, in its present blindness, can be guaranteed not to accept. Already the pattern has become evident. There has been from Congress not a whimper of protest about President Kennedy's military budget. Almost certainly the armed forces will get every penny that has been asked. But Congressional pruning knives are being sharpened to operate on those sections of the budget that bear the opprobrious label of "welfare" programs. It is taken for granted in Washington that nothing very startling is going to be accomplished toward Medicare and that any massive new educational-training program is almost a dead issue.

Even such a veteran and ardent cold-warrior as the ultra-conservative columnist David Lawrence sees the issue. In a column in July, 1962, Lawrence wrote:

How can the armament expense of the United States . . . be materially reduced so that an era of business growth and a sound economy can be achieved in America?

This question is more important than a tax cut or any other "gimmick" being advanced as a cure for the stagnant economy of today. For the truth is America cannot absorb the present-day expense for armament and grow productively at the same time.

Here then is the first basis, only now beginning to be perceived and discussed, for the eventual creation of a politics of disarmament. Given time, it may perhaps be highly persuasive, for business itself, which has been committed ideologically and financially to the aims and rewards of the cold war, must come to see that this commitment no longer serves—that the economic welfare of the nation demands a civilian, not a military, employment of the nation's best brains and resources.

Such an awakening to hard economic fact is certain to be speeded by regional jealousies and frustrations arising from the highly in-equitable distribution of the multi-billion-dollar bounties of the War-fare State. California, hogging an incredible 24 per cent of those pro-curement billions and still insatiable, has become the envy of the other forty-nine states. New York, which lost as California gained, has established agents on the West Coast to try to woo some of the business back. The great industrial heartland of the Midwest, the arsenal of the nation when the major materiel consisted of tanks and guns and trucks, has since seen its share of procurement contracts cut from 27.4 per cent to 12.6. Its cities are burdened with heavy un-employment; its best scientific brains are being steadily lured to California; and "piracy" is about the kindest epithet its Congressmen and Senators can apply to the burgeoning military colossus of the West Coast.

The issue erupted into bitter debate in Congress last summer. Senator Frank J. Lausche, the conservative Democrat from Ohio, revealed that a group of Ohio Congressmen had conferred with Secretary of Defense Robert S. McNamara, pointing out that their state was receiving only 2.3 per cent of defense-research contracts and that the bulk of the business was all going to the East and West coasts. Why? "After some discussion," Senator Lausche told the Senate, "the Secretary of Defense made the sweeping indictment— and I call this to the attention of Senators from the Midwestern states —that the Defense Department is sending its contracts to the states where the brains are located. The Midwest does not have the brains to do the job, and therefore, he said, the assignments go to the East and West coasts." Then Lausche, after stressing the number of excellent Midwestern universities, charged that there had been "a migration of scientists and a pirating of them from Midwestern states" by the states, principally California, which the federal government had set up in the missile business.

In response, Senator Thomas H. Kuchel (R., Calif.) took the position that the safety of the nation was at stake and that defense contracts went to California in such numbers simply because California was best equipped to defend us. It was not an argument that found favor with legislators representing the deprived. Other Midwest Senators and Senator Jacob K. Javits (R., N.Y.) joined in the verbal barrage. Senator Humphrey, opening the hearings of his Small Business Committee, fairly sizzled. The Defense Department, he said, was giving so much of its business to California because high officials want "to get out there in the sunshine" and "just flit around there on the beaches." As for brains, "How do you think they got so smart in California?" he demanded. "The Government started putting out money to the University of California. It was not such great shakes a few years back. . . . I never heard of anybody who stood on their head when they were offered a university contract in California."

Senator Humphrey's bitterness stemmed from the fact, as he himself admitted, that only a few states were really dining to repletion on those defense contract billions. Cape Canaveral, he noted, was only a stretch of "sand dunes" until the federal government sent scientists and engineers there and made it the nation's No. 1 missile-testing site. The federal government, Humphrey pointed out, starts the build-up, and once a key installation or research center is established, naturally more contracts, more business, flock to it—"those who have, get more; the richer you get, the more you get."

The significance of this for the rest of the nation was underscored by some of the testimony presented before Humphrey's committee.

This established, for example, that hard-hit areas of the country—the so-called redevelopment areas—contain about 19 per cent of the population, but have 30 per cent of the jobless; they produce about 10 per cent of the nation's goods but get only 3.7 per cent of defense contracts. Even provisions to allow such areas special treatment in the awarding of defense business are honored more in the breach than in the observance, for in the last half of 1961 they received less than one-fifth of 1 per cent of the total of prime contracts awarded.

Why hasn't more defense money been funneled into areas of desperate need like West Virginia or Detroit? Dr. Conley H. Dillon, consultant to the Governor of West Virginia on unemployment, put it this way:

> . . . It is difficult to divide some procurements into two parts. This automatically eliminates a considerable percentage. Second, the contracting officer does not like to take the time and trouble to divide procurements and do the extra work necessary to utilize this procedure. He also prefers to deal with his old customers.

Senator Humphrey charged that the present method of distributing military contracts has served only to turn hundreds of thousands of workers into nomads, following the path of technology west to California and other fortunate areas.

> This is what is happening in our own state [he said]. This is why many of the states in the Middle West have not had population growth. Their birth rate has been high; their health rate is good; mortality rate is low. But they look around and the plant has left town. The industry has gone. So they have to sell their house, leave their family, frequently break up a family, a husband leaving his wife and children home, charging off to some distant place, chasing after what?—the scientist, the technician, the new plant, and the government contract. They move 2,000 miles down the road.
>
> The social disturbance this is causing our country is incredible, the lack of stability. It seems nobody has looked at it; we have just said, 'Well, it is free enterprise, let it go.' Communities were disrupted; government tax bases upset; families divided; children changed schools; delinquency increased. And you end up with these hard-core areas of unemployment.

Such is one face of the Warfare State. The question arises: Can we keep the Warfare State and change the face? Senator Humphrey and other members of Congress from deprived areas obviously hope so. They all vote, virtually without dissent, for ever costlier military appropriations, and when they indulge in verbal combat on the floor of Senate or House with the representatives of California, it is always in the hope of raising enough ruckus so that they can get a few more contracts for Ohio or Minnesota or West Virginia. Patent in Senator Humphrey's attitude in the hearings before his Small Business Committee was his desire to get a larger slice of the pie for his state, not to threaten the multi-billion-dollar military-procurement program.

But every Senator's hope that he can cut his constituents in on the gravy train is doomed to failure. Research and technological skills, concentrated in one area, perpetuate themselves there to the exclusion of other areas. Research, for example, is a continuing program; many valuable contracts are "follow-up" contracts, sustaining projects already started. Even new research, when it is initiated, tends to go to the areas where scientists and engineers are already established. Moreover, production tends to concentrate in the same area, close to the brains and facilities that created the blueprints.

Anyone who feels inclined to dispute this needs only to look at the last Defense Department summary of the allocation of research millions. The Pacific Coast and Mountain states have been awarded 54.8 per cent of all research contracts; California alone had 41 per cent. What this means is that California, despite all the anguished outcries, still has a hammerlock on the vital research which will lead to the military contracts of tomorrow; and these contracts, in turn, will go to California, precisely because the research was done there and the facilities and manpower are there.

California's representatives in Congress sometimes try to argue that a lot of the state's primary contracts are subcontracted, and that these subcontracts flow into every state in the union. But *Aerospace Management* magazine, after an exhaustive survey of 6,000 industrial plants across the nation, reported late last year that while California firms did subcontract a lot of work outside the state, their subcontractors sub-subcontracted much of it right back to California! The state wound up doing more than a quarter of the entire aviation-space business in the nation.

The *Los Angeles Times* chortled happily over this discovery and noted that, if Eastern Congressmen had really known the full story, their outcries "would ascend like a siren's," for what had been demonstrated by the *Aerospace Management* survey was "that California eventually gets more work than the Defense Department's figures show." The *Times* went on to exult that California has a lock on the brains and talent of the space age. "These experts are in California not only because the physical climate tempts them, but because the intellectual climate is one of the most salubrious in the United States and the world," the *Times* boasted. ". . . The envious Eastern Congressmen need more than federal money, they need talent—and they can't get that by voting for it or soliciting sympathetic testimonials from the President and Vice President of the United States."

That California intends to woo and keep this talent becomes evident when one reads the California press. In a single edition last November, for example, the *Los Angeles Times* ran fourteen solid pages of advertisements from major aviation-space-electronics firms pleading with scientists, engineers and technicians to flock to "lotus land" and partake of its luscious fruit. "The Sky's the Limit for Scientists, Engineers & Technicians," screamed an eight-column banner over one such page of advertisements. "Reach New Heights in the Space Age—Enjoy a Challenging Future," proclaimed another.

There is no disposition here to challenge the thesis that this country needs an adequate defense system. But the fact is that our swollen military budget is only partly related to legitimate defense needs, as Senator Proxmire has noted (see *The Nation*, August 25, 1962), and the best proof of this is the incessant sparring that goes on in Congress over what-state-should-get-how-much of the defense pie. The upshot has been that we have achieved, and are constantly adding to, a *needless overkill capability* at the expense of our national economy.

This is the issue as it is beginning to present itself to some, at least of our politicians and economists. And it is aggravated by the fact that the largess of military procurement is distributed in such a way that those who already have much, get more, while those who have little get less. Economics, in other words, has begun to throw its powerful arguments behind the idealistic and humanitarian pleas of those who are seeking to stop the arms race.

A MERGER OF MOVEMENTS: SIT-INS AND MARCHES

by Carleton Mabee

THE STUDENT MOVEMENTS for racial integration and for peace—the two major campus causes of the sixties so far—are similar in that they both use nonviolent, direct-action methods such as picketing, marches and civil disobedience. The student movement for integration centers in the South; it is directly related to the compelling personal concerns of its chiefly Negro participants. The student movement for peace centers in the North; it is more remote from student daily life and politically more sophisticated.

It is natural to ask whether the youth who take part in the more immediate integration struggle are being led by their experience toward taking part also in the similar, but more nebulous, peace struggle.

The present nonviolent movement for integration grew during the 1940s and early 1950s, out of pacifism; that is, the movement for nonviolent resistance as a substitute for war. Moreover, it is also related to the peace movement in that the wave of sit-ins which flooded the South in 1960 released energy that helped produce, in 1961 and 1962, a corresponding wave of student peace demonstrations.

In the North, students in both movements are usually white. The number of colored participants in Northern integration demonstrations is sometimes embarrassingly small; it is even smaller in peace demonstrations. One Negro taking part in a Washington peace march widely supported by Northern students could count only seventeen Negroes among some 5,000 marchers. Evidently many Negroes feel that participating in peace marches doesn't help them win middle-class acceptance.

Northern whites who participate in one movement often also participate in the other. According to Walter Lively, a colored field secretary for the Student Peace Union, most of the union's members are whites who first became active in liberal causes through supporting the sit-ins. At a recent integration conference in Baltimore, sponsored jointly by CORE and the Student Nonviolent Coordinating Committee (SNCC), a considerable minority of the delegates were involved in both movements.

If you were to query Southern Negroes on whether their participation in the nonviolent integration struggle has led them to take an interest in the peace movement, they are likely to say that they never even thought of any connection. A Southern region American Friends Service Committee representative, Tart Bell, explained it this way: Negro students become so intensely involved in their local desegregation struggles that many of them think only of the immediate crisis. "If a man's in a lion's den," said CORE National Director James Farmer, "he's going to worry about the lion." As the much-jailed North Carolina Negro minister, Elton Cox of the CORE staff, put it, most Negro youth don't think intellectually about the non-violent movement for desegregation, and therefore don't see any relation between it and the conscientious objector's position.

Nevertheless, there has been more discussion of peace among Southern students since the wave of sit-ins began in 1960 than before, according to Ella Baker of the National Student YWCA, Atlanta. Workers for peace organizations occasionally appear even in the middle and lower South, hoping to attract students who are already in the integration movement. Some integration leaders have resisted on the ground that integration should be the first concern of students in the South; it is hard, they say, to be effective on two fronts at once.

When Leo Lillard, a Florida-born Negro, first became a college student in Nashville, he thought like the rest of his class—"only of money, money, money." Taking part in sit-ins, however, changed him. "If I had not been in the sit-in movement, I would never have been concerned about my fellow men," he explains. Now he is active on many fronts. "I see no difference in explaining to critics why I picket for peace or civil rights," he told me as he left a picket line; "I just can't see any separation between peace and freedom." It is possible that the sit-ins have produced more changes in the sitters than in the segregationists whose businesses they seek to affect.

Another colored student who has come to believe that peace and integration are indivisible is Jan Triggs of Howard University. "If there is to be a genuine turn toward peace in the world," he said in a speech to peace marchers, "our society, like that of the Soviet Union, needs reconstructing. In this task there are many posts to be manned. The peace marcher who is too busy to join in a sit-in deludes himself if he thinks he is fighting for peace. Sitters who will not demonstrate for peace are likewise deluded if they think they are fighting for freedom; they are only acquiescing in the drift toward the ultimate solution of the race problem—the extinction of the human race."

Both North and South there is now a small, vigorous group of students in the integration movement—especially among those who circulate outside their own campuses—who have become peace-conscious in varying degrees. The variety of views among them is suggested by a recent conversation in the church-basement headquarters of the student integration movement in Cairo, Illinois, a town with Southern-style segregation.

The chief conversationalists in a group around a table were both twenty-two years old and had both recently been arrested in Cairo while demonstrating for desegregation. One was the very blond Jim Adams of Southern Illinois University, and the other the very black John Lewis of Fisk University.

Someone recalled that Robert Williams of Monroe, N.C., had advocated Negroes' using force against vigilantes.

"I agree with Williams," Adams said, "that if no police protection is available, the law of survival justifies Negroes defending themselves."

"We have the protection of the law in the United States," Lewis replied, "so fighting is not justified." Lewis, born of a poor family in the Alabama black belt, is a ministerial student and chairman of the student integration group in Nashville.

Someone by the table asked: "Is violence to defend yourself from cannibals justified?"

"Violence in no sense is justified," Lewis replied. "I have no right to destroy any human beings because they are sacred."

"Your own life is as sacred as the next person's," Adams broke in. "You should at least defend yourself enough to get away. We were taught that in the Army."

Then Adams asked the inevitable question: "If someone attacked my wife, I would risk my life to save her; if someone attacked your wife, what would you do?"

"I would try to defend her by nonviolence," Lewis answered. "I would try to attract violence to me away from her. I would offer the attacker clothes, food or money to prevent physical violence. Non-violence involves sacrifice. You must be willing to suffer, even to die."

Lewis has applied for draft status as a conscientious objector. Adams, like most students in the peace and integration movements accepts nonviolence as a tactic as long as it works. While he believes that armies are unfortunately necessary for defense, he regards nuclear weapons as essentially aggressive. He wears a nuclear-disarmament button.

Among the integrationist students inclined to pacifism, some have come to this position by the road of rebellion against society. When Negro students enter the integration movement, they are likely to be thinking in terms of middle-class demands for equal status, such as the right to eat in restaurants with whites. In time, they are likely to realize that equality in public places is not enough. They become aware of the power structure which prevents equal opportunity in jobs, housing and politics. As they knock up against that power structure, some of them become more and more alienated from the institutions that support it, such as education, business and government. They become emotionally "anti-respectability," "anti-boo-beousie." When asked whether they would fight for the United States, some may snap, as does Dion Diamond, of Petersburg, Va., a much-jailed member of the SNCC staff: "The only ultimate defense against communism is the complete realization of the American ideal of equality for all. Otherwise what is there to defend?" Or, as a student at Tennessee Agricultural and Industrial University says, "I don't think any second-class citizen should fight for his country."

Other integrationist students incline to pacifism because they have come to regard nonviolence as a way of life. These tend to be religiously oriented.

White theological student Bob Zellner, SNCC staff member from Alabama, is still struggling with some of the fine points of nonviolence theory. For instance, he is not certain whether, when police are brutal to him, as they have been, it would be vengeful of him to sue them. But on some questions he is sure: "Violence in international relations simply can't be permitted any more," he says, "so the nonviolent movement must be made strong enough to act in international relations as well as in race."

Because the Nashville-to-Washington peace walk included colored as well as white personnel, its story suggests both the problems and possibilities involved in putting integration and peace into one package in the South.

The walk was planned by the Committee for Nonviolent Action (CNVA), a group known for its demonstrations against nuclear testing. During the planning, Freedom Rider Jim Peck, of both CORE and CNVA, urged that the walkers should not make a point of challenging segregation in the towns through which they passed. It is simply not feasible, he urged, to expect many Southern Negroes, with their overwhelmingly personal concern in integration, to get involved in peace; nor many Southern whites, with their deeply ingrained feelings about color, to get involved in integration. Robert Gore, who took part in sit-ins while in college in North Carolina, and who was the only Negro to participate in the whole walk from Nashville to Washington, agreed, and it was so decided.

Last April, in Nashville, where the walk began, the walkers were invited to take part in a sit-in. They declined, according to plan, but did schedule their walk to pass by the site of the sit-in. The sitters, resenting the fact that the walkers did not join them, stayed away from a meeting the walkers had planned.

Quite differently, when the walkers were still twelve miles from Lebanon, Tenn., they "were absolutely astounded"—Gore wrote in his log of the walk—when Negroes from the Lebanon integration movement joined them. "We proudly walked into town about thirty strong," he wrote; and they "passed through the hostile crowds with no worries."

In both Lebanon and nearby Carthage, the walkers "established a perfect integration" with sitters, as Brad Lyttle, another walker, put it. The sitters understand nonviolence, he said "because they have practiced it."

Later the walkers met a group of colored students on their way home from a SNCC conference in Atlanta. One of them, Clarence Glenn of Louisville, was startled by the walkers. "I had never heard anyone talk like they did before," he said afterward. "But it's pretty much like what we are working for in the South. We think love and nonviolence can change the South; they think love and nonviolence can change the world. I think we are working for the same things."

The walkers often slept overnight in churches and held meetings there. By the time they reached Virginia, Gore decided that most Negro ministers they met seemed to be vaguely attracted to the walkers' peace program, while most white ministers didn't consider it worth discussing.

When the walk was over in June, it seemed to have been largely the fact that the walkers were integrated which had brought hostility down on them, including arrests, cursing and pelting with stones. Nevertheless, while Peck emphasized—with justice, as Gore's log shows—that many Negroes initially welcomed the walkers because they thought they were demonstrating for integration, Gore decided that the walk proved that those who are using nonviolence in the integration struggle are at least open to the possibility of using it in international relations as well.

Now that during the last three years the two "terrible meek" movements have achieved new stature, some participants believe that the present unobtrusive ties between them, if developed, would strengthen both. It would be helpful, they say, if the peace forces would point up their effort to educate for integration as an essential ingredient of peace, and if the integration forces would point up their effort to educate for peace as an essential for making integration meaningful. As Lawrence Scott of the Washington Peace Action

Center says, "There is no great value in desegregated coffins." It would do more good than harm, they argue, if Martin Luther King, James Farmer and other nonviolent integration leaders would be more vocal about the peace issue.

Robert Gore has come to believe, as a result of the Nashville-Washington walk, that the two movements should openly support each other. George Willoughby of the CNVA and Carl Braden of the Southern Conference Educational Fund believe that a manifesto by both colored and white leaders on the relationship of the two movements would be timely. Walter Lively of the Student Peace Union thinks that, while to promote the formation of peace organizations among student integrationists in the South would be divisive, Southern students should be aware that the integration movement in the South *is* the peace movement in the South; and, to encourage this awareness, he recommends experimenting with such devices as peace study groups within the integration forces, a magazine about peace for integrationists, and a peace secretary for integration organizations. The problem, as he sees it, is to show students that it is necessary to retire Senator Eastland from Congress because he is both a racist and a militarist—and that he is both for the same reasons.

Meanwhile, the two movements have already been cooperating in ways which hint of further possibilities. In Northern cities, they sometimes coordinate the scheduling of peace and integration demonstrations to encourage participation in both. The War Resisters League has released its executive director to give about half his time to integration. Peace marchers, with the encouragement of their sponsoring committee, have sat-in at segregated restaurants. Both movements have been promoting the purchase of women's leather tote bags produced by Negroes in Haywood County, Tenn., to help offset the economic retaliation they have suffered for registering to vote. Both movements are beginning to look for ways to support political candidates who favor both desegregation and a search for alternatives to the cold war. And both movements are assisting, along with nonviolent forces in India and Britain, in the creation of a nonviolent army to operate across international boundaries in Africa on behalf of both national freedom and racial integration.

WHAT THE PEACE MOVEMENT NEEDS

by Charles D. Bolton

THE PERIOD SINCE MID-1961 has seen the greatest proliferation of peace activities since the 1930s, perhaps in our history. Reasons are not hard to find: the Berlin crisis, the deterioration in the U.N., and the Soviet test resumption (which suggests that Russian leaders now consider nuclear war so likely that urgent preparation for it outweighs any propaganda considerations). But I think the major reason is the realization, yet hazy for many, that powerful elements in American society are mentally and morally capable of starting a nuclear war, or at least of knowingly taking actions involving the highest risk of one. Three experiences brought about that realization. First was the shock of the failure of the Kennedy Administration to take the significant initiative for peace that many liberals, rightly or wrongly, had come to expect during his campaign; second has been the *rapprochement* of so much of respectable conservatism with a resurgent extreme Right, which has shifted from a policy of defending the *status quo* to a policy of urging the eradication of communism, even by war if necessary; the third, and most focal, was the Administration's shelter proposal, with the subtle first-strike implications being further promoted by assurances from major news magazines that nuclear war need not, after all, be so bad.

Until this recent period, the peace movement had consisted of ingroup stimulations by disparate groups ranging from pacifists to one-worlders; occasional acts of public witness, and essentially critical stands by liberal groups like SANE. Now community groups have sprung up in great numbers—the San Francisco area alone has over a dozen. There has been a contagion of women's marches and protests. Symptoms of the shaking of student apathy have appeared, most strikingly in the form of student cooperation within adult peace groups.

Many professional and academic people have begun to speak up for peace. A new spirit has also emerged. The upsurge has the character of an authentic mass movement, with an ignoring of traditional social and organizational lines and an emphasis upon individual initiative. Very few institutional organizations have played a significant role. The actions have been essentially expressions of individual sentiment, gropings by concerned people for meaningful action in a world which, as David McReynolds puts it, is rational but no longer sane.

Unhappily, the lasting power of the movement is in doubt because of the very individual spontaneity which has been its initial strength. These new peace workers direct their anguish at crises of the moment; few look beyond to any specific program for attaining peace. The extent to which the Kennedy shelter program has become the focus of attack is symptomatic. Winning the peace will almost certainly require persistent effort over a period of years. Can individual responsibility be sustained simply by crises, without the morale and ideology of organized groups? Will it operate during periods of low international tension, which is actually when the most political progress can be made? The new peace workers have been concerned largely with registering their own protests and encouraging like-minded people to register theirs, without, for the most part, addressing themselves to the organizational and tactical questions involved in influencing the thinking of the general public. The movement still thinks in terms of the $2 contribution. There are no spokesmen who speak in ringing terms, no symbols of evil, no enemies decried.

Perhaps the fundamental internal problem of the peace movement is the character of its leadership. There are no important political names among its active leaders. Clergymen and union officials, with certain notable exceptions, have provided little leadership; and considering their organizational contexts, not much can be hoped from them. A major source of leadership remains with pacifist-oriented groups like the Friends, and their record of quiet, consistent effort is admirable. Their approach is one of persuasion by personal example, a reluctance to see other groups as enemies or to question motives, and a strong individualism emphasizing each person's own peace-directed form of action rather than striving for any group stand. It is extremely difficult for persons ultimately committed to nonviolent resistance to accept a conflict-group theory of influence. Yet it is doubtful whether political decision-makers can be swayed without concerted organizational persuasion, whether popular stereotypes about international affairs can be changed without publicly raising questions about the integrity and commitment to democracy of the power blocs promoting the ideology of the military state.

Intellectuals, too, find it hard to provide the leadership required. The academician has a distaste for the rough and tumble of competitive persuasion. The scientist's trained tendency to doubt operates against commitment to action for political ends, with their inevitable uncertainties. The intellectual's aversion to black-and-white thinking makes him, paradoxically, reserved about any action which is apt to polarize issues and, at the same time, antagonistic to the "public relations" concessions necessary to enable the peace movement to become a genuinely popular movement.

The division and reluctance in leadership is reflected in the movement's inability to agree on specific goals. Various elements urge pacifism, unilateral disarmament, general disarmament, arms control, initiation of reciprocal steps in tension reduction, world government, etc. They agree only in being against a general nuclear war. But the issue is not whether people *want* war or peace—almost everybody, publicly at least, is against war. The issue is what specific course of action as an alternative to the current unstable balance of terror has a reasonable chance of preserving both peace and the values of civilization. Symptomatic of the problem is that, while there are peace groups galore, scarcely one among them is pleading disarmament as its special cause. Disarmament has never been an issue of serious public debate in this country.

Perhaps a by-product of the very desperateness of the current international situation is that it may bring some unity and hard-headed realism to the peace movement. If members of the movement hope to affect the course of history (or make future history possible), they must agree on three general points.

POINT 1. The jam in which the world finds itself, and which will likely be accentuated in the next years, is too critical to justify any but practical, i.e., conceivably effective, peace activities. Any alternative to the military posture must have reasonable credibility for the general public, as well as for some—though not necessarily all—of the major power hierarchies in society. Such approaches as pacifism and unilateral disarmament, though appealing to many peace workers, have no likelihood whatever of being accepted by the bulk of the American people within the future in which the decision of war or peace must be made. The unacceptability of any alternative that would leave the door open to a Communist takeover would be so great to the political, economic and military hierarchies that they would almost certainly disrupt democratic processes to block it.

The alternative must require international cooperation, empathy for the legitimate concerns of other nations, and a commitment to an accelerated effort to stabilize the relations among peoples by raising the standard of living in underdeveloped countries. But it cannot imply a narrow political or economic ideology which would divide the peace movement, alienate significant potential support, and enable opponents to denounce it as subversive—thus barring the movement from access to the mass media and institutional structures essential to bringing about change in mass society. For example, an alternative such as world government—a worthy, long-run goal —is not a practical possibility for promotion by the peace movement in the decisive future.

These considerations leave the peace movement with no feasible alternatives to the balance of terror except arms control or general disarmament. The arms-control theory is, as a matter of fact, not a realistic alternative at all; it cannot be viewed as anything but a smoke screen for a continuation of the arms race [see "How Not to Disarm: The Arms-Control Doctrine," by Seymour Melman, pp. 225–231]. Hence, there is left no realistic course for the peace movement except to throw its weight toward the goal of general disarmament with appropriate inspection and controls. Disarmament has no particular ideological content, has a large body of respectable scientific support, and is the avowed goal of both Russia and the United States as well as the neutralist nations. Though no one should overestimate the depth of commitment they represent, these public testaments bespeak a climate in world opinion that can be appealed to.

Such a course implies further that proposals for solving East-West crises should be evaluated primarily on the basis of their contribution to preparing the ground for a disarmament agreement. For example, an opportunity exists in the case of the German issue to press for a policy that would at once solve that political impasse and start the U.N. toward disarmament-control activity. It seems reasonably possible that Russia would accept a solution involving the disarmament of both West and East Germany and a withdrawal of all NATO and Soviet forces, both goals to be achieved under U.N. supervision. Reunification of Germany would in time almost certainly occur, but justifiable Soviet fears would be relaxed by Germany's disarmament. A crucial accompanying step would be to extend U.N.'s opportunity to serve other countries in a similar role. Thus there could evolve, in a short time, a U.N. framework for inspection and maintenance of disarmament applicable to general disarmament when the time came.

Similarly, the peace movement cannot realistically urge any approach toward the China question other than the abandonment of present U.S. policy, aimed at reinstating Chiang Kai-shek on the mainland. Peiping's current strained relations with Russia should be exploited to bring about modifications in the relations of China to the rest of the world that will make its Communist government more responsive to world opinion and to the dangers of nuclear war. With its rapid industrial growth and bitterness at world ostracism, China may well turn out to be the critical question on which disarmament turns.

POINT 2. It is by no means enough for the peace movement merely to stress the horror of war and to propose a vague disarmament ideal. A disarmed world is as inconceivable to most people today as was a world without a hereditary ruling class to our medieval ancestors. Not only must a credible political program for disarmament be presented, but peace workers must think through the implications, especially economic and social, of disarmament. I believe it will be possible to appeal to the majority of articulate Americans only if universal disarmament can be portrayed, not just as an escape from the "Red or dead" dilemma, but as the door to a new vision of socio-economic life. To avoid ideological bogs, the vision, for the peace movement itself, must be vague. But to generate the required enthusiasm there must be promise of something more inspiring than just averting depression and relaxing tensions.

As an initial step in making disarmament plausible, the popular stereotype of the manner in which decisions leading to war or peace are made needs to be exposed as false. Advocates of the balance-of-terror deterrent must logically make the assumption that decisions will invariably be made, in rational fashion, by objectively informed political and military leaders. This assumption is invalid. Such decisions reflect primarily the collective climate in which the decision-maker operates. One need not turn to our witch-burning ancestors or to the collective insanity of a highly civilized people under Nazism to illustrate the power of collective climates. That non-rational social contagions shape the climate of thought of elite groups, as well as of the general public, can readily be seen in twelve years of American policy toward Communist China, the gross miscalculations of the Cuban fiasco, and the way in which the international crime of the U-2 incident has somehow been converted into an American moral triumph. A political elite sharing the premise that history is irrevocably moving in its favor overlooks contradictory evidence and miscalculates the will of opponents. An elite which habitually refers all social upheavals to a conspiratorial causation comes, in time, to perceive all social change as a gigantic conspiracy against civilization and reaches the ultimate ethnocentrism of preferring the eradication of mankind to the triumph of the conspirators.

This is not to say that rationality is not predominant in *most* decisions. It is to say that there is no ground for faith in the *invariability* of rational, accurate calculation implied by the balance-of-terror deterrent. It is to say that, whereas the tensions of an arms race inevitably generate irrational social contagions, premises of distrust and collective insanity, disarmament would foster a climate of opinion which would minimize thinking in terms of military solutions and encourage hope that international differences could be resolved by negotiation.

While the details of disarmament are voluminous, the general framework is ordinarily overcomplicated by its proponents. For a considerable time into the future disarmament can and, because of ideological differences, must be worked out with a minimal modification of the existing U.N. structure. Unquestionably some system of world law must eventually evolve to handle genuine conflicts of interest between nations.

But we must recognize, I think, that it is simply not true that most conflicts that produce war in modern societies can be resolved by judicial action. The interests of the Nazis could not have been adjudicated by any court. The conflict of interests between the United States and the USSR is an ideological conflict, not one subject to legal decision. The American Civil War demonstrates that the rule of law alone does not prevent war. Nations compete in many fields (as in seeking markets for trade); but, with rare exceptions, it is the existence of the capacity for, as well as the will to, military action that raises resultant tensions to the conflict level. Since it is beyond our capacity to bring about a worldwide fabric in which there are no clashes of interest, the only alternative is to eliminate the capability for military action. The fact that the kinds of weapons that create the real danger today require the skills of highly trained scientists makes this goal easier to attain. The internationalization of the high moral standards which characterize the best of the world's scientific-technical community must for some time be the key to the maintenance of disarmament. Given general disarmament, the U.N. and the World Court have a high likelihood of evolving a system of law adequate to handle the kinds of disputes which are subject to adjudication.

What modifications in the U.N. are necessary to prepare it to serve as a disarmament apparatus? The first is to change the Charter —if that is necessary—so as to assure universality of membership. Clearly no universal disarmament plan is viable which does not include all the peoples in the world.

Since the disarmament agency would be an executive function, the major structural modification necessary would be in the Secretariat rather than the Assembly. Required would be a large inspection commission of scientists recruited from the various nations. Peace workers should give more attention to Dr. Leo Szilard's belief that faith in the honor of the scientific community may be the world's best hope. I mean no blind faith in scientists as persons, but rather an awareness that the character of science as an organized activity exercises a form of moral control over its members that is different from the amoralities operating in political and economic realms. (It is instructive, here, to compare Bronowski's *Science and Human Values* with Mills's *The Power Elite*.)

It is generally proposed that a U.N. police force would be the major enforcing instrument of disarmament. But the problem of control and use of such a force against major powers poses difficulties of the same order as immediate world government. While no doubt a medium-sized force capable of preventing wars in underdeveloped areas would be essential from the outset, I think we must candidly admit that, until the world has evolved further toward a common political frame of reference, maintenance of disarmament would have to depend upon the unanimous voluntary support of the major nations (though, of course, subject to full inspection and all non-military types of controls). Fortunately, it is from the major powers that voluntary adherence is most easily maintained. For it is there that the community of scientists is most advanced; and it is on the major nations that the eyes of the world would be focused. The free international communication among scientists in a disarmed world —which it is crucial to establish in the first stage of the disarmament process—would lessen the likelihood of a technological breakthrough giving one nation an advantage over another in rearmament potential. In addition, once the commitment of its scientists to a disarmed world had been obtained, no major country could move toward rearmament without provoking so deep a split in its own scientific community that large-scale rearmament efforts would be paralyzed.

POINT 3. Since any plan of universal disarmament involves uncertainties and risks, advocates of disarmament face a difficult educational problem. Peace workers can win their case only if, at the outset, they can convince people that the question is one of choosing between alternatives which involve varying degrees of risk. Disarmament must be shown to involve less risk to civilization and humanity than a continuation of the arms race.

The most fundamental risk in disarmament involves an intellectual judgment: that Communist leaders are not men of undiluted and *unchangeable* evil. I cannot agree with those who say we must take the pessimistic view of communism. It is a thin line between success-fully answering this challenge and being declared "soft" on com-munism. The problem is not to defend communism at all; it is to make clear that the Communist world is changing, that the direction of this change depends very much on our response to it, and that communism would change even more under disarmament. While it would be naive to expect Communists promptly to give up their belief in the ultimate triumph of their system, history makes clear the falsity of the premises of ideological invariance and the un-changeability of national orientations. The form taken by applied Communist ideology has been shaped in large measure by the para-noid logic of an arms race with modern weapons, by the grinding context of forced-march industrial development, and by the world-wide anti-colonialist revolution. Under disarmament, it is highly plausible to believe that the loss of effectiveness of fulminations against the West, combined with an increase in the consumers' share of an already impressive rate of economic growth, would accelerate change in Communist societies and hasten their evolution away from the police state and their efforts to export revolution.

The problem posed for a disarmed world by the tenet of Com-munist ideology that internal revolution is a legitimate political technique is indeed serious. However, the inspection and control apparatus that would be set up in every country under disarmament would work strongly against outside interference in the domestic affairs of any state. Revolutions not dependent upon outside influ-ences, or threatened by counterrevolution from outside, would be likely to develop in a more moderate direction. Communist revolu-tions have rarely directly succeeded; they have succeeded by radicalizing moderate revolutions which stalled, or were threatened from without.

Ultimately, the peace movement's answer to the risk of revolution is similar to the one which must be given to the danger that, in a world where the gap between the "have" and "have not" nations is so enormous, real grievances between nations might mount up to an overthrowing of disarmament. The answer must be that disarmament is the *beginning*, not the *completion*, of the solution of the problem of war. But it is a beginning which would enable us to move meaningfully to further steps. A crucial advantage of the contemporary point in history is that the level of technology for the first time makes possible extremely rapid closure of the economic gap between the "have" and "have not" peoples. The primary barriers are social and political, and many of these barriers would be reduced under disarmament. The vista of technological possibilities opening beyond the road block of militarism is one in which the political symbols of communism would have little appeal. Indeed, the advantages to mankind of a disarmed world are so great that it is time we cease just timidly proposing disarmament as a less risky alternative than the arms race; it is time to make clear that human societies should seize this precarious moment in history to liberate the potentialities of our technical knowledge. And this can be brought about only when man vacates his self-made community of fear.

BASIC RESEARCH FOR PEACE

by Donald N. Michael

In order to do a special study, we trained up a team of highly specialized young scholars with extraordinary combinations of skills in mathematics and statistics, Chinese and Russian languages, political science, psychology and computer disciplines. It took the better part of six months to put this team together, and with funds we could have kept them at work on problems of disarmament, international crises, alternatives to war and the like. As it is, we have had to terminate nearly all of them and scatter the research team to the four winds.

The irony is that during the period of disorganization I was asked to consult with several peace groups and individuals who wanted dreadfully to "do something" *right now* about the frightening state of world affairs— but not to contribute or raise funds for basic research into the processes of conflict and integration—how wars break out and grow and how laws and institutions take root. These same people complain about the vast sums of money being spent on missile research and development, but they cannot perceive that alternatives to war may require something more than good intentions, may indeed require large-scale financial support for a parallel kind of research and development.

In THESE TWO PARAGRAPHS in a letter to the author, a distinguished scholar sums up the problems and purposes of peace research. This article will examine both in more detail.

In the last few years, there has gradually grown a new state of mind in some whose profession it is to study man's individual behavior and that of his institutions. What once were, for example, simply studies in international affairs, political science and the psychology of decision-making are now viewed, in a few quarters, as peace research. In the past, scholars in these fields might have been motivated to seek knowledge and understanding, or to improve our capability for conducting world affairs in traditional ways. Today, the professional peace researchers seek to discover the criteria and conditions for viable alternatives to the looming annihilation toward which traditional perspectives and operating styles are driving the world.

Given this state of mind, the range of studies defined as peace research is steadily broadening and interdisciplinary studies have blossomed in what were traditionally the special, usually non-overlapping, provinces of the students of international law, the psychology of behavior under stress, arms-control inspection and so on. Joint effort —or at least the awareness of the need for joint effort—is the methodological order of the day. Evidence of this is found in the above-quoted letter from a political scientist—and in the growing number of summer seminars, study groups and working conferences, such as that sponsored in 1960–61 by the American Academy of Arts and Sciences, the special seminar on disarmament in 1960–61 held at the California Institute of Technology, the disarmament seminar composed of Harvard and MIT scholars which is now in its third year, and the arms-control seminar which meets regularly in Washington.

An illuminating example of the multi-disciplinary approach is a research program on the meanings of "deterrence," supported by the Naval Ordnance Test Station at China Lake, California. Working on grants from NOTS, historians, mathematicians, psychologists, anthropologists and physicists in several universities are gradually evolving a systematic understanding of the assets and liabilities of deterrence as a generalized concept and, thereby, the extent of its applicability for helping to attain a reasonable state of world affairs. (This example is also important in that it demonstrates an underlying difference of opinion in the research community. Some scholars feel that peace research is by definition never undertaken by the military and that such studies should have nothing to do with weapons of any sort, even if they are part of a carefully planned carrot-and-stick approach. They would therefore not accept the NOTS program as being part of the peace-research effort. But other researchers feel that, given the state of our present ignorance about plausible alternatives to annihilation, such studies are necessary and can be usefully applied to other problem areas as well.)

Whatever philosophy is emphasized, there are, in fact, only a few organizations established for the specific purpose of conducting research on peace, though there are a number doing related studies: the Carnegie Endowment for International Peace, the Institute for International Order in New York, the Center of International Studies at Princeton, the Center for International Affairs at Harvard, the Center for International Studies at MIT, the Institute of War and Peace Studies at Columbia, the Institute for Defense Analyses in Washington, RAND and the Hudson Institute. Organizations established specifically to do or support peace research include the Center for the Study of Conflict Resolution at the University of Michigan, which also publishes the highly professional *Journal of Conflict Resolution;* the Committee on Research in International Conflict at Washington University in St. Louis; some of the work of the Research Foundation at Colorado State University, and the Peace Research Institute in Washington. Small groups of informally organized researchers are to be found at a number of universities and in a few private organizations; some professional groups, notably in the legal and psychological disciplines, are also active.

And, of course, there is the Arms Control and Disarmament Agency. (It's worth noting that while ACDA will study many aspects of arms control and disarmament, its responsibility for providing a basis for negotiations means that there will be strong pressures to emphasize short-term, immediate pay-off research rather than long-term; and for a variety of reasons it will be slow to emphasize political, psychological or sociological studies.)

. In Europe there are the Institute for Strategic Studies in England, the Institute for Social Research in Oslo, and a few other groups in France and Denmark. And there is the newly formed Canadian Peace Research Institute.

In spite of the impressive titles and the number of interested groups, these peace-research facilities (even including ACDA) are pitifully financed and pitifully small. The reasons are several, and they say much about the present state of private peace research and the limits on its future possibilities. Money is perhaps the greatest single limitation. At present, efficient peace research needs only relatively modest funding. Nevertheless, the disparity seems disproportionate between the billions spent on military research and the $6 million proposed budget (fiscal 1963) for ACDA, overwhelmingly the best-financed peace-research effort.

What makes peace-research people bitter and discouraged is not the lack of large-scale financing, but rather the fact that there are no reliable and easy sources of funds to cover projects that may cost from $2,000 to $200,000. It is in this range, and particularly at its lower end, that fundamental contributions can be made. And for this situation, individuals and organizations directly involved in peace action (as contrasted with peace research) must shoulder much of the blame. In their preoccupation with immediate "action," most of them continue to overlook the imperative need for future action programs based on systematically derived and validated knowledge.

The fact that it takes ten years, an army of scientists and engineers and a large bureaucracy to develop a weapons system, and that it will take at least the same order of time to develop the ideas and knowledge needed for evolving peaceful alternatives, has yet to stimulate these groups to support research on an adequate scale.

The picture is not wholly discouraging, however. A few peace action groups, for example the Fellowship of Reconciliation and the American Friends Service Committee, have cautiously begun to support small studies. The Canadian Peace Research Institute is sufficiently optimistic to be mounting a grass-roots fund-raising campaign on its own behalf, and is basing it on the assumption that funds will be forthcoming from peace action groups in that country.

So far they have managed to collect some $250,000; how much more they can tap remains to be seen. The big foundations so far have not arranged their programs to encourage peace research as such, but an ingenious researcher can sometimes translate his particular project into one which does fit the going programs of the foundations. And there are some smaller foundations whose purposes, in principle at least, admirably lend themselves to the support of peace research. But the foundations, big or little, grind slowly. All in all, funds from all sources have been too small and too slow in materializing to meet the growing need.

The present and future of peace research is not entirely a matter of money. There are scholars in the universities and industry doing studies which have profound significance for peace action, but who are not aware of the implications of their studies for this area. There are also scholars unaware that there are crucial problems needing study which would interest them professionally. Away from Washington, the subtleties and ramifications of the endless problems which must be solved, if we are to work our way out from the present maze into a reasonably sensible world, never reach much of the research community. Even a sophisticated reader would be hard put to understand, for example, that a major unsolved problem in a weapons-control inspection system is: how does one nation go about providing highly convincing information that it is doing what it says it is to an opponent who distrusts it deeply? It isn't only the paranoid who can read malevolent intent into charitable actions. To the scholar not intimately informed about arms-inspection problems, it is unlikely that the variety of profoundly important basic- and applied-research projects implied in this question would be evident.

Also, many scholars are under the impression that finding solutions to major problems requires secret information. In fact, most of those with access to classified information deny this. Thus, for example, important contributions to the systematic study of means for recruiting, maintaining, training, controlling and using an international police force can be made without any secret information, and yet this problem so far has received very little attention. This applies also to the profoundly important area of decision-making in crisis (though here familiarity with the Washington scene and access to discrete, if not classified, information would be necessary for checking out theoretical formulations).

To help close this gap in appreciation of what needs study, the Institute for International Order commissioned and published in 1960-61 five documents outlining many of the problems in need of research: *The Technical Problems of Arms Control, Economic Factors Bearing Upon the Maintenance of Peace, The International Rule of Law, National and International Decision-Making,* and

Communications and Values in Relation to War and Peace. These and the journal *Current Thought on Peace and War* (originally started by IIO and now independently incorporated and struggling for lack of funds), along with the new Peace Research Institute in Washington, now provide much of the broad-range professional background materials for alerting the potentially interested peace researcher. But in the professional research community, there is still too little understanding of what needs study: and for this reason, too, there is a shortage of good people doing peace research.

One uncomfortable and crucial question is whether the findings from peace-research studies will be applied in any systematic manner. Even the recommendations of RAND and other "hard-nosed" contributions to the prevailing approach to world affairs are not always applied. Bits and pieces of studies are used, and occasionally large chunks of programs; but research findings as such serve chiefly as swords or shields in internecine battles for power and apppropriations. Peace-research products can hardly expect more careful or sympathetic attention or application. In fact, the hurdles are higher, since much peace research heavily involves the social sciences, which are still thought intellectually dubious—in some cases rightly—by leaders and decision-makers in government, private institutions and peace action organizations. However, in other cases the findings are solid and crucial. Indeed, sometimes the findings so decisively challenge favored viewpoints or beliefs that the information is, and will be, used only reluctantly or be suppressed or ignored—whether those who should use it be devout counterforce proponents or unilateral disarmers.

Indeed, the very people who should be most eager to use the findings from social science in general and peace research in particular, namely the peace action groups, seldom use what already is known. Rather than basing their case on validated studies and research about human behavior in crisis, the characteristics of nations, their weapon systems, their values, etc., many action-oriented groups rely chiefly on emotion-based arguments. This is not to say that such appeals do not have power, but rather that knowledge now available from peace research and related studies is not used effectively by the very groups who should make the most of it.

This is not a new state of affairs in the ways of human action, but it is a particularly disturbing and inadequate approach to peace action. Grass-roots support is needed and is impressive in governmental eyes; but in the end only by using the formal knowledge we have, and only by increasing that knowledge, will the peace movement develop the sophisticated arguments which can move leaders of government, inspire members of Congress and encourage private-opinion leaders to support the positions espoused.

It is by no means clear at this time that the peace-research effort will grow strongly enough and in a sufficiently organized fashion to provide information fast enough to contribute significantly to a way out of the present terror. It will take much money and time. If we haven't the time, it doesn't matter. If we do have time, those committed to developing a peaceful world cannot afford to leave the support or conduct of peace research to someone else. It's chiefly their job to support this effort. Professional competence is needed. Sympathetic and sophisticated understanding of the role and utility of research is needed from those who cannot themselves do it. Those who wonder what they personally can do to help in the search for peace might well consider contributing hard cash for the hard study which seeks answers to the world's most pressing problem.

SOCIAL SCIENCE IN THE
CAUSE OF PEACE

by John Cohen

ARE WE FORCED to accept the *political* picture of a world irreconcil-
ably divided to the bitter end? Eight Pugwash conferences [now
known to American scientists as COSWA—Conference on Science
and World Affairs.—Ed.] have made it plain that in the domain
of science the ablest men from East and West can come to terms
on what must be done to root out the hazards of war. And they have
shown how the resources of science can be organized on an intercontinental scale for the common good of mankind. This demonstration that the state of the world is not to be taken at its political face
value carries a spark of hope for the future.

Less than two hundred men have taken part in these meetings.
But behind them stand thousands of other scientists waiting to take
part in a constructive enterprise. And there are countless people
everywhere equally eager and well disposed. How can all this good
will be harnessed to a common goal?

The idea of a Human Pugwash was conceived in an attempt to
answer this question. It calls for a world "organ" which could bring
the full strength of the biological and human sciences to bear upon
the challenging problems of the contemporary world; to pursue, with
indefatigable zeal, the goal of realizing the potentialities of man and
nature—biological, psychological and cultural in the fullest sense
of the word.

The voice of Pugwash science in world affairs, in the past, has mostly been confined to issues dictated by the political situation; in the main, to problems of disarmament. The time has come to put the boot on the other foot—for politics to take its cue from the issues raised by science in the exploration of human and natural resources.

That such a change in initiative is imperative becomes clear if we face the fact that the energies of our shrewdest statesmen are locked in ceaseless wrangling over one seemingly futile issue after another; the moment Berlin is at peace some other such issue will rear its dreary head. In the meantime, the helpless individual stands demoralized by this spectacle. And scientists are ready to offer an escape from the desperate impasse, not by entering a competition to solve *political* problems, but rather by seeking a *non*political course of action, by trying to shift attention from the arid desert of futile disputation to the fertile pastures of productive action, by changing the subject of conversation from "how to die" to "how to live."

The overriding interest of Pugwash in disarmament was doubtless essential at the start. Latterly this interest has extended to questions of international collaboration, chiefly (though not exclusively) in physical science. Scientists outside the Pugwash movement are also becoming increasingly aware of the importance of international collaboration. This is exemplified, for instance, in the expanding scope of activities of the International Council of Scientific Unions. But however vital a high-energy accelerator is judged to be, or a program for deep-drilling into the earth's crust and mantle, or an investigation of the biological potential of the Indian Ocean, these leave untouched the actual problems of people in their daily life: first and foremost, the nature and conditions of their work, the character of their dwelling places, their aspirations and conflicts, their opportunities for "fulfillment."

Scientific collaboration faces a multiple of "human" tasks. To feed six billion gaping mouths (twice as many as there are now) before the end of the century calls for a single global authority; and the pathetic squalor of contemporary Mauritius gives us a foretaste of what awaits us all, when our children reach maturity, unless farsighted measures are soon taken. But the provision of food may turn out to be one of the less intractable problems. It is true that people have to eat, but they also need homes, cities, schools, colleges, hospitals, systems of communication and transport, and ten thousand amenities of civilized life. Let Pugwash assemblies discuss the scientific implications of *these* needs.

Consider the task of *speedily* raising the standard of education in backward countries to the level of the more advanced parts of the world. Merely sending a handful of teachers to Indonesia is to tinker with a problem of such a magnitude that it can be overcome only by full utilization of modern techniques of communication. Here we might bear in mind the large-scale experiment in educational television recently conducted in France to meet the shortage of teachers of mathematics. This type of problem was examined in detail at the first International Conference on Visual Information at Milan in July, 1961, and is continuing to receive expert study. What is lacking is a central authority which could feel a sense of extreme urgency about these matters. Also lacking for this reason is the relatively small sum of money needed to put the requisite scheme into effect.

Or, looking ahead, reflect on the form that work will take in an epoch of automation, when men will no longer be subject to the indignity of doing what can be done by a machine. What meaning will his occupation bear for the worker? And will it elicit his talents and efforts? How will he devote his leisure after a four or five-hour stint of labor? And what, indeed, will be the significance for him of his leisure? Even if industry of the future could be purged of its monotony and meaninglessness and infused with some of the spontaneity of play, there will remain scope for *re-creation* by immersion in the imaginative life, in art, drama, dance or other ways of transcending the space and time of daily life. *These* are also urgent matters that deserve the attention of international science.

In an illuminating article in *The Nation* of September 30, 1961, Margaret Miller described a variety of industrial, social, medical and educational difficulties which beset the Russians in their struggle to cope with the complex tasks of their huge country. These very human difficulties bear a family resemblance to those encountered in the United States and other capitalist countries. What could be more fruitful than a joint scientific attack on these shared problems?

The incalculable waste of human potentialities and natural resources in the world today is a fact of life that has yet to impinge on the minds of statesmen, who are busy with other things. Think of the treasures of intelligence and imagination, of skill and talent, which lie untapped in the countless millions still living ill-fed, ill-housed and illiterate. Even in the affluent countries, there is a lopsided interest in mere technological ingenuity to the neglect of what might be described as the imaginative life of man. The patent defects of our so-called educational systems, with their relatively primitive schools and many antiquated centers of higher learning, bear witness to this. We must not speak as if all that mattered were the product of technological ingenuity, while disregarding the art and enjoyment of living.

Nor must we forget how thin is the civilized veneer which conceals the dog beneath the human skin. The nature of man is better apprehended by a study of his history, just as his history becomes more intelligible by a study of his nature. A Human Pugwash could seek a scientific understanding of the way man's nature, such as it is, and his history have conspired to generate the unimaginable brutality manifested in the wars and exterminations with which our generation is so familiar, but to which it reacts with indifference and apathy.

Man, I suggest, is primarily an *imaginative* rather than an *intellectual* animal. Yet there is an exclusive concern in modern education with the manner in which children acquire a representation within them of what happens in the world outside. To perceive, to learn, to remember the outside event, that seems the be-all of our educational effort. What of that inner world of creative imagination which equally requires to be tended, and to be represented? Possibly it is only by the cultivation of the inner realm of experience that we shall overcome the callousness which allows us to ignore human suffering that does not occur under our noses; we are enormously more affected by a slight accident which happened round the corner than by a terrible castastrophe a thousand miles away. In the long run, the survival of the species may depend on discovering the psychological "antidote" to such callousness.

Each branch of social study may have something worth contributing to a Human Pugwash—sociology, demography, economics and anthropology; even psychology is not entirely to be despised in this connection. For although psychology disclaims any magical methods for resolving international tensions, it may make useful suggestions for raising the effectiveness of international debate and for clarifying the relationships among hostile groups. The principal task of psychology, however, as I see it, would consist in revealing the extent to which our mental and emotional resources are still unexplored and uncultivated.

It may be said that the success of the Pugwash venture will depend on the help of politicians and that nothing would be gained by antagonizing them. I entirely agree. But more will be needed than the sympathy of politicians. An informed and enthusiastic public opinion will have to prod its political representatives into action to translate the dreams of science into a waking reality.

If an abstract Human Pugwash is to be quickened into life, it must take a form which appeals to those in the East and West alike—and to the "neutrals" into the bargain. It must be heralded not so much as a *novel* ideal, but as an endeavor to *implement* those ideals which are already universally acknowledged. Its participants must come as individuals and not as parrots dressed like men; in this way, the greatest cultural variability would more likely be allowed for. The outcome would not be yet another international agency to share the alphabet with those which already exist—although the latter (and I include the specialized agencies of the United Nations) might well be rendered far more effective by becoming linked to a *single focus* of world interest.

The ideological affiliation of individual participants may vary widely, but this need not be a barrier to cordial cooperation. If theoretical reconciliation is out of the question, for the present at any rate, let them devote themselves to those tasks which they agree must be discharged if the world is to survive and flourish. Let them stop singing hallelujahs to their particular Way of Life and begin instead to talk about the many things that can be done together.

The ultimate function and structure of a Human Pugwash must be left to its members, and premature crystallization of the formative notions is therefore to be shunned; a *fait accompli* is unlikely to win worldwide cooperation. My personal view is against a mass movement of scientific workers, which would be cumbersome and diffuse in its effect, and hence unlikely to achieve a powerful impact on legislators or public opinion. On the other hand, an exclusive Nobel Prize-winners' club may become out of touch both with the rank and file of scientists and with public opinion. Some synthesis is desirable which would allow close contact between the most distinguished men of science on either side and, at the same time, enlist popular scientific support, as well as the active interest of other groups alert to the issues, especially groups which feel themselves directly affected and involved. While the "input" to Pugwash should come predominantly from the biological, medical and human sciences, the "output" should be directed, as and when appropriate, to receptive audiences everywhere, including industrial, professional, administrative and trade-union organizations, student groups and, of course, political leaders, government administrators and the United Nations.

A last word. The image of science presented today is overwhelmingly that of a dark and sinister Frankenstein monster threatening to destroy mankind and engulf the world. Much weaker by contrast is the presentation of science as a benign, healing and creative influence. Films, fiction and the press conspire to produce a double image in which the dark overshadows the light. This betrays itself in a basic ambivalence of people towards nuclear power, with its inexhaustible possibilities for good and evil. This is a distortion of what science *could* be, and it cries out for correction. If, in the minds of the impressionable young and their even more impressionable parents, science were to be represented as a beneficent force, this in itself might help to make it so in fact. The abuse of science for ends inimical to man might then become a thing of the past.

THE ECONOMICS OF DISARMAMENT

by William S. Royce

COMPARATIVELY few economists in the United States have had either the opportunity or interest to think through the broad question of disarmament and its economic impacts in terms of the real world. Most of those who have considered the question at all take positions at one of two extremes: they do a quick double-take at the thought of an America that is suddenly bereft of all defenses, and rush back to the arms race, or they mentally abolish the defense budget overnight and then become overwhelmed by the $46 billion question: How to replace that huge gap in the gross national product?

These people see either a hopeless defense problem or a hopeless conversion problem. In either case, they forget that neither a "defense" nor a "gross national product" is a single entity. What really would happen throughout the economy in the wake of an approach to disarmament can be known only if one examines the separate reactions and decisions made by a host of persons—individuals, corporations and agencies—each of them motivated by differing goals and preferences.

The hasty conclusion that elimination of the defense budget would mean ruin for the "aerospace industry" or the "electronics industry" is wholly unwarranted. It would have great impact, to be sure, on such companies, but the extent of the impact would depend on how well each company had prepared for such an event, what alternatives were available to it, and what other conditions affected its ability to carry out its plans.

Similarly, the impact on any given community would be not just a simple subtraction of defense dollars now poured into it from military contracts, but the complex result of numerous actions taken by the official agencies, business firms, families and individuals that compose it.

The assumptions that must be made by any person having a planning function related to some future disarmament move are of several types: timing, or the schedule of specific actions; the nature of the world that will exist at various stages along the timetable; the division of responsibilities among government, industry, labor, communities, for coping with specific problems; and the policies to be followed by government regarding various alternatives open to defense industries converting to non-defense activities.

I consider it grossly unrealistic to assume that a transition from the present arms race to a condition of general and complete disarmament (GCD) would take place in as abrupt a span as five years, despite the fact that certain proposals under international negotiation call for such "fast" action. International agreements of so vast and profound a nature simply do not get implemented so quickly. Realistic planning for adjustment to an eventual state of disarmament should be based on a series of transitional steps—stages of arms control— each of which would have its own impact on the economy.

Given three to five years in which to prepare disarmament plans, and a span of five to ten years during which they would be carried out, both public and private agencies should be able to make the necessary adjustments without undue hardship on any major sector of industry or segment of the population.

This brings us to some consideration of the nature of a world in which two great power blocs, each totally opposed to the other's socio-economic-political system, may have achieved a negotiated state of disarmament. Very little thought has been given to the subject: most people mentally say "good riddance to the military" and assume we could relax. But is this realistic?

In all their proposals for GCD, the Soviet leaders have never once renounced belief in their destiny to rule the world. On the other hand, they have repeatedly promised to "bury us"—if not militarily, then in the political, economic and social graveyards. Let me recall the official statement of Soviet doctrine on "peaceful coexistence":

... The chief force of aggression and war is U.S. imperialism. ... The policy of peaceful coexistence is a policy of mobilizing the masses and launching vigorous action against the enemies of peace. Peaceful coexistence of states does not imply renunciation of the class struggle ... [it] is a form of class struggle between socialism and capitalism.

Clearly, even in the event of a retreat from the arms race, we must anticipate continued Soviet-Allied confrontation across other segments of the spectrum of conflict. There is grave question whether the American people have yet faced up to this fact and to its inevitable consequences. We seem always more ready to spend money for weapons and uniforms than for less forceful ways of resolving conflict. In the fifteen years since World War II we have spent, with little hesitation, more than $450 billion on military forces. (This investment can be evaluated either way: that it deterred the Soviet bloc from launching a worldwide aggression or that it failed to bring us peace.) During this same period, we have spent about 10 per cent of that amount on the non-military foreign aid and information programs—and the expenditure of nearly every dollar has been contested.

Can it be some mark of heritage that we are more willing and able to fight with our fists than with our brains, with military force than with friendly persuasion? The Communists have made it quite clear that, if we are to forswear the use of arms and still prevent them from taking over the world, we will have to change our attitudes rapidly and commit substantial investments in ideas, money, manpower and resources to the battle on the economic, social and political fronts.

Now there are two economic questions involved in this. The first is the extent to which a condition of GCD actually enables us to reduce the defense budget. The second is what compensating expenditures will be required to enable us to win the conflict on the non-military front.

Even the most far-reaching proposals for disarmament make provision for retention by each country of forces for maintaining internal order and for contributing to an international peace force. Implementation of any secure disarmament agreement would also require establishment of sophisticated and expensive systems for insurance against cheating.

The Bureau of the Budget estimated in 1960 that the effect of GCD ten years after adoption of the plan then proposed by the United States at Geneva would be to reduce major national defense expenditures by $30 billion per year from the levels that would obtain if the arms race continued. If agreement were reached today, the amount of reduction would come to about 4 per cent of the gross national product estimated for the year 1970 (this does not account for displacement of the multiplier effect attributed to defense spending). The defense budget then might be between $20 and $25 billion per year, instead of between $50 and $60 billion if the arms race continues. And we know already that this timetable cannot be kept.

As I have indicated, it is most unlikely that any agreement on general disarmament can be implemented fully in as short a span as five years. During much of that period, while procurement of arms was tapering off, military spending would be gradually replaced by expenditures for inspection and communications systems to monitor the process of demobilization of forces and destruction of weapons. The equipment to assure conformance with a nuclear-test ban alone would cost between $20 and $25 billion, spread over three to five years (one estimate on the cost of enforcing a ban on orbital bombers runs to about $15 billion). Enforcement of a ban on production of nuclear weapons probably would cost more than the $2 billion annually we have been spending on production of nuclear warheads. I have, as yet, seen no estimate on the costs of an over-all international inspection system that might be set up to prevent cheating on a general disarmament agreement.

Of perhaps greater significance to the economy, but more difficult to predict would be the changes in allocation of the remaining defense expenditures. Presumably, the procurement of nuclear-missile weaponry would be ended, as would the deployment of long-range air and naval strike forces. But much of the industrial capacity now devoted to producing these items might be diverted to satellite monitors and electronic-detection systems. Heavier dependence on militia and international police forces would possibly mean a larger share of total defense expenditures for pay and support of ground forces, reversing the trend since World War II. These are only a few of the many possibilities, but they indicate the kinds of information that industry and communities must have if they are to prepare for adjustments to a GCD situation.

Beyond this, we need better planning guidance on the efforts required to carry on the non-military aspects of the struggle against communism and the specific contribution that can be made by various industries, communities and classes of people in the country. To most Americans, foreign aid has been nebulous and remote. Before it can mean anything to most citizens, the Alliance for Progress, for example, must become a program in which individual Americans can feel they have a personal stake—through participation in activities like the Peace Corps, through business relationships with their counterparts in newly developing countries, by realizing that some portion of what they produce (other than taxes) has a direct influence in demonstrating to people in other lands the advantages of our system.

There is a real need for study of means whereby we can not merely match the Communists in appealing to others, but can seize the initiative with programs of peaceful development that will be of lasting benefit both to them and to ourselves.

It is heartening to see that President Kennedy has included the functions of planning for economic and social adjustment to disarmament among responsibilities assigned to the new United States Arms Control and Disarmament Agency. It may be noted that the National Security Act of 1947, which set up our present mobilization-planning agencies, gave these agencies authority to plan only for war, not for conversion to peace.

Neither corporations nor communities can do much realistic planning toward economic adjustment to disarmament until the federal government provides them with some reasonable guide lines on a number of vital questions. These include such problems as alternative rates of curtailment of specific arms programs; probable rates of government procurement of civilian products similar to those used in defense (communications satellites and related electronics, for example); provisions for conversion of government-financed war plants and machine tools to non-defense production; government attitudes on encouraging major private investment in and patent protection for new industries growing out of defense-supported research; and the possible priorities for instituting new government public-works programs.

One problem of considerable importance is how to reallocate the $30 billion or so that may ultimately be saved in the annual federal budget. Three alternatives, or combinations of them, are open: reduce the national debt, reduce taxes, or increase expenditures on social welfare and economic development programs. It is not possible to go into this question here in detail, but the potential for controversy is obvious. A partial answer has already been given by the decision to press forward with the national space exploration program. Expenditures in this category were nearly $3 billion in fiscal 1963 and may reach $10 billion per year by 1970. These could rapidly replace much of the military business of the missile-electronics and related industries.

Of perhaps greatest concern to the industrial planner trying to set strategy for a period in which defense contracts would no longer be available is the question of the government attitudes toward "monopolies." There are firms today with the capital and the desire to diversify outside of military business that have difficulty selecting investments they would be allowed to make. An example is the current situation in which American Telephone and Telegraph finds itself. The Justice Department has disclosed its consideration of a plan to force AT&T to get rid of its overseas communications network. At the same time, other government agencies are playing a major role in AT&T's plans to get into outer space communications.

Perhaps it is time we review our whole attitude on the antitrust question and start developing positive federal policies to encourage the growth of competing companies, instead of merely negative efforts to hamstring firms that are already successful. In a related direction, maybe we should concern ourselves less with an arbitrary estimate of a desirable total tax bite and more with the effect of specific tax rates on the ability of young corporations to blossom into healthy competitors.

Finally, the defense agencies have the problem of preparing adequately for the curtailment of their own operations—the reduction of military forces and return of their members to civilian life; shutdown of bases, depots and arsenals; and the redirection, hopefully, of many of their resources to constructive, peaceful efforts to strengthen the Free World in a continuing struggle. None of these tasks would be simple; the manner in which they are performed will have great impact on the country, on local economics and on our international relations.

Military procurement at present accounts for about 10 per cent of the nation's total output, and production for the military has grown at about twice the rate of growth of the economy as a whole. Moreover, studies of the Stanford Research Institute have indicated that a large proportion of the "growth" companies in the United States during the past twenty years have concentrated heavily on defense products, while companies primarily dependent on consumer goods have experienced much slower average growth.

But these studies also indicated there is more than mere coincidence here. The "growth" companies were also characterized by organized research and long-range planning efforts, proven competitive ability and the courage and aggressiveness to take risks in new ventures. Under changing conditions resulting from the transition through arms control to disarmament, most of these companies can be expected to take the conversion in stride, provided they have assurance of a generally prosperous economic climate and are given adequate advance data on which to base orderly planning.

There are other firms that are less capable of meeting the challenge. These are mostly small and medium-sized firms specializing in narrow product lines. They will need more guidance to help them reduce their vulnerability to sudden changes in the nature of military requirements, since they lack the flexibility of plant, capital and management to switch rapidly to other products.

Many of the adjustment problems resulting from disarmament are likely to be related to workers rather than corporations. In an age of specialization and security-seeking, workers have become much less versatile and less mobile than companies. "Retraining" seems an obvious answer. But retraining for what? By what techniques and in what type of institutions? Under what auspices? The proposed retraining program, now before Congress, will have to meet these questions.

For many years, our major effort in industrial research and technology has been in the direction of "labor-saving." Perhaps it is time to mount a counter-effort toward "labor intensive"—not by outmoded means of featherbedding, but by stimulating development of economic activities that would result in useful work at competitive prices.

Industrial firms are not likely to finance the research and development necessary to this end. But labor organizations should do so. There is an urgent need for identification of functions that will be in demand a decade from now, and for the application of new techniques for educating and training workers to be ready for them. Government and business *both* must help, but this seems a fertile field for a new brand of labor statesmanship.

By the very nature of present programs for employment security, vocational retraining, urban renewal and housing, highway and other public-works construction, the major responsibility for planning and executing measures of direct benefit to those affected by shutdown of defense facilities falls first on city and state officials. Federal activities are mostly in the form of national planning and guidance and the furnishing of financial support to state-administered programs.

It would seem, then, that a very real need exists for development of a much better understanding of the whole range of possibilities both at the federal level and, through federal guidance, at state and local levels. State and local officers need to begin thinking also about how their areas and people would be affected by various actions the federal government might take. For instance, actions to increase economic opportunities in Eastern depressed areas may help to slow down migration to the West Coast and ease the conversion unemployment problem in Los Angeles.

But such things take time; we cannot wait to start until military spending is cut off.

The American economy has already made at least four major adjustments since World War II approaching or exceeding the magnitude that would be required following a possible GCD agreement. First was the reconversion of 1946 and the tremendous surge to satisfy pent-up consumer demands while accommodating the mass migration of servicemen, war workers and their families to new homes throughout the country. The television revolution came next, with impacts—many of them adverse—on a host of other industries. We hardly recovered from these before the Korean buildup sent us back to a new defense effort, much of it patterned along World War II lines. Just about the time this was completed, our whole defense system made the massive switch from surface carriers and human-aimed explosives to nuclear-electronic-missile weaponry. Coincident with these changes came the pervasive movement toward automation and the geographic relocation of several major industries.

These adjustments have not been simple and we are still living with some of the residual problems in the form of depressed areas, chronic unemployment among certain classes of workers, comparative stagnation of some industries and a complex host of problems at the metropolitan levels of government. Nevertheless, we have made these adjustments within the framework of a dynamic, regulated-enterprise economy and, compared to what people in other parts of the world have gone through during the same period, the worst hardships were hardly more than inconveniences.

A rereading of Galbraith's *The Affluent Society* should be in order whenever people start to list the things that should be done to take up the slack left by cutting off defense spending. The problem is not so much one of listing new peacetime spending programs that could total the same federal budget as before. It is more one of political economics and behavioral science—how do we manage it so that the mechanisms to meet the real needs of the people can be geared up to the already fantastic capacity of our production machine?

What this all adds up to is a plea for recognition of the fact that conversion problems are complex, that they are as much political as economic, and that the federal government does not now have the capability or even the organization to make plans or to carry them out or even to guide others on how to plan for disarmament. There

is still time in which to do a proper job of research and planning
before we run into the "danger" of a real disarmament situation.
The challenge is before us to begin now examining the alternatives
and to be ready with acceptable solutions when, as I hope, the time
does come.

HOW NOT TO DISARM:
THE "ARMS-CONTROL" DOCTRINE

by Seymour Melman

DISARMAMENT IS STILL a professed goal of American policy. But for several years now a growing and influential group of American strategists, while continuing for the most part to give lip service to disarmament as an "ultimate" goal, in reality are working toward an entirely different one—arms control, i.e., a permanent, regulated international military-deterrence system.

This shift in aims has been apparent in a spate of publications, debates and forums which have come to public attention in the last year. Notable, in this regard, were the Conference to Plan a Strategy for Peace held at Arden House in 1960, and the "Collected Papers" presented at the Summer Study in Arms Control, published in 1960 by the American Academy of Arts and Sciences.

The new doctrine evolves logically from the "hard-headed, realistic" thinking that produced, first, the theory of "superior military strength" and then, on its wreckage, the doctrine of "massive deterrence." The theory of superiority became obsolete, for all practical purposes, with the application of a bewildering number of technologies to military problems; no one country could count on being ahead of all others in every technology. Now massive deterrence is falling into obsolescence. Both sides have it, and it has resolved nothing; it has simply made the brink, on which both sides continue to teeter, more frightful.

So the "hard-headed realists" have come to the conviction that if we cannot have superiority in arms, we ought, at least, to have equality. This is the basis of the doctrine of arms control. And it is the more dangerous because, while remaining a salable theory to the Pentagon and to the arms industry, it can—and is—being sold to the public as a kind of disarmament.

The fathers of the new doctrine—a vigorous, intelligent collection of scientists, scholars and military professionals—arrived at the idea for varying reasons and with diverse approaches to it. Some among them, as government advisers or weapons technologists, had played important roles in the arms race and had become fearful that it was getting out of control. For them, arms control reflects a crisis of conscience; they are well aware of the Armageddon to which a continuation of the arms race could lead.

A second trend favoring arms control can be recognized in certain military and political theorists, together with munitions makers, who found in the doctrine a method for heading off the growing public pressures for disarmament. This group finds the dual appeal of arms control entrancing: it can be presented to the public as disarmament, yet in some views of arms-control requirements it need not close down a single major military establishment, nor put any obstacle in the way of the Pentagon's war games and strategy planning.

Then there is a group of men, many of them in government service, who tried repeatedly to implement disarmament measures, and found themselves stymied by the opposition of the Pentagon and the Atomic Energy Commission. (Saville Davis, managing editor of *The Christian Science Monitor*, has marshaled impressive evidence on the persistence of this opposition in an article written for the fall, 1960, issue of *Daedalus*.) Wearily, this group has now decided that it is futile to buck the military any longer, and has turned to arms control.

Finally, there are those who fear disarmament because "it would leave the United States naked." (Fear of "nakedness" has become a national phobia. The fear is present even with our current high level of armaments; the mere prospect of disarmament heightens it. The phobia is the price we are paying for our apolitical attitudes of the last decade.) For these men, who have no explicit theory of society which they are prepared to match against Bolshevik doctrine, the sword is their only shield. Indeed, they know no other politics but the sword; and if, by the mischance of ubiquity, technology makes it impossible for us to be certain that we have the bigger sword, at least we should make certain that we have one just as big.

It is at this point that the ultimate fallacy of arms control—in fact, of all military-deterrence thinking—is exposed. Wars generally serve political ends; one may go further and say that not all battlefields are military. Of what use is it, then, to exhaust our energy and resources on weaponry if the Soviet Union chooses to fight on the political and economic fronts? Or do we attack militarily, anyway, destroying ourselves in the process of destroying the enemy?

The strongest supporters of the theory that military power is the best foreign policy are those who are out to "destroy communism," to "get it over with"—even at the cost of our own destruction. The theory finds merit with those who see it as unbearable that the military deadlock should continue while the Soviets succeed in extending their political system. Such are the tensions reflected in a military strategy which envisages the destruction of the Communists at whatever cost to ourselves. This is not really strategy; it is defeatism, a counsel of despair—all the more marked because it involves a yielding of the political and economic initiative to the Soviet Union.

Arms control, say its supporters, will provide for both military stability and the factor of deterrence. Will it? To achieve military stability, i.e., a stable balance of military strength, it is necessary to agree not only on the numbers of weapons-in-being, but to freeze (a) the ability, and (b) the will, to make new ones.

But the only way to freeze the ability to develop new weapons is to disband major research-and-development facilities and to put their personnel under appropriate inspection and control. No arms-control scheme yet put forward contemplates any such step.

And the only way to freeze, or to destroy, the will to make new weapons is to achieve a relaxation of the present fear-ridden mentality, engendered by distrust, which grips the world. This distrust, which is basically a political factor, will not be dispersed by agreements that are designed to regulate, but not to terminate, the arms race.

Arms control, therefore, will not achieve military stability. Military technologies will continue to be developed in the customary way, with first one side and then the other seeming to have the advantage.

We turn now to the factor of deterrence. What exactly will arms control deter? Presumably, a major missile attack by one of the great powers upon the other. But equality in missiles, for example—i.e., arms control—will not necessarily deter a "first strike" if that promises advantage to one side or the other (assuming the will to strike is there). Obviously, the more nearly equal two opposing forces are, the greater the role surprise and evasive maneuvers can play in the outcome of the conflict. In this sense, arms control might well increase, rather than decrease the danger of surprise attack.

Of course, there is the deterrence implicit in retaliation "from the grave." This is based on the premise that the Russians know that, if they attack first and, in the process, utterly destroy our country and every living soul in it, our weapons-control systems would nevertheless go through their grim, automatic ritual and destroy their country and their people. The picture of death dealt from an uninhabited wasteland is surely a piece of insanity beyond reckoning; but it is an insanity to which both sides must subscribe, else there is no operative deterrence.

Yet in other respects the promise of stabilized deterrence through arms control is based upon the premise that governments always behave with substantial regard for rationality. That this is not true, history amply demonstrates. Under conditions of recurring international tension, irrational decisions, based on erroneous estimations of the moves or intentions of the opponent, are more likely to occur than rational ones. Each side, equipped with an arsenal of strategies for outwitting the other, can readily impute to the other side his own intentions (which may not always be of the very best). Conditions of crisis are a standing invitation to national leaders to make human errors of judgment.

Moreover, error—human or mechanical—could precipitate catastrophe in another way: through accident. Arms control would not perceptibly lessen this danger, which is inherent in the very existence of the complex missile weapon and the equally complex warning and response systems that are its necessary adjuncts. And it must be stressed that, in a massive missile stalemate, even a single accident could be fateful for mankind.

All of these complexities would be multiplied by the appearance on the world stage of new members of the nuclear club, to say nothing of new ways to deliver atomic warheads. These altogether realistic possibilities underscore the importance of reaching some sort of test-ban agreement quickly which would put a limit to the number of nuclear powers. But this inference is not generally made by supporters of the arms-control doctrine.

In a subtle way, "national security," "stability" and "deterrence" —all promised by the new doctrine of arms control—have come to imply, to many persons, *political* security, *political* stability and *political* deterrence. This is self-deception. As I have already indicated, schemes for balancing military power can be outflanked by political and economic methods. Arms control could well become the political Maginot Line of the West. Political and economic competition must be met on its own terms; it cannot be evaded by alignments of missile systems and the self-deception involved in them.

It is precisely in this field that inspected disarmament, with objectives and methods basically different from those of arms control, offers important hope. It opens to the West alternatives to a policy of sole, or major, reliance on military power; it presupposes that the West can indeed deal with political and economic competition on its own terms—and do so successfully (the economics of disarmament would strengthen the West in this non-military competition). If reliance on arms—controlled or not—to solve all problems is a counsel of despair, then reliance on inspected disarmament is an article of faith.

Inspected disarmament holds out other realistic hopes. The inspection process would reduce the technological capability of war-making —a result impossible to obtain through arms control. By creating confidence in international political processes, it would reduce the intensity of the fear and distrust implicit in the cold war. The reduction would be cumulative. The first disarmament agreement (necessarily the goal would be arrived at in stages), which might provide *inter alia* for an international inspectorate and a method for adjudicating disputes, would in itself help to create an atmosphere of confidence in which subsequent agreements would be easier to achieve. (The feverish efforts of groups with an occupational or political stake in the arms race to prevent a bomb test-ban agreement may well be explained in this context. Obviously, a mere test-ban agreement would not affect present military capabilities; but the arms-race supporters can justifiably argue that such an agreement would encourage subsequent and more far-reaching ones.)

Inspected disarmament would certainly stimulate the pro-peace and pro-freedom segments of society in the Soviet Union and the United States. There is evidence that in both countries there exists a vast, latent sympathy with the disarmament ideal. While there is little evidence of anything other than private debate on the subject in the Soviet Union, the very fact that the discussion there parallels ours suggests that an operating disarmament process would strike fertile political roots among the Russian people.

Public debate in support of disarmament invariably runs into the objection that no inspection system can be foolproof, and therefore the whole business is too dangerous to risk. But what is sauce for the goose is sauce for the gander. Where are the assurances that an un-hampered arms race, or even one under a system of controls, would save us from being blown to smithereens? The most that proponents of arms control can offer us is a dubious, short-range hope of avoid-ing immediate catastrophe. But none among them has seriously ad-vanced the argument that arms control can have any long-term value in safeguarding this country, or the world, against a calculated or accidental nuclear holocaust.

Proponents of the arms race are willing to risk the destruction of civilized society in the name of defending it. The development of the arms-control doctrine may be regarded as the partial response of conservative theorists to the growing strength of the disarmament idea. The weaknesses and dangers of the doctrine are the weaknesses and dangers of the arms race—and of conservative thinking in the West.

This much is clear: arms control is a theory of armament, not of disarmament.

There is risk and uncertainty attached to every political policy. For each person in a free society, the choice of where to take one's chances is determined by one's values. If these values include a high regard for human life, a desire to develop man's potential for peaceful living, and the will to extend the boundaries of freedom, then the strategy of disarmament, with its allied political and economic goals, is the preferred course. But if one's values place human life at low worth and include a preference for man's destructive potential and for authoritarian relations in political life, then some variant of conservative military theory, such as arms control, is preferable.

The pity is that so many of us make our choices without awareness of the ends, or values, that are being served.

SECURITY THROUGH DISARMAMENT

by Louis B. Sohn

THE RACE IN ARMAMENTS is spiraling beyond the stratosphere. The nuclear stockpiles of the major antagonists have reached the horrendous size of an equivalent of some 60,000,000,000 tons of TNT—twenty tons of explosives for every man, woman and child in the world. Tremendous missiles, many stories high, can cross distances of more than 5,000 miles in half an hour, and no nation can any longer feel safe behind vast ocean ramparts. Very soon even a small and poor nation may afford to have a very few citybusters to threaten its neighbors.

The nations of the world are spending some $100 billion a year on arms which are supposed to guarantee their security, but there *is* no security. By design, by miscalculation, by accident—a war can start at any time. Some quiet morning when most of us are asleep, hundreds of missiles may rise from the depths of the oceans and destroy all the major cities within several hundred miles of our shores; half an hour later, the big missiles will arrive across the oceans and destroy the inland cities. With luck, a few of them will be destroyed on the way, but enough will get through to change most of our cities into radioactive rubble, and to kill on the spot some 40–80 million people. All our military might cannot save them, nor protect the remainder against fallout and starvation. The only thing we can do is to retaliate on the enemy, thus further increasing radioactive fallout and multiplying the chance that even innocent bystanders in other nations will not be able to survive.

232

Our great array of weapons is extremely important as a deterrent, but if war should start they would no longer give us any real security. By increasing further the size and quality of our armaments, we can increase our chance to retaliate and thus diminish the possibility of a premeditated attack. The grave danger lies, however, in a nuclear war developing from a limited war through gradual increase in the destructiveness of the weapons used in it by the losing side, or from accident or mistake. With growing reliance on intricate devices and push-button weapons, the chance of a mechanical failure increases at a rapid rate. This is accompanied by an increase in tensions and an accumulating desire to get rid of them at whatever cost. Finally, even if the present possessors of nuclear weapons can be expected always to make wise decisions, adequate caution may not prevail in the other nations which are likely to acquire these weapons in the near future. As an eminent scientist said recently, there is no longer just a probability, but a certainty, of a nuclear war in the next ten years.

It is the duty of the President of the United States to make these facts and danger clear to the people of the United States and to Congress. Otherwise it may not be possible for them to accept the drastic remedies needed. President Roosevelt, writing before the advent of the atomic age, instinctively grasped the basic requirement of a peaceful world: *a comprehensive reduction in armaments.* The road to American security no longer lies in the direction of an arms race toward an illusive point of superiority in destructive power; we can obtain more security only by obtaining a cut in our potential adversaries' power to destroy us. Such a cut can be obtained in one way only—by an agreement on a reciprocal reduction of armaments to the point where neither of us will be able to destroy the other.

We must, of course, maintain our present strength while we try to find some mutually acceptable terms for such an agreement. It might even be a good bargaining point to threaten an increase in our military establishment, and in the deterrent strength of our allies, if an agreement is not reached within a reasonable time. But the main effort must be in the opposite direction. We need to start thinking about disarmament as the only remaining way of increasing our security. The question is no longer whether we can "risk" disarmament; not to risk it is to run a greater risk.

The main thing that seems to stop us is that we know the risks of the arms race, however frightening they may be, but we have really no idea what are the actual risks of reciprocal disarmament. In a disarmed world, national power will depend not on arms, but on other factors elusive at present and, therefore, looming as dangerous. Can we compete with the Russians in areas other than armaments? Can we win a race for the hearts and minds of men in a world free from the fear of a devastating war? Is our system sufficiently dynamic to devote as much to winning the peace as to deterring a war? To all these questions the answer is yes, if we are ready to buckle down to work and if our President is willing to lead us into this exciting world of peace.

Assuming that we are ready to explore the path to peace, where shall we start? In the first place, we need an agreement not with the Russians, but among our own people with respect to disarmament. While our government has accepted "the goal of general and complete disarmament under effective international control," there is a strong feeling in this country and abroad that we are paying only lip service to the idea. The doubts would be largely removed if the President would officially proclaim his willingness to do all in his power to make considerable progress towards this goal during his Administration. His declaration should then be submitted to Congress for endorsement, and Congress should appoint a special committee, composed of leaders of both parties, to work closely with the President on the preparation of plans to realize the goal. The best brains in the country should be mobilized and alternative routes should be explored. While it is not necessary for the general public to know the details of the plans under preparation there should be sufficient disclosure of general outlines to test the sentiments of the country.

Once the President has Congress and the country behind him, then the time will arrive to get the agreement of our allies and their suggestions for improving our proposals. Once our allies are satisfied, we will be ready to talk seriously to the Russians, and they will be forced to believe that we are actually ready to arrive at a meaningful agreement. For as long as there is serious doubt that anything proposed by our government will be approved by Congress, any proposals will be considered as sheer propaganda; once there is preliminary approval by Congress and the people, the other parties to the negotiations will no longer be able to avoid the issue and will have to bargain in good faith.

The ideas suggested here are not novel. They are based on two of our most important past experiences: the preparation of the United Nations Charter and the North Atlantic Treaty. From the Fulbright Resolution to Dumbarton Oaks, and from the Vandenberg Resolution to the Washington Conference, this method was followed with success. We ought to try it again in seeking to obtain an agreement on disarmament.

It would be presumptuous on my part to attempt to anticipate the exact details of the agreement that might be finally reached on disarmament, but some possible alternatives may be outlined. All of them are based on the assumption that the United States will not abandon the goal of general and complete disarmament, under effective international control, that was endorsed in all the principal draft resolutions presented at the fifth session of the General Assembly; and that the main problem relates to the method by which this goal can be reached.

Over the last few years, we have been trying to proceed by small steps, hoping that an agreement, for instance, on nuclear tests will establish a more favorable atmosphere for a more comprehensive agreement. It cannot be doubted that such an agreement would brighten the horizon for future negotiations; but if the next small step should require the same amount of time and patience as did the first, many years would elapse before we could reach any actual disarmament agreement. It seems desirable, therefore, to abandon this preliminary fencing and to start thinking instead about some big steps toward controlled disarmament. In fact, such a big step might be easier for the Russians to accept, as it would involve an amount of controls which would be more proportionate to the amount of effective disarmament. We have seen that a nuclear test is worth, according to the Russians, only three inspections a year, with important limitations as to the size of the territory to be inspected. If we want more inspections, we have to accept more meaningful disarmament measures.

Almost thirty years ago, President Hoover proposed that all armies and navies be reduced by one-third, and that certain specific weapons (heavy artillery, tanks and bombers) be abolished entirely. Over the years the Soviet Union repeatedly made similar proposals; in particular, it picked up a French proposal for the abolition of all means of delivering nuclear weapons (missiles, military aircraft, naval vessels, submarines and artillery), and suggested that they be abolished in the first stage of the disarmament process. Other measures to be taken in the first stage, according to the Soviet plan, would include: reduction of the armed forces of all states to fixed levels (for instance, of the United States and the Soviet Union to 1.7 million men each, equivalent to a cut of about one-third); a corresponding reduction in conventional weapons and military expenditures; withdrawal of all forces to national territories and the elimination of foreign military bases; launching of rockets for peace purposes only; prohibition of transfers of nuclear weapons to states which do not possess them and of the manufacture of such weapons by these states. (The only important measures missing from these proposals are the abolition of nuclear weapons and the prohibition of their manufacture.)

The Soviet proposals also contain provisions for a control organization which "shall at each stage have powers in conformity with the scope and nature of disarmament measures involved." In particular, international inspection teams would be permitted: to watch over the destruction of prohibited means of delivery and the abolition of foreign bases; to insure that airfields and ports are not used for military purposes; to establish permanent controls over factories previously engaged in the production of prohibited means of delivery, and to examine documents pertaining to the budgetary allocations of states for military purposes.

The United States proposals for the first stage, also presented in 1960, included the following steps: prohibition of placing nuclear weapons in outer space; notification of all launchings of missiles and space vehicles; establishment of a zone of aerial and ground inspection in agreed areas of the United States and the Soviet Union; cutting of military forces of the United States and the Soviet Union first to 2.5 million and, after the verification of this reduction, to 2.1 million, and of the forces of other militarily significant states to agreed levels; stopping of production of fissionable materials and transfer of thirty tons of weapons-grade uranium from weapons stockpiles; and, to prevent a surprise attack, exchange of observers at agreed military installations, including missile and air bases at home and abroad.

Both groups of proposals are clearly deficient from the other side's point of view. The United States proposals contain an extremely small amount of actual disarmament and a relatively large amount of inspection. The Soviet proposals, on the other hand, are deficient in their inspection provisions, though they contain more effective disarmament provisions. While the United States puts strong emphasis on measures to prevent a surprise attack, the Soviet Union considers that these measures are designed to obtain information about the location of Soviet air and missile bases. On the other hand, the Soviet proposals do not seem to contain inspection provisions adequate to insure that all bases, means of delivery and factories have been actually opened to inspection, and that no means of delivery are hidden in other places or that no other factories are engaged in producing them.

It would seem desirable to combine the good features of the two groups of proposals and to eliminate their deficiencies. There are three basic difficulties. In the first place, it is not likely that the inspection system in the first stage will be so efficient as to guarantee complete compliance with the provisions of the agreement. A margin of safety would be necessary, therefore, and each of the two sides might wish to keep a number of means of delivery roughly equal to the hypothetical number of means of delivery which might have been hidden by the other side and which are not likely to be discovered immediately by the international inspection teams. (Since an aggressor needs more than a 200 per cent superiority in weapons to destroy the ability of the other side to retaliate, a number of weapons equal to the size of the possible error in inspection checkup should constitute sufficient insurance against a premeditated attack.)

In the second place, it is not practicable to declare that on a certain day all means of delivery will be suddenly abolished. Even the first stage will have to be subdivided into several phases, during each of which certain measures will be taken. But if this proposition is accepted, then a third difficulty will arise, due to Soviet insistence that controls be proportioned to disarmament. The Russians might be willing to allow inspection of *all* their territory only *after* all means of delivery have been abolished. Otherwise, the Soviet air and missile bases which are now protected by their efficient secrecy will become vulnerable to a sudden attack by the other side. During the various phases of abolishing the means of delivery, only partial inspection would be permitted, preserving the rest of the territory from foreign spying.

To get around this difficulty, it has been suggested (e.g., see American Academy of Arts and Sciences, *Summer Study of Arms Control 1960, Collected Papers,* pp. 265–69), that disarmament and control measures should be phased on a territorial basis. For instance, each side might divide its territory into six areas, in each of which there would be an about equal number of its means of delivery. One of these areas would then be chosen either by the other side or by the international control organization, the selection to be based on a random choice by lot, or on a suspicion of the likelihood of evasion in a particular area. If both sides should try to apply the game theory, the first method of selection might be safer, as otherwise one side would try to outguess the other. (If B thinks that A is likely to choose area "a," B would transfer all extra weapons to area "b"; if A thinks that B might think so, it would choose area "b" instead of "a"; if B thinks that A might think that B might transfer the weapons to "b" because it thinks that A might choose "a," B might put them in "a"; etc.) In addition, military intelligence experts might prefer not to have the task of deciding which area should be chosen, as too many variables and inadequate data would make a decision extremely difficult. Thus choosing by lot might be better in the long run, and with each subsequent selection the odds against a successful evasion increase considerably. On the other hand, in the early phases, a certain amount of possible evasion is not too dangerous, as the other side would still retain most of its retaliatory force.

To prevent sudden shifts of armaments after an area has been selected, inspection teams could be stationed temporarily on the

borders between all the areas prior to actual selection, as well as at
rail and road centers and at airfields. After an area has been selected,
the inspection teams on the boundaries of the selected area would
remain there, but all the other teams would be withdrawn from the
boundaries of other areas and would be brought to the selected area
to aid in inspection.

Prior to the selection of an area, each side would be required to
submit a general list of all its armaments and other objects of inspection, subdivided by areas; and after the selection of the area, it would
be obligated to submit a more detailed list of armaments and other
objects of inspection located in the selected area, the totals of which
should not differ from those contained in the general list submitted
in advance. Meanwhile inspection teams would be entitled to check
the accuracy of the list and to check whether any non-listed control
objects are located in the selected area. They would also supervise
the actual process of disarmament within that area, and would see
to it that all the armed forces, armaments, military installations and
production facilities in the area would be reduced by the end of that
particular phase to the numbers agreed on in the disarmament agreement.

This process would be repeated in the second phase with respect
to the second area, and go on until by the end of all the phases of
the first stage all the territories of both sides would become permanently subject to inspection and all the components of military
strength would be reduced to the minimum specified in the disarmament agreement.

Subject to the acceptance by the Soviet Union of these or equally
effective control provisions, the President should propose a big step
toward disarmament which would establish a bilateral balance between both sides, on a level much lower than the present one, with
respect both to weapons of mass destruction and other weapons.
Once this balance is established and satisfactorily verified, it should
be easier to scale the armaments still further to police forces needed
merely for the maintenance of internal security. In this second stage,
an international police force would be simultaneously built up, effective means would be provided for dealing with international disputes
and the United Nations would be strengthened to the point neces-

sary to maintain peace and to enforce world law in the limited field of freedom from fear.

But progress toward the second stage depends on the successful completion of the first stage. This stage must contain a sufficient amount of disarmament to compensate for the Soviet acceptance of the amount of inspection which we deem necessary. It is suggested, therefore, that the American proposal for the first stage contain all the following elements.

1. The number of means of delivery of nuclear weapons should be reduced to an agreed small number needed as an insurance against the possibility that one side has hidden a similar number of weapons.

2. The production and testing of new military missiles should be prohibited, and the production, testing and use of rockets needed for space research should be permitted only under strict international control.

3. Military stockpiles of fissionable materials should be reduced in the first stage to an agreed amount, proportionate to the number of authorized means of delivery. (If, for instance, the number of means of delivery should be reduced to 100, the military stockpile of each side might be reduced to two metric tons of fissionable materials. While it might be more difficult to check on possible evasions of stockpile limitations, the size of the actual stockpile is not very important if there are strict limitations on means of delivery, as was well stated in the French proposal of 1959.)

4. All fissionable materials not needed for the authorized military stockpiles would be either destroyed, denatured or used up for peaceful purposes. The production of new fissionable materials would be limited to those needed for peaceful purposes. Both this production and all the peaceful uses of fissionable materials would be subject to strict international supervision. (Necessary safeguards for that purpose have been drafted in 1960 by the International Atomic Energy Agency.)

5. Testing of nuclear weapons would be prohibited.

6. All existing stocks of biological, chemical and radiological weapons should be destroyed, and new production and testing would be prohibited.

7. The armed forces of the Soviet Union and the United States

should be reduced to 1,000,000 and no more than 100,000 of them should be stationed outside their national territories. The remaining naval forces should be restricted to specified ocean areas. Flights by remaining military airplanes should be restricted to national territories and specified foreign areas. (If the United States should agree to a limitation on its main armaments, i.e., nuclear weapons, it must require a corresponding drastic reduction in the chief Soviet asset, i.e., the Russian Army. While most foreign air and missile bases should be deactivated, and all airplanes and missiles should be removed from those remaining, not all foreign troops need be withdrawn if the allies in whose territories they are stationed required the presence of some to guarantee immediate assistance in case of attack.)

8. Simultaneous reductions would have to be arranged for the military forces of other nations, in particular in Europe and Asia, taking into account in each region the need for maintaining a proper balance among various possible antagonists. The limitations in Africa and Latin America, where the arms race has been relatively limited, can be even more drastic.

While it is not possible to estimate exactly the time needed to put all these measures into effect, there would be four main periods of varying length during which the following steps would take place: (1) the preparation of the United States plan for controlled disarmament; (2) the negotiations with other nations; (3) the first stage of disarmament to a level of an insurance force sufficient for retaliation against a violator, and (4) the second stage of disarmament to such a point that, to quote President Roosevelt, "no nation will be in a position to commit an act of physical aggression against any neighbor."

During World War II, the preparation of the United States plan for the Charter of the United Nations took three years and involved many redrafts in the light of comments from various government departments, Congress and special consultants. With proper leadership by the President, and in view of the urgency of the situation, this period may perhaps be cut down to a year. The negotiations with the United Kingdom and the Soviet Union at Dumbarton Oaks took less than six weeks, and negotiations with China required only nine extra days; the Mexico City Conference with our allies took two weeks, and the San Francisco Conference itself required two months. The Charter of the United Nations came into effect on October 24, 1945, fourteen months after the start of the Dumbarton Oaks conversations.

It might be difficult to emulate this part of the United Nations record, but it is conceivable that the Russians are going to be more cooperative if we present to them a really effective and reasonable plan for disarmament, well thought through and sufficiently detailed. The bargaining position of the United States would be much better if our negotiators could go to an international meeting with an agreed plan rather than with a few vague ideas requiring more precise formulation during the negotiations themselves. If the President can persuade the country and the Congress, he may find out that it might not require much additional effort to persuade the Russians as well.

The two actual disarmament stages must fulfill two basic conditions: all steps must be taken as rapidly as possible, but at the same time each phase should be long enough to allow sufficient inspection to insure that no large evasions are taking place. Six phases of six-month duration would allow the completion of the first stage in three years. The second stage, in which most weapons would be scaled down to zero, might be a little more dangerous, and would require a slowing down in the tempo of disarmament. A five-year period, composed of ten six-month phases, should nevertheless provide sufficient time for the further improvement of inspection methods and the creation of an additional element of security through the establishment of an international police force.

Thus, general and complete disarmament under effective international control could be accomplished safely in eight years from the coming into effect of a disarmament agreement.

This is a drastic program, but desperate times require drastic remedies. It is for the United States to take the initiative, as it has done with respect to the United Nations Charter, the North Atlantic Treaty and the Marshall Plan. All these great steps forward were done under Democratic administrations. The new Administration should take the logical next step, and there can be but little doubt that the country would follow a vigorous leadership in this direction. If we want to survive, we must take the necessary risks, and these risks are certainly smaller than those involved in the present arms race.